JOURNEY OF
THE EMPOWERED HEART

BY KATIE GRAY

Copyright © 2021 Katie Gray

All rights reserved. With respect and honor for the many years and countless hours invested into the creation of this body of work, no part of this publication may be reproduced, distributed, or transmitted in any form without the prior written permission of the author/publisher, except in the case of brief quotations embodied in critical reviews and certain other noncommercial uses permitted by copyright law. For permission requests, contact Katie Gray. www.katiegray.com

ISBN: 978-0-578-25462-3 (softcover) 978-0-578-25711-2 (hardcover)

Cover design, Empowered Heart diagram, layout by Erica Ekrem
www.loombound.com

All original illustrations (The Empowered Heart) by Masha Pimas

All other book illustrations licensed through Creative Market

Author photograph by Kurt Baumann

Cover photograph by Keith Hardy

Printed in the USA

This book represents actual events in the life of the author as truthfully as recollection allows. Occasionally, dialogue consistent with the character or nature of the person speaking has been supplemented. The names and details of some individuals have been changed to honor privacy and anonymity.

Everyone is welcome here.

CONTENTS

INTRODUCTION *1*

Part I: THE STAGES OF SUFFERING *14*

1. **HEART** *15*
   The Unraveling • The Sacred Sphere of Being • The True Self • Before the Pain • Home in the Heart

2. **WOUND** *25*
   Wounds Cannot Be Rated • Our Tender Youth • Collective Wounding • Creating Wounds • Lost Memories

3. **PAIN** *40*
   The Crack of Division • Fear • Insecurity & the Wolf • Hidden Wound, Hidden Pain • The Backpack of Shame • Taking a Life • Sadness & the Undercurrent • Grief & the Heavy Bucket • The Different Forms of Grief

4. **NEED** *56*
   The Echo of Pain • Hunger & Longing • The Insatiability of Social Media • The Need for Inclusion & Attention • The Need for Control • A World in Need

5. **PROTECTION** *72*
   Ego: The Great Divide • The Illusion of Avoidance • The Facade of Fine • The Lullaby of Distraction • The Lure of Screens • The Wall of Desensitization • A Global Problem • The Loss of Intuition • The Disconnection of Dishonesty • Dishonesty with the Self

6. **DEFENSE** *93*
   A Fist in Slow Motion • Fierce Mother Instinct • The Harshness of Judgment • Self-Judgment • The Survivalism of Competition • The Fire of Anger • The Slow Burn of Passive Aggression

7. **SUFFERING** *112*
   Stuck in a Pattern of Avoidance • The Wave of Compulsion • The Cycle of Addiction • The Cloud of Depression • The Story of Rose • The Broken Branch • One Billion Rising • The Storm of Violence • A Suffering World

A MOMENT OF PAUSE *133*

8. **REALIZATION** *134*
   The Hidden Benefits of Suffering • Learning from Our Struggles • Letting Go of the Past • The Decision • Commitment • Intention: The Direction Home

INTRODUCTION *149*

Part II: **THE PATH TO EMPOWERMENT** *153*

9. **OBSERVE** *154*
   Confronting Fear & Avoidance • The Gift of Learning • Opening the Doors • The Cleansing Light of Awareness • Finding the Patterns • The Investigator & the Witness • The Higher Self • Judgment Awareness • Self-Awareness • Following the Trail of Pain

10. **FEEL** *185*
    Understanding Feelings • Going into the Uncomfortable Places • Collective Desensitization • Learning to Feel • Honoring the Sensitive • The Physical Sense • A Shift in Senses • Every Feeling is Welcome at the Table • Acknowledging Anger • Remaining Present Through the Feeling • The Hidden Language of Intuition • Intelligence of the Heart • Leaning into the Feeling

GETTING YOUR NEEDS MET *217*

11. **CONNECT** *219*

    Seeking Connection • A Familial Network • Friendship • Plants & Animals • Friendship with the Self • Journaling : A Sacred Doorway • Anonymous Sharing • Present Listening • Social Media with Intention • Counsel • Plant Medicine • The Elders • Opening to Life

12. **RELEASE** *257*

    Coming Clean • Voicing Your Truth • The Intentional Space of Sharing • A Good Cry • Wash the Pain Away • The Power of a Man's Tears • The Child Behind the Mask • The Flow of the River • The Apology • Write a Letter • The Language of Music • Artistic Freedom • Expression Through Movement • Gentle Through the Detox • Letting Others Find Their Own Way

13. **COMFORT** *298*

    Temporary Comfort • Being Comfortable • Creating Meditative Space • The Soothing Relief of Sleep • Home is Where the Heart is • Divine Mother Nurturance • Warmth • Kindness • The Almighty Hug • A Breath of Life • The Natural World • Receiving Comfort

14. **LOVE** *332*

    A Powerful Force • Self-Love • The Woman in the Mirror • Stepping Back with Love • The Gift of Compassion • Empathy & Feeling Bad • Self-Compassion • The Light of Forgiveness • Along the Highway • Self-Forgiveness • Your Body, Your Friend • The Choice to Love is the Choice to Live

15. **EMPOWERED** *370*

    False Confidence vs. True Confidence • Strength & Power • Anger vs. Empowerment • Overpowering Addiction • The Subtle Rewards of True Happiness • Gratitude is a Choice • The Return Home to Presence • Greater Intelligence • The World Around You • The Power of Purpose • The Unknown

GLOSSARY *400*

REFERENCES *403*

INTRODUCTION

IMAGINE YOURSELF ON A LONG WALK. You're calm, present, and enjoying the beauty around you. Then, a small stone tosses itself into your shoe. At first, it upsets you, but you figure to yourself, *I can manage; it's just a little pebble.* So, you continue.

However, the little stone manages to shift over beneath your heel, and it hurts. You thought maybe the little stone might break up on its own and turn to dust. It didn't. It's still there inside your shoe and randomly piercing your flesh.

I need to stop and get this out, you think to yourself, *this hurts.* Yet, you don't. Instead, you continue walking and strategize a solution of leaning your body's weight to the outside of your foot to avoid stepping on it. It seems to work. The pebble of pain is near your arch and if you walk with pressure on the outside of your foot, you don't step on it.

Perfect! You've found a solution! A way to avoid feeling the pain! However, now your knee is hurting from walking out of sync with your body's natural posture. This twists your leg, which throws off your hip and lower back muscles and they now feel very sore.

Where once you were present and enjoying this walk, now your face is scrunched up and your eyes are peering at the ground. *This walk is ridiculous. Why would anyone ever come here? It's boring and there's nothing to see. When will it be over?* you think to yourself. Instead of feeling at peace and grateful, now you're disgruntled, uninspired, and in pain. You're suffering.

Whether you can relate to this story or not, chances are that you know what it's like to be in pain. But rather than a stone in your shoe, you've been traumatized in other ways. Through abuse, divorce, neglect, bullying, judgment, breakups, illness, death, and the many other ways we humans experience heartbreak, you've been through trauma and you know what it's like to feel uncomfortable as a result.

Sadly, you probably also know what it's like to not want to think about those things. To avoid them and try to keep moving without getting slowed down by the shame, sadness, fear, and discomfort that naturally accompanies them.

Unfortunately, when you avoid pain, like the stone, it doesn't go away. It just stays there, digging into your being, creating more problems and more pain, and you end up suffering as a result of it.

At some point, you've got to stop avoiding where the pain is really coming from and take the time to look at it so you can understand it and heal from it. You've got to sit down, untie your laces, pull off your shoe, find the rock, and shake it out.

Why? Because it's hurting you, and you don't deserve to be in pain. You've suffered long enough. You've spent enough of your life carrying the heavy backpack of shame, hobbling in self-doubt, avoiding the pain in your heart, and pretending to the world that you're enjoying the walk and everything's ok.

It's not ok. It's not ok to suffer and it's not ok to give up any more of your precious and valuable life moments, missing the beautiful view along the way because you're in too much pain to enjoy it and you're too afraid to look at where the pain is really coming from.

It's time to sit down and deal with the discomfort because you're done struggling and you're ready to start enjoying the journey of life. You deserve to be healed from suffering and empowered in your heart!

Ok, hold on, let's pause... is any of this sounding too good to be true? Maybe a little cliché? Like *another* self-help book promising freedom from all of your troubles?

If so, I'm cringing a little bit. I fully mean every word I say that *you can heal from your suffering* and yet, I don't want any of this talk of *healing* to sound unrealistically optimistic. I also don't want it to sound quick and easy. It's not easy. Going through everything you've been through wasn't easy and healing from it isn't easy either.

To be honest, that's one of the reasons I've been so turned off by self-help books for much of my life, because so often they make healing sound really quick and easy. *Just follow these five simple steps and you too can be as happy and healthy (and beautiful, popular, sober, wealthy, and perfect) as me!*

When you're exhausted, ashamed, or addicted, and doing everything you can to stay emotionally afloat and then hear about healing being quick and easy for others, it can be deflating. You begin to feel like no one understands and like you really are alone; like something really is wrong with you. That's how I felt for a very long time.

It was also hard for me to find an author who I naturally and genuinely wanted to spend weeks or months hanging out with (I'm a slow reader). I needed help but more so, I needed a friend, someone who could really relate to what I was going through and someone I really trusted. Reading is a very intimate experience. It's like spending time in your bed, or on your sofa, or in a car with someone who's sitting *really* close to you, speaking directly into your head. That's a relationship to choose discerningly. So if I sensed that an author was dishonest, egocentric, or had ulterior motives, I quickly lost interest and closed the book.

Now, you might be wondering: *why did you write a self-help book if you're not really into them?*

Good question. To be really honest, I didn't write this book because I wanted to; I wrote it because I felt like I *had* to.

My experience of healing from suffering (compulsive eating and bulimia) was unique and somewhat unconventional. While a lot of people find healing through psychotherapy, rehab centers, or organized programs, I didn't. The support I needed to break the thick shell of my unconsciousness and suffering was found through shamanic plant medicine, daily meditative self-inquiry, and *years* of personal research and study. Through devotedly studying and analyzing my behavior, patterns, and tendencies, I not only understood what I needed to do to heal, I understood why I was struggling.

Why was I struggling? I had been wounded. Like stones in my shoes, I had experienced traumas and rather than dealing with them, I had avoided them. I had distracted myself from the pain and in doing so had become separated from myself; from my heart. This left me in a confusing, lonely, and painful place for many years.

In order to heal, I had to honestly look at my life and all of the uncomfortable and unpleasant experiences I had been through. I had to really understand where my insatiable hunger was coming from: all the needs that hadn't been met. I had to step out of fear and talk to someone about my struggles. I had to be more gentle on myself and rather than constantly judging and shaming myself, I had to be a better listener and better friend to myself. I had to let go of the tears I had been holding in for so long and I had to forgive myself. I had to love myself.

Once my needs were finally met, I wasn't hungry or anxious anymore. I didn't feel like I needed to hide or be secretive about my past. I didn't feel like I was a bad, dirty, broken, or pathetic person. I felt clean, whole, strong, and empowered. Essentially, I felt healed and my decades of shame, insecurity, and addiction were done.

After spending so much of my life suffering, I had discovered a treasure trove of perspectives and tools that transformed my life and freed me from pain, and it wasn't right to keep that treasure to myself; it was my duty to share it with others.

So I did. Over the past 12 years, I have become experienced and confident in walking the pathway out of suffering, so I started helping others find the pathway too. With that, I developed *The Empowered Heart*. Through inspirational talks, guided meditations, workshops, retreats, and working closely with countless individuals, I passed the light on to hundreds of people.

Then, I realized it was time for that light to be passed on to anyone who needs healing, regardless of whether I'm there to help facilitate or not. For months and years, I heeded the call by studying counselling session notes, journal entries, epiphanies, and notepads filled with everything I've learned over the years of healing myself and helping others heal themselves. Eventually, I weaved those insights together into something portable, accessible, and digestible—namely, this book.

Through the experience of mapping out the suffering and healing process, I've come to understand that a lot of us are going through very similar cycles of suffering and struggling with similar pain. Regardless of what we are personally struggling with (insecurity, grief, self-judgment, lack of purpose, alcohol dependency, eating disorders, anger issues, etc.), we're often hurting from deep, internal, emotional wounds.

Again and again, I've witnessed how this powerful work of consciously and lovingly going within helps people heal. No matter our personality, age, gender, race, or sexual preference, we all have the power to heal ourselves through this deep, explorative work.

I've also come to understand that we all have a lot more in common than we realize. Each and every one of us is innocent, caring, and compassionate in our heart of hearts, and given the right space, permission, and encouragement, we can open ourselves up to be our true selves.

THE JOURNEY OF THE EMPOWERED HEART

THE GOAL OF OUR WORK TOGETHER is to bring you safely back to your true self: honest, kind, loving, confident, compassionate, and comfortable in who you are. Essentially, for you to feel safe and comfortable here in this present moment and enjoy life again.

But to get there, we've got some work to do: the work of *The Empowered Heart*, which is a methodology and also a map. As very specific events and occurrences caused us to end up in a place of suffering, the cycle of the empowered heart doesn't just offer solutions for *how* to heal, it also offers deep awareness of *why* we need to heal. For that reason, this isn't a "5 easy steps" process. It's more like a *14-stage circular odyssey*.

THE MAP OF
THE EMPOWERED HEART
–A pathway through suffering and back to the heart–

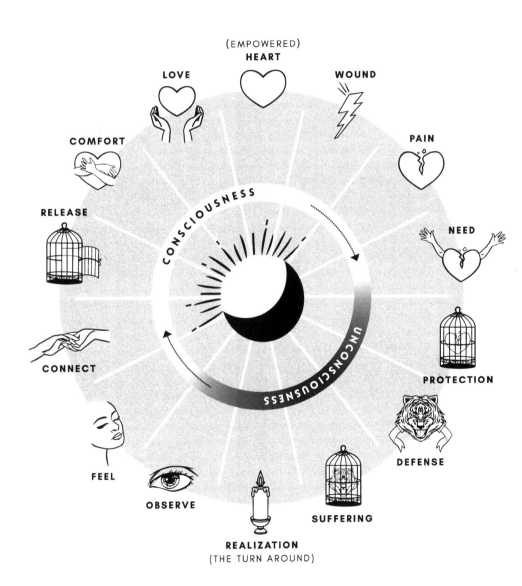

First, it begins with the *Stages of Suffering*:

- Heart
- Wound
- Pain
- Need
- Protection
- Defense
- Suffering

In this part of the journey, we start with the precious and pure being of our true selves (heart), then look at the traumas that happened to us (wound) and the fear, discomfort, and anxiety that emerged as a result (pain and need). Next, we'll explore what happens when we don't get our needs met (protection) and how we've adapted to prevent future wounds and pain (defense). Finally, we arrive at the place where we're furthest from our true selves (suffering).

Next, we'll take a moment to pause at the turnaround (realization). We'll decide whether it's serving us to be so disconnected from our hearts. We'll assess the journey and make the powerful change to return home to ourselves.

Then, we'll enter the *Path to Empowerment*:

- Observe
- Feel
- Connect
- Release
- Comfort
- Love
- Empowered

This part of the journey will be like entering through the dawn into the daylight. By applying the wisdom and awareness from the first part of our journey, we'll develop skills and tools to create a healthier, more sustainable relationship with ourselves, one that is free of suffering.

First, we'll look at the truth of what's going on now and what happened in the past (observe), then resensitize and access the deeper feelings and sensations we may have separated ourselves from (feel). From there, we'll learn about getting our needs met, beginning with connection (connect), then letting go of all that's held inside (release). Next, we'll learn about the art of receiving and being more comfortable in who we are (comfort), then get clear on what it feels like to truly honor ourselves and others (love).

After traversing the mountain of suffering and getting home to our true selves, we'll awaken to new levels of confidence, compassion, and resilience (empowered). With an empowered heart, we'll see that our challenging life experiences haven't made us broken and weak, but given us the potential to liberate and empower ourselves to live our life's purpose.

I imagine we'd like to skip straight to empowerment, right? Yeah, me too. However, healing takes time. It requires presence, patience, knowledge, willingness, and the commitment to show up. Though it's not always fun, it's necessary to have a deep awareness of why we're not feeling good and develop the skills to feel better. Otherwise, we soothe the suffering for a moment, but without knowing what happened to cause it, we run the risk of falling into the same places and patterns again and again.

I don't think that's what you really want. I sense that you're completely done suffering and ready to live life. You don't want to temporarily lessen the pain, you want to permanently uproot it. You want to get to a place where you don't need any more books to help you because you could write your own book... because you're so healthy and empowered that people are asking *you* for support.

For those reasons, this journey is not quick and it's not easy. But it is worth it. I will do everything in my power to make it comfortable for you, but there will likely be moments that are not a lot of fun. There may be moments on the journey where you're ready to put the book down and not pick it back up, especially through the first half of the journey where we climb up the mountain and into the suffering.

In those moments, remember that you didn't get to this place in your life overnight. It took a long time to get where you're at and it will take time to get where you're going. Take deep breaths. Keep going. Ahead of you on the horizon is the other side of the mountain; the other side of the journey. There, you'll be met with the long-lasting rewards of relief, kindness, compassion, forgiveness, and happiness.

Along the way, I'll be your guide, lighting the path. I'll share my personal life experiences and stories to give you a reference and feel for the essence of each stage and help you to look within yourself at similar experiences you have had.

As well, there will be extra treasures of awareness to add to your satchel of wisdom, such as:

- How insecurity derives from not feeling safe
- What emotional hunger is
- Why we feel jealousy and envy
- Why crying might be the healthiest thing we can do for ourselves
- How to regulate our relationship with social media
- Why "feeling bad" isn't healthy
- How to be better friends to ourselves
- Why forgiveness is so beneficial
- What true confidence is
- The difference between false power and true power

GUIDELINES

IN PREPARATION FOR THIS JOURNEY, here are some guidelines and ground rules to keep in mind:

1. **Be honest with yourself and with me.** We humans are very good at lying and pretending. Many of us learned to fib from a very young age to protect ourselves but you don't need to do that anymore, especially not with me. Whatever you've been through and whatever you're going through, I'm not going to judge you. I also ask that you don't judge yourself. Each dishonest tale you tell comes with the heavy burden of shame to carry and there are too many things to see and places to be to let shame slow you down. The more open and honest you can be with yourself, the sooner we'll get to our destination.

2. **You're the healer. You're the leader.** No one is forcing you to read these words, at least I don't imagine they are. No one can do this work for you. Only you can do it. While I will be here guiding you along, holding the light, and pointing out the signs, I'm not

the one who will be turning the pages, nor the one who deserves acknowledgement for you doing this monumental work for yourself. You deserve that credit and recognition. You are the one making this happen. Not everyone is ready to courageously delve deep into their pain to find and rehabilitate their broken heart. You're about to heal yourself and I'm going to be here beside you, *helping* you do it.

3. **You're ready.** It's nearly impossible for me, or anyone else, to help someone who isn't ready to be helped unless *they* are ready. You're the one who is ready for change and you're the one who has overcome your fears and followed your intuition enough to arrive at this important place and time. You're ready, and by just showing up and being here right now, the healing is already happening.

4. **It's ok to stop and rest.** Like climbing any mountain, there are vistas to take in and breaths to catch. We're going to visit some tender areas that may awaken contemplative self-reflection. Like opening a closet and pulling everything out, we may come across old boxes of trinkets, memories, and treasures—things you'll want to take a seat and reflect on for a moment. Do that. Take a moment. Take five. Take a year. Life moves quickly and we're often racing frantically to keep up with it. Too often, we don't stop to breathe, feel, and reflect. This book is an opportunity to slow down and take it in for yourself. There's no rush and no expectation. This is your journey and you can turn the pages at whatever pace feels right for you.

SYMBOLS, SIGNS, AND SELF-INQUIRY

WE'RE ALMOST READY TO START our journey together, but before we do, I want to point out a few unique qualities about this journey we're going to take.

In both the *Stages of Suffering* and the *Path to Empowerment*, I use very simple symbolic images to represent each step. These images are signposts to help you understand and identify what's going on within you. As we continue our journey, the map will be revealed to you. Ideally, these symbols are tokens of support that continue to serve you long after you complete the Journey of the Empowered Heart.

While I will often speak to *you* directly, I will also speak of "us" as two friends on a journey together. I think of us doing this *together*, you and me. But it's not just the two of us who suffer and struggle in this world. As you'll soon find out, most of us on the planet are in some way suffering. So at times, I will refer to "we" in reference to the whole human species. For that reason, we'll look closely at "ourselves" as individuals, then pan out to look at what "we," a planet of suffering people, are going through. This might seem unusual at first, but as we grow on our journey together, it will become natural to you to see "us" and to see all humans as "we."

While much of this journey will be me speaking and you listening, it's essential for *your* voice to be heard as well. We will intentionally go into areas that may have you thinking deeply and asking yourself questions, and that's a good thing! While I plan to be a strong and stable friend, it's our goal for you to build a strong and healthy friendship with *yourself*.

What makes a great friend? Someone who's honest and caring, and knows how to listen. So, as a way to strengthen your inner friendship and ability to listen to yourself, I will offer self-inquiry questions in each chapter. These are moments to pause and hear your own voice, instead of mine. While it's not necessary to write about what comes up for you, it might support your healing process.

For this reason, you might consider getting a notebook or journal for our time together. This is a great way for you to speak openly and honestly while also listening and being heard. If you're not comfortable with writing or find it unfamiliar, that's not a problem. There are no rules and no requirements.

As you will find out, journaling has been a major component in my healing and a vehicle that brought many insights into my life, and now into yours. I offer the encouragement to write knowing that you may benefit from the act of writing, finding your voice, freeing your thoughts, and being heard, which are all things you deserve.

INTENTION

LASTLY, ONE OF THE MOST POWERFUL and important steps when entering any sacred space of transformation and healing is to align with intention. This involves *knowing* and *understanding* what you are seeking. It's important to understand where you're going, like an invisible cord that connects your heart and your thoughts to a future reality. The more clearly you can visualize where you want to go and why, the easier you make it to get there.

It's ok to feel fearful and uncertain. However, there's a deeper reason why you're here. There's a vision of healing that speaks to you from inside your heart. It's important to listen to that voice inside.

What does it say when you ask yourself these questions?

- *What am I seeking?*
- *What am I ready to let go of?*
- *What am I ready to welcome into my life?*

Sometimes, when given the opportunity to imagine what we want in life, we think of financial wealth, career success, or a better body. In reality, what we're often really seeking are the quiet subtleties of presence, better sleep, healthier relationships, improved communication, emotional balance, confidence, feelings of worth, or a sense that we belong right here, right now.

•

When you feel ready, let's get started!

Part One
THE STAGES OF SUFFERING

1.
HEART

The central and innermost part of something; the vital essence.

M̲y mom used to wake me up slowly. She would gently lay her hand on my arm and whisper, "Kaaatie, time to wake uuuu-up." My eyes would gradually open as her warmth welcomed me to the day.

Without losing the gentle, loving qualities that were so central to her nature, she would quickly enter a constant, steady swirl of *doing*. She would pack the lunches, go to work, cook the meals, clean the dishes, pay the bills, and do everything else that was needed to raise three girls as a single mom on a meagre income.

She was a very gentle, caring, and incredible mother—and also incessantly nervous, busy, and distracted. She rarely showed her vulnerability and regularly kept her heart closely guarded, and often felt a little out of reach.

From the outside, you might think that's who my mom was—a busy, anxious, single woman who was closed off and didn't have the time. However, there was far more beauty, love, and life beyond the monotonous wall of her day-to-day routine, beyond the desk where she sat answering questions about auto parts.

In one lifetime, she was a beatnik and an activist.

In another lifetime, she was a ceramist and an artist.

In all lifetimes, she was curious and a steady listener; someone who would undoubtedly create space at her dinner table for you.

I think back to her gentle and careful method of waking up and it feels so reflective of how gracefully and gradually she is dying right now.

Years ago, my mom experienced a stroke. While it didn't take her life, it did take much of her memory and in its place, left the life-altering effects of dementia. Like a body being laid into water with slow motion and ease, she is gradually, carefully transitioning from her life's waking state to the rested spaciousness of death.

Over the years, I've lost loved ones to cancer, and with each of them, it felt so abrupt and unforgiving—as if I was being rushed through an airport and forced to say farewell to someone whose plane was about to depart.

I have friends who lost their loved ones to car accidents, and I can imagine how many prayers and years it took to finally come to peace, feeling that their last goodbye was good enough.

Now, I face a different kind of loss, and while dementia is a long and painfully drawn-out process in many ways, I can't imagine a more generous goodbye.

THE UNRAVELING

WHILE THERE IS A LOT that we as a family (and dementia researchers) understand, there is also much that we don't understand. Strangely, dementia has a way of unraveling the mind and peeling back the layers of thought, story, and memory... like layers of clothing being unwrapped from a child who is brought in from the cold.

First, her unraveling happened through the loss of friend's names and birthdays. She forgot how old she was and all of the years she had spent working. She couldn't remember being married or the places she had lived over the years. She forgot how many kids she had and slowly, the names of those kids. Recently, she has been forgetting her own name.

Although the loss of her memory has been a profound tragedy, it has also been a mystical unfolding. Through this strange and bizarre separation, she has pulled entirely away from the tether of her identity and become completely separate from who she *thought* she was—the ego—and reunited with what remains—presence.

With each of the stories and memories that have come undone, so too have the layers of protection that were wrapped so tightly around her for so long. She doesn't know to be worried about money or concerned about her appearance. She doesn't know to turn away and avoid staring deeply into another person's eyes for fear of being rude. She is unabashed, untamed, and unafraid. Like a nameless, sexless, ageless being who doesn't know about the past or have concerns about the future. It's as if she has *unlearned* the awkward, polite conduct of being human and simply resides in the spaciousness of what's happening right now.

No longer is she my *mom*, who I can reflect on a lifetime of memories with. No longer does she live in the realm of memories. She lives here, in this moment. Now, she is a being who wakes up each day to greet the wonder of existence—pointing out of the window in awe of the "big… there… those… things…"

Clouds.

While it's been *deeply* painful for me, my sister, and our spouses to be her full-time caregivers for seven years now, it's also been a profoundly enlightening experience to walk beside her on her journey of transformation.

In many ways, she has cycled through the journey of life and come full circle to the place of presence that she first embodied having initially beamed into her suit of humanism. She has been stripped of her layers and returned to her original state of being: the state of presence and spirit that remains if and when each of us is relieved of our memories and stories.

If this state of being could speak, it might look around at life with wide and curious eyes, saying, "I am here, experiencing life."

THE SACRED SPHERE OF BEING

ESSENTIALLY, THIS SACRED SPHERE of being is the heart of who we are inside, and it's something that you and I will talk a lot about. We'll reference it again and again, and while the word "heart" also means the hard-working, life-giving organ that beats from your chest, we'll be referring to your heart to describe the *spirit* of you. It is the tender orb of consciousness at the center of your being, having a very unique and sometimes very challenging human life experience.

Here are some examples of what the true HEART of you is like:

- Honest
- Present
- Loving
- Conscious
- Innocent
- Trusting
- Vulnerable
- Caring
- Curious
- Unafraid
- Enthusiastic
- Whole

Though you may feel quite separate from this profound and radiant spirit of truth within you, it's still the heart of who you are—infinitely and unconditionally—with no exceptions. It's the core and base of your being. Regardless of how angry, troubled, addicted, wrong, or messed up you feel and see yourself at times, the fact will always remain that the heart of who you are is an innocent spirit having the temporary experience of being human.

In a book that embodies a devoted mission to understanding and transforming pain and struggle, it might seem like we should begin our journey talking about the past and asking, "what happened?" In other words, looking at the traumatic wounds you've gathered along the way.

However, if we make the pain-filled problems our starting point, then somewhere inside, you might associate yourself as the problem. You might see your timeline of dysfunction beginning with the painful sources of your pain and have difficulty tethering and understanding who you are *beneath* and *without* the pain.

For that reason, our journey begins here, with the heart. The place where you started. The orb of presence and consciousness that is the true nature of who you really are.

Why? Because, it is our sincere and devoted mission to get you back home, here, to this place of your true self. The fearless, confident, honest, present, pure, and conscious being that is truly you.

THE TRUE SELF

SADLY, IT SEEMS THAT SOMEWHERE along the way, we humans have forgotten who we are. Like a giant, collective case of amnesia, we've misplaced this understanding and remembrance of our true selves. Perhaps from thousands of years of cycled and recycled pain being passed on from generation to generation, we've acquired a concept that in order to be present, conscious, and free from our suffering, we have to become something different; something better.

So, we try. We frantically do this, learn that, buy these, fix those, and continually attempt to change ourselves so we can somehow feel closer to a sense of peace, completion, and worthiness. But we don't need to. We don't need to strain our arms, reaching outward in the hope of altering ourselves into a state of wholeness. Why? Because we're already whole. We're already complete.

The golden jewel of what we seek—healing through love, presence, peace, and conscious awareness—is and has always been right here, accessible within us. It's literally what we're made of. It's the heart of us. Like the molten rock that fills the depths of the Earth, the very heart of our beings is light. It's the embryo of life force and love, which exists at the core of our beings: consciousness.

But, what is consciousness?

Consciousness is the infinite awareness and aliveness of life. It's the light matter of the universe, the thing that gives existence a pulse. It's what stimulates our eyes to open and our minds to have realizations. While you might see yourself as a separate individual with a body, a name, a job, and an age—you're also something infinitely greater and more expansive. You're the formless, uncontainable spirit of life and wholeness that exists within the physical embodiment of you.

How do we access consciousness?

Through presence. Through allowing ourselves to re-engage with the natural, open essence of our true selves. Whether we remember it or not, being present is a sacred experience and one we all know. Like a language imprinted and communicated through our hearts, it's something very familiar to each of us.

Similar to a drop of water yearning to be connected to the ocean, we don't need to see ourselves as separate beings who have to work hard to become something greater. We're already made of something so much bigger and greater than us.

How am I so certain and confident about the true nature of the self?

Because you weren't always hurting and suffering. You weren't always bogged down by fears, emotions, struggles, and stories. Back when you first entered the cycle of living, you embodied the true essence of yourself: consciousness and love. You were the original version of you, embodying the purest reflection of that true nature.

BEFORE THE PAIN

A LOT HAS HAPPENED TO YOU since you first started your journey, but it doesn't mean that the core of who you are has changed. Just like the buildings, cities, and pollution happening on the Earth's surface doesn't change who the Earth is; it just changes what's happening to the Earth. Regardless of how painful or destructive those things may be, the reality of what exists at the core is still the same.

Perhaps the best way to understand this original, true spirit is to ask:

Who were you before you were hurting?
What were you like before you learned to be afraid and protect yourself?

We may not know exactly what you looked like, but we do know a few things...

- Your body was very, very small and you had clear, curious eyes.
- Your heart was open and you had not yet learned to fear or hold back.
- You were extremely vulnerable and needed support from others to survive.
- Your mind was uncluttered and spacious, clear of stories and thoughts.
- You were honest, authentic, and unashamed of feeling or crying.
- You told people when you needed something and let people know how you felt.

- You cared deeply about those you loved.
- You lived completely in the moment.
- You were the embodiment of presence, awareness, and consciousness.

This is who you were when you first entered the world, when you embodied the highest concentration of your true nature. Yes, your body has grown quite a bit since then, and you may (or may not) have more hair now, but you are essentially the same essence of being that you were when you were born—a conscious, innocent, tender miracle of life.

Is it challenging to think of yourself in such a majestic light? Maybe you're no longer fearless and open with your tears? Maybe you find it difficult to speak up when you need something? Maybe you don't consider yourself special, vulnerable, or innocent anymore?

Well, what's interesting about being human is that even though you may act and think differently than you once did, you're still the same loving, caring, sensitive being as when you first started. You're just as innocent and vulnerable, just as in need of and worthy of support and connection.

What has changed over the years isn't *who* you are but the experiences that you've been through. Unfortunately, many of those experiences were probably very painful and challenging—and as you identify with them, they formed layers and layers over who you truly are.

Being human can be such a painful experience, so you developed the ability to withstand intense and painful challenges while doing your very best to preserve the gentle and pure nature of your heart.

Do you have remembrance of being a small child and feeling present, clear, and without fear?

HOME IN THE HEART

YOU CAN SPEND A LIFETIME SEARCHING for that beloved sense of connection, presence, and wholeness, which you know so well in your heart, but you won't find it out there. It's not hidden on a bookshelf or tucked in the depths of your fridge. It's not resting in a job promotion or stacked up in your bank statement.

It's right here—inside you. It's covered up and hidden beneath the layers of pain, fear, stories, and protection that somehow got mangled in with your understanding of the self.

What this means is that you don't have to carry on judging, seeking, and scrambling to be better than you are. You don't need to search to "find yourself." You just have to *let go* of the toxic, fear-infused resistance holding you back from being your true self. You have to give yourself permission to remember who you are and always have been inside.

Our journey will take us many places and through many experiences together, and it will be my honor to bring you back here, to this sacred place of life and bewilderment within you.

Remarkably, you are your own destination.

❦

Who are you without your stories and your words?

Who are you if you aren't ashamed or embarrassed?

If there is no resentment for the past or fear of the future, what is left?

You.

The real you.

*The you who is only temporarily having
this experience of being a human.*

*The you who doesn't filter love
or hold back your feelings.*

*The you who has no need to excuse your failures
because you don't have any failures.*

*The you who stands in awe,
marveling at the miraculous wonder of the sky.*

*The you who you have always been inside,
formless and infinite,
simply here in this moment,
doing your very best to be alive.*

❦

2.
WOUND

Injury caused by impact.

The daytime was often calm and still in our relatively humble house. My mom spent most of the day there, and if you happened to see her, you might witness a woman who looked naturally exhausted from raising kids. She would probably smile and say something about the weather, avoiding too much eye contact and keeping the door not too open—just like how she guarded herself for so much of her life.

As the evening approached and my dad came home, the winds of distress would sweep through the rooms. A thick haze of nervousness and apprehension filled the air, like blood filling a mouse who seeks refuge in safe corners and behind heavy furniture.

The thing is, my dad was kind, loving, very sensitive, and generous with his care. However, he was working long hours to uphold his business and provide for his wife and young children. He was a foreigner in foreign land, scrambling frantically to embody the striving manner of the American dream. And stress is a poison that can taint and cloud even the purest of streams.

While it's definitely not the case for every family in India, there is a cultural pattern that often deems it permissible for men to release their aggression on women and children. And, my father was immersed in this perspective of consent. United with his pain and stress, it erupted in anger, which intensified with each sip of alcohol. The storm of pain and rage overcame him many times, and many times he inflicted those wounds on his wife and children.

Suddenly, there were doors slamming and fists swinging. There were put downs and regrets viciously yelled back and forth, in the halls, up the stairs, and through the walls. The painful voices and tears of my mom and dad—two lovers who had become opponents—echoed through the nights.

Without knowing how to change this cycle, my mom gradually formulated a plan to escape it. Late one afternoon, as we were playing in our rooms, we heard her voice shrieking up the stairs, "Girls!" We ran closer to hear her. "We're going on a trip. Each of you, grab one toy. Hurry! We've gotta go."

Frantically, we ran outside and loaded up the car she had borrowed from my older brother Paul, from her first marriage. With our hands gripped tightly around our toys and hers around the steering wheel, we left before my dad came home. We left the house, we left the cat, and we left our life there in Virginia. We drove all the way to Michigan and never returned. My mom became a single mother, and we—the wide-eyed and wilted children—followed the path of division laid out in front of us.

Though I was only a young child at the time, the trauma of those years and our dramatic departure were wounds etched deep into my heart. For many years, I was intimidated and embarrassed by it all. I felt ashamed that there was a heavy cloud lingering over my family. I felt like everyone else was clean and put together, while we were stained with a painful past that was too heinous to admit. Somehow, we were wrong, broken, and unworthy of fully participating in the effortless joy of life.

However, as I moved forward through life, reconnected with my dad (as you'll see in Chapter 14) and provided counsel and support to many others on their journey of healing, it became very clear that it wasn't just me or my family. Every single one of us knows what it feels like to experience the impact of traumatic wounds, the bolts of lightning that strike the peace of our minds and hearts. Wounds are something we *all* have in common.

I used to refer to these painful flashes and explosions as "traumas," which they definitely are, but it's easy to underestimate or misinterpret what is classified as a trauma—the deaths, rapes, accidents, and natural disasters. The term "trauma" comes with so many preconceived notions like this that people often overlook the real root of their pain—feeling that it's not justified as a trauma.

While these monumental events are deemed significant enough to be "legitimate trauma," in reality, it's also the let downs, put downs, and breakups that can cause a lot of pain. This is why I use the terms "wounds" and "hidden wounds" instead, so we can look across the wider field to find hidden bits and pieces of debris from the storm that are unknowingly creating severe distress and discomfort in our lives.

Examples of WOUNDS:
- Physical and/or emotional abuse
- Rape or sexual abuse
- Death of a close loved one
- Racial oppression, inequality, judgment, and/or abuse
- Poverty
- Cancer or a major illness diagnosis and recovery process (self or loved one)
- Sexual harassment
- Addiction
- Having a disability
- Vehicle accident

Examples of HIDDEN WOUNDS:
- Separation of parents
- Alcoholic parent
- A lineage of abuse and addiction
- Being separated from parents
- A parent siding with an abusive step-parent or not standing up for you
- Being bullied in school (verbally or physically)
- Experiencing verbal or physical abuse from a sibling
- Controlling parents
- Controlling spouse
- Being put in a foster home
- Complications at birth
- Undergoing surgery
- You or your partner undergoing an abortion
- Experiencing a miscarriage
- A breakup or divorce
- Feeling pressure to fit in at school

- Experiencing governmental oppression
- Verbal judgment and put downs from a loved one
- Not making the cut for a sports team
- Financial insecurity
- Being a woman in a male-dominated industry
- Being black in a white-dominated environment
- Being indigenous in a land overtaken by settlers
- Living on a reservation
- Witnessing deforestation
- Having a lack of friends
- Having absent parents
- Having parents who argue
- Moving to a new school
- Getting low grades in school
- Comparing oneself with others on social media
- Coming out as homosexual, bisexual, asexual, pansexual, or transgender
- Watching stories in the news
- Trying to get off of drugs or anti-depressants
- Being bitten by an animal
- Being a single parent
- Being abandoned
- Having a disability
- Not having the ability to see, speak, or hear
- Being encouraged or forced to hunt and kill an animal
- Finding out how many tons of plastic are dumped into the ocean each day
- Learning that you were adopted
- Experiencing dental visits and procedures
- Not having enough money to pay for groceries
- Being ignored
- Being feared by someone else
- Birthing a child
- Experiencing body teasing and judgment
- Having social anxiety
- Unintentionally causing harm to someone else
- Being wrongly accused of something
- Being told not to cry or express emotions
- Being continually interrupted
- Being fired from a job
- Losing custody of your children

- Feeling trapped in a profession
- Losing a beloved pet
- Being told "I hate you"

Maybe you've experienced more than one of these wounds? Maybe you've experienced a lot of them? Maybe you've even experienced some of these wounds today? This is just a small glimpse of the thousands of ways that you learned this world can be an unsafe place.

Examples of **what wounds feel like**:

- Trauma
- Shock
- Fear
- A jolt
- Intense impact

Remember the whole and loving heart of our original state? The one where we're naturally open, trusting, and present? Well, when we're wounded, we shift from feeling present and open to feeling scared and shocked.

It's as if our heart says, "Ouch! That hurts."

Together, it would look like:

HEART: *I am here, experiencing life.*
WOUND: *Ouch! That hurts.*

Suddenly, through stinging words, hot stoves, heavy hands, sharp teeth, startling accidents, and the painful wrath of those who couldn't heal their own pain, we're struck by the shocking blows of the human life experience.

As we make our way up and down this mountain of pain and healing here, I'll often refer to these wounds. While they're not comfortable to look at or think about, it is important to do so. Especially as we move into Chapter 9, where we embrace honesty and observation, it's important to be open about what we've been through and look at the roots of our pain.

With that, let's allow ourselves to step forward and begin getting a clearer idea of the wounding in our hearts. Eventually, through knowing where the pain is coming from, we'll have a better understanding of how to heal ourselves and return to the wholeness of our hearts.

WOUNDS CANNOT BE RATED

THE MOMENT WE PLACE OUR WOUNDS on a scale and determine them unfit to qualify, we lose the opportunity to better understand them, and we lose touch with the stem that connects to the root of our pain. In doing so, we overlook very important clues that would unravel the mystery of our struggles.

Ignoring our wounds is an act of self-protection, but it desensitizes us and leads us down a troubled road to suffering. For this reason, it's essential that we don't judge or weigh our traumas, or those of others. We'll never truly know what it's like to be someone else or live their life, so it's not up to us to judge what's *significant* or *insignificant* to them—that's up to each individual. Nor should we self-judge or feel ashamed of ourselves for what we have been through.

For example, maybe you're not very passionate about animals, never had pets growing up, and don't understand why some people are so attached to their pets. For someone else, they may feel a close sense of connection with their pet that is similar to a best friend or family member. If and when that animal friend dies, you may not think much of it and feel that the person's grieving is an overreaction. But to them, they've lost the closest friend they ever had.

Just because our hearts don't all love, open, or hurt in the same way as one another, it doesn't mean we haven't all known and experienced the similar aches and wounds of life.

When we're convinced that someone else doesn't deserve compassion, understanding, or validation for their pain, then we reveal how deprived *we* are from the healing, support, and attention that we desperately need and deserve. It's possible that you've disconnected from your own painful life experiences and the necessary sensitivity of feeling and working through them.

I saw this first-hand during a very moving meeting with a man who I initially made a strong and wrong assumption about. Having spent time in Delhi, Los Angeles, Detroit, Washington D.C, and other places where I perceived suffering to be tangible, visible, and authentic, I underestimated the suffering of a wealthy man living in a prosperous ski town in Colorado.

At the time, I perceived Mike to have a privileged life, one that greatly contrasted the struggles I was dealing with. I imagined that having been raised by seemingly happy parents and coming from a family who had spent generations swimming in financial abundance, that Mike had no idea what *struggling* was. I compared his white skin to my brown skin, and I compared his prosperous bank account to my empty pockets.

Then, thankfully, I was proved wrong. The more I got to know him, the deeper I saw into his world, where I observed a young boy who was ignored and neglected by parents who were too busy. They were swept away with an insatiable hunger for fulfillment—more so than being emotionally available to their child. I saw how he longed for approval and a heartfelt connection with his dad. I saw how he felt like he never really knew his mom.

I saw how deeply insecure he was and that money had been his lifeline in making friends. But beyond dollars, he didn't seem to understand the true value or worth in himself. I watched as he drowned out the cry of his sorrows through substances, clinging to them like a child grasping for the maternal warmth he never had. I felt a loneliness in him as sad and cold as a boarded-up, empty room. Although I could relate to his feeling of loss, it was only to a certain extent because I'm me, not him.

While, yes, I had experienced violence, abuse, addiction, racism, and sexism, I hadn't lived his life and I didn't know his sorrows. On the surface, his life may have looked abundant with riches, but inside he struggled with depression and a constant feeling of loss and loneliness. On the contrary, those who live in poverty and don't have enough food to eat may still have family and feel loved, and who's to say that love isn't worth more than anything in the world?

This was a moment of growth for me because I realized that we *all* suffer and that our suffering will be different. At what point are we willing to see beyond our tightly enclosed walls and stories of suffering to look up and realize that every one of us has experienced pain and challenges?

Some of us wear bruises on our bodies and some in our thoughts, but *all* of us have them in our hearts. At some point, each of us have stumbled, fallen, and grappled with the human life experience. If we're unable to fully witness and understand that, we cut ourselves off from truly understanding ourselves. We also deny ourselves the feeling of being included in the undeniable force of connection that weaves us all together.

Can you remember any experiences in your life (whether significant or trivial) that you may have talked yourself out of acknowledging as deeply jarring or traumatic?

OUR TENDER YOUTH

WHEN WE WERE JUST ENTERING this life, we were so tender, wide-eyed, and present. The pores of our being were expanded and open, absorbing every moment with the intense purity of presence. It's *because* we were so open, so present, and so aware that any wounding during our beginning years was especially shocking and sculpting of our understanding of life.

When we're young, we're not yet trained in the hardening act of carelessness. Caring is our natural, birth-given state and it's within that tender, open-hearted essence of our caring that we experience the most authentic and raw impact of the pain. If we didn't care, we wouldn't hurt, but we do care, and it does hurt.

While we were once surrounded by serene warmth and safety, experiencing a wound is the cold and chilling breeze of being human. It is a stark reality of contrast and intensity that reveals how scary and unsafe this life experience can be. Like so many of us, I was very young when I learned *it's not safe*.

My mom tried so hard to not let us know what was going on throughout the separation to protect us from being more traumatized, and yet I knew. I was four years old and I knew.

In fact, when I was in my mid-20s, I reunited with an old family friend who we had stayed with the night we left my dad. I hadn't seen her since that night, but with tears in her eyes, she said, "Do you know what you said to me that night? You looked to make sure your mom wasn't watching and you leaned in and apologized. You felt so concerned for imposing and said, "*Thank you so much for letting us stay with you. I'm sorry for all of this. We probably won't ever see you again because we're moving far away to be away from my dad.*"

How often do we discard the experiences that the youth endure because we think they're unaware of what's going on? In fact, they know *exactly* what's going on. Maybe they don't quite understand *why*, but they can see and observe *what*.

I didn't want my mom to know that I knew because I understood the pain she was in, and I didn't want to contribute to her feeling more stress and discomfort. Not only that, I was concerned about imposing on the kind woman whose house we were staying in.

How many of us learned to carry the stress, pain, and discomfort of others in the hope of somehow relieving them from the burden? How many of us are *still* doing it today? How many of us withhold our own expression of pain for fear of making others uncomfortable?

Our apprehension of being with or speaking the truth of our discomfort is reflective of the fear initiated in those early years of wounding. Like premature birds being pushed from the warmth of the nest, we were forcibly removed from our feeling of safety. With that harsh, abrupt fall to the ground, we were severed from our feeling of trust.

In those years of development, we also aren't offered the reward of choice, and our opinions often make little impression on the conclusions of the decision-makers. Like bystanders in situations beyond our control, we are in many ways powerless, forced to participate in the stories that play out from other people's unresolved pain.

Can you remember any emotionally painful experiences that happened in your youth?

COLLECTIVE WOUNDING

WITH THAT SAID, NOT ALL WOUNDS and traumas are something we have personally experienced ourselves. We can be equally cracked open by what occurs in the destructive and violent nature of the environment and the world at large. You might not live in a country that's in a state of war, but by watching the news and seeing bombs being dropped, homes being shattered, and children becoming orphans—you may experience the emotionally jarring impact of it.

Maybe you've never been personally threatened by gun violence but there was a shooting at a nearby school that left you feeling shocked and anxious. Hearing about trees being cut down through deforestation may be a painful occurrence happening to an entirely different life form thousands of miles away, but because you *care*, you may experience discomfort and sadness when hearing about it.

It's also very likely that within your lineage and ancestry, there's the imprint of war, violence, and abuse. Perhaps you don't recall experiencing the trauma, but because your parents (or their parents) survived something extremely traumatic, you still carry the echo within you. The imprint of that pain has been cycling (and recycling) for generations, all the way down to you.

Unfortunately, if someone can't understand and heal the pain inside of them, nor understand the pain inside their parents, it's likely they will one day be the parent who causes pain to their children. For generation after generation, we've been lost in cyclical patterns of collective avoidance and distraction. We've been causing pain to our sons, daughters, brothers, sisters, lovers, spouses, friends, community, and environment—all the while not looking at or talking about the tender wounds that are buried and guarded within ourselves.

CREATING WOUNDS

WHAT IF IT'S *you* WHO CREATED THE WOUND in someone else? Because the nature of our true and authentic selves is genuinely caring and loving, the act of causing pain to others can be a very traumatic experience. Maybe it was an accident where you were driving and someone was hurt? Maybe you used to tease and pick on your younger sibling? Regardless of whether it was an accident or something you regretfully meant to do at the time, it's possible that what you're feeling is the strong, shattering feeling of regretful wrongdoing.

Shame and regret is something that many of us feel, whether we're comfortable acknowledging it or not. As we'll talk about in the next chapter, there are many ways that we experience pain after a wound, and whether or not we are the ones to inflict it or receive it, we are likely experiencing the pain and remorse from it. In fact, it's not uncommon to suffer from the wounds we inflict on others more than those that have been inflicted on us.

However, *what if you're not feeling it?* What if you're aware that you caused a wound and *don't* feel the painful effect of your actions? You don't necessarily have to be a sociopath to be dissociated from the pain you cause others. In fact, it's extremely common for us to disengage and numb ourselves to the pain we cause the world around us. Look at what we're doing to the environment and the bee population. Most of us are actually *really* good at not feeling the pain we cause to others.

Also, it's likely that somewhere inside, you *are* feeling it but aren't aware because it shows up in ways other than shame or remorse. It's also possible that because we each carry the gift of an internal *conscience*, when you're ready, someday you will feel it. At some point, we must inevitably acknowledge and feel the deeply impactful effect of our actions.

What happens when the person you've been hurting is yourself? How many times have you said something to your body that you would *never* say to someone else? How many times have you judged, beaten, or reprimanded yourself with hurtful words, neglect, or punishing actions? For many of us, this is a daily way of life—feeling hurt, insecure, ashamed, and beaten down from our own painful and judgmental relationship with ourselves. Just like any other experience of abuse, it can leave us feeling deeply wounded, shocked, and traumatized—requiring an honest and healing confrontation with ourselves to transform the relationship.

As we move further into the book, we'll get onto the path of empowerment and talk a lot about strengthening the awareness and friendship we have with ourselves.

Can you remember any experiences in your life when you may have caused a damaging wound to yourself or someone else?

LOST MEMORIES

MAYBE YOU WOULD ADDRESS YOUR WOUNDS if you could, but you just don't know where they are or what they are? You've tried and you can't find what created so much upheaval in your life and heart? Maybe you remember a few rough patches as a kid but can't recall anything really severe or traumatic? Instead of a logbook of personal wounding, you just have a blank sheet of paper that has "I can't remember" written on it?

This is understandable. In fact, a common response to trauma is to block it out and erase it, in avoidance, denial, and distraction (we'll talk more about this when we get to Chapter 5). It's like our brains are caregivers who quickly rush to our aid, covering our eyes and cupping hands over our ears.

We're protected by the nature of survival and separated from the memories and experiences that could potentially cause us emotional harm. Basically, we forget. Intentionally and unintentionally, we disconnect and dissociate from the truth and forever find ourselves with tilted heads and looks of confusion when trying to recall the cause of our wounds.

If your mind has created a safety buffer of separation between you and your memories, it's done so out of care for your wellbeing. While the forgetting may not necessarily be serving you, it was done with intention for safety. Those memories are painful, so it makes sense why you've separated yourself from them. While they may seem forever gone, they've not been erased; they're just hidden. If you genuinely desire to pull back the curtain to expose them, this intention is a reflection of your readiness for change and healing.

As we move further along our path together, we'll learn more about the different ways we protect ourselves and eventually learn skills to heal the pain instead of avoiding it.

*The storm has passed,
yet the windows are still broken.*

*Dispersed throughout the lawn
like bones,
the shingles lay from the wind.*

*This place hurts.
There's so much work to do.
Too much.*

*A breath.
A sigh.*

*It will take time,
but not forever.*

*One day, this house will be
a home again.*

3.
PAIN

The experience of distress and discomfort caused by injury.

"Give this to them when you get there," my mom said as she handed me a signed note for my elementary teacher explaining, "Please be aware that Katie suffers from motion sickness in vehicles." While I imagine that most kids were overjoyed to take a break from the classroom and go on a fun-filled field trip, I was absolutely distraught. Yes, being on fast-moving buses didn't help, but it wasn't motion sickness that caused my severe stomach aches, diarrhea, and sleepless nights prior to the trip. It was the fear and anxiety of being separated from my mom.

It makes sense. She represented safety and had been my tether to survival through the tornado of trauma. While we had seemingly made it through the storm, we were hurting and distressed. We were insecure and holding onto our freedom intensely, uncertain whether it was ours to keep.

Especially in those early days right after the separation, life was still very stressful and very uncomfortable. As my mom feared my dad finding us, we lived in a state of secrecy. Whether it was a valid concern or just my mom's trepidation, she believed that we were under threat of kidnapping, so our babysitters, teachers, and principals were notified to keep a close eye on us at all times. There was an air of caution surrounding us at school, on the playground, and in the babysitter's yard. To remain protected and hidden, we changed schools numerous times. Like scared and wounded animals, we clung together in grocery stores and had trouble making eye contact with people we didn't know or didn't trust, which was almost everyone at the time.

Personally, I was sad, scared, and grieving. I was confused about what was going on but I was also ashamed of how others perceived us. I felt like it was written on my sleeve. Even though my mom was white, I wasn't. I had the brown skin of my dad and felt uncomfortable and ashamed when people stared at us, sometimes asking, "What race is the father?"

Of course, this brought up the deeper question—*where is the father?* Where is the once beloved member of our whole that was now cut out of family photos? Well, he was on the outside, 500 miles away, peering in longingly through the barbed wire fence of a restraining order.

As for us kids, we followed along and did our best not to ask too many questions. We watched silently and uncomfortably, unaware of what to do. While we didn't voice it, we acutely felt the stress of the situation.

This is what happens when we humans are cracked open by the traumatic happenings of life: we're in pain and we're uncomfortable. We hurt, we grieve, we ache in our hearts and in our bodies, and we lose sleep tracing and retracing memories of the past. This aftershock of pain and discomfort is the *post-trauma*, and it can last for weeks, months, or even years.

<u>Examples of feeling PAIN:</u>
- Discomfort
- Fear
- Sadness
- Shame
- Loneliness
- Insecurity
- Grief
- Disappointment

I often refer to these feelings as the "undesirables," because as natural as it is to feel pain after a wound, it's also a profoundly uncomfortable experience. As a result of that, it can be equally uncomfortable and undesirable to look at, think about, or talk about. Yet, because pain is often what lies beneath the surface of our unhappiness and suffering, it's vital that we look at it, understand it, and talk about it.

Why? Because pain is an alert. You see, we go from whole and open hearts to wounded to in *pain*, like this:

<u>HEART</u>: *I am here, experiencing life.*
<u>WOUND</u>: *Ouch! That hurts.*
<u>PAIN</u>: *I don't feel good. I'm in pain.*

Pain notifies and alerts us that we don't feel good. This makes it a powerful signal to pay attention, to lean into the wound, to find out what happened, and to discover what we need to feel better. Without pain, we can't fully understand how to heal ourselves back to wholeness. So, regardless of how unpleasant the experience and thought of pain may be, there is so much we can learn from it.

As we move forward on our journey together, we'll explore the importance of embracing discomfort in order to relieve it (particularly in Chapter 10.)

For now, let's awaken our bravery and start talking about the infamous, undesirable pain.

THE CRACK OF DIVISION

LET'S THINK BACK TO YOUR ORIGINAL and whole self—and visualize a whole heart within you. When you're inflicted with trauma, it's like a lightning bolt striking your heart. It creates a crack, a wound, a broken heart.

Because of that break, we feel a sense of division and disconnection inside. This internal sense of division affects the way we connect with the world around us and with ourselves. Rather than feeling whole, united, and confident—we feel hurt, insecure, and weak.

Does this sound overly dramatic? Let's think of it another way. Imagine that instead of your sensitive and emotional heart being broken, it's your arm. What would happen then? Your arm is designed to pick things up, so what happens if it's broken in two?

Well, you would likely be in a lot of pain and be unable to fully function or physically operate. You might lose confidence and trust in your abilities and feel insecure.

You see, experiencing emotional pain is a lot like experiencing physical pain. Your heart is made to love, so what happens if it's broken in two? When your heart has been impacted by the harsh intensities of life, you are weakened and not operating at your full capacity. You might feel uneasy, insecure, and disempowered, rather than feeling confident and whole.

FEAR

THERE IS ANOTHER MAJOR ASPECT OF DISCOMFORT that emerges from being wounded: *fear*. Like being torn away from our calm, safe, and trusting selves, fear enters our lives. We no longer feel safe and comfortable—in fact, when we've been hurt, we often feel the opposite. We feel uncertain, apprehensive, insecure, distrusting, and on edge.

Our natural state is to feel at ease and relaxed, and when we experience something jarring and painful (like a wound), our natural and automatic response is fear. Just like experiencing pain, fear is a very useful tool provided by our beings. It alerts us of something or someone "not safe" to keep us from harm. Pain doesn't feel good, so fear is there to prevent pain from happening again. Unfortunately, while fear is something we experience in the initial moment of trauma, it can easily intensify and grow over time.

What exactly happens when we experience fear?

We shift into alert mode. Our breathing rate increases and our heart rate rises. Our adrenal glands are triggered and we go into fight or flight mode, feeling anxious and unsettled. These feelings can last a short while after the impact of the wound or much longer depending on how traumatic the environment is.

Say you're living with someone aggressive, alcoholic, or unpredictable—you're likely living in a constant state of pain and fear. Each week, or each day, you feel shocked and afraid, automatically feeling unsettled, anxious, discontent, unsafe, and insecure.

What if it was years ago that you lived with that person and now, they're a memory from the past? Well, because fear is such a natural and automatic response from our bodies and beings, you can remove yourself from the traumatic situation and still feel that you are not safe. Unless the wound is properly acknowledged and tended to with the soothing relief needed, you can easily find yourself living in a constant state of fear.

This is something that many of us experience without even knowing it. Because we may not know to look directly at the original wounds as the culprit, we can feel continually anxious, insecure, and uncomfortable for a very, very long time. In fact, we can understand that to be who we are and how life is.

It's not true. Living in fear and discomfort is not your true state and life is not to be feared. While there are valid things to be cautious and mindful of in this world, it's very important to understand where the pain and fear originally stem from so you can experience life without feeling continually uncomfortable and insecure.

INSECURITY & THE WOLF

INSECURITY IS AN INTERESTING THING. I've found that we humans often relate insecurity to our physical appearances and our bank accounts, when really, insecurity is a direct response to the fear and pain that results from being wounded.

To better understand this, let's talk about security first.

What is security?

By definition, **security is: to be safe and free from danger or threat.**

When something is secure, it's intact, in place and stationed in safety. "The dish is *securely* placed on the shelf"... "The lock is *secure*." When something becomes *in*secure, then, it's no longer firmly fixed. It's liable to disassemble or break.

Just like anything else that experiences security and insecurity, so do we humans.

When you think back to the original wholeness of your heart, in that true and genuine state of being, your emotional self is intact. Intact meaning whole, complete, and unbroken. You are secure in yourself, secure in your family, and secure in your body.

What happens if you experience painful and impactful wounds that injure you and damage your heart? You become insecure. You are separated from your understanding of wholeness, belonging, and safety. Then, you feel a residual response of feeling threatened, unsafe, and not secure.

For many of us, our deepest wounds happen within the home, within the family, within a seemingly loving relationship where the shared space of trust and safety was compromised or eliminated. With that, our understanding of the security of the human life experience is divided and pulled apart.

We might think it's the big, heavy wounds like divorce, abuse, and death that are worthy of bringing on the aftermath of sadness, shame, grief, and insecurity. Not necessarily. The subtle and hidden wounds—the sharp slash of hurtful words, let-downs, and breakups—can also cause deep pain and discomfort.

Imagine a wolf in the wild. The wolf is part of a pack, a familial network of support. It works together with the pack to access safety, nourishment, and protection. Now, imagine the wolf is picked on and attacked by other wolves in the pack. Where there was once an internal sense of trust, inclusion, and belonging, there are now feelings of exclusion and separation.

The wounded wolf goes from a place of feeling *secure* to feeling *insecure*. Rather than feeling a sense of connection and safety, it feels displaced, excluded, ostracized, and fearful for its wellbeing. Without the protection and support of its loved ones, it feels vulnerable, exposed, and at risk of more wounding.

Maybe you weren't physically attacked (or maybe you were), but like the wolf, you too can feel excluded and insecure because of hurtful words, neglect, abandonment, or painful emotional assaults.

Maybe it was a step-father or a sister? Maybe it was someone at school who said or did something that generated your feelings of exclusion, remorse, or insecurity? Maybe it was you telling yourself something hurtful and judgmental that caused your feelings of insecurity?

Whoever it was, without a sense of trust and inclusion, we become disconnected and internally separated, and we drift further into the realm of fear, unconsciousness, and eventually, suffering.

Hidden wound, hidden pain

I once worked with a woman named Gina, who was seeking counsel to heal herself of compulsive eating. We spent months searching like two detectives through her childhood, her relationships, and her lunch breaks to find the hidden stones that wounded her and eventually led to her feeling insecure and anxious in her body. We were on a mission to find out *what happened* to create such insecurity and feelings of unworthiness in her.

Her parents were relatively happily married. She was never physically or emotionally abused (that she could remember). Her family lived modestly, but comfortably. Yet, something caused her to feel extremely insecure, and unworthy. Something caused her to have a constant need to feel accepted and included.

One day, she said, "There's this memory that's been coming up lately, but I never say anything." Instantly, it felt important, so I encouraged her to continue. She said, "Honestly, I'm so embarrassed about it that I don't even want to say anything. It was so long ago and so small that I feel pathetic that it's even a thing I think about, but… I have a recurring memory of being about 11 years old and at recess on the playground."

Then, she began to cry. She was having trouble speaking because so much emotion was beginning to release itself.

"My best friend—like, best friend in the world—had just made friends with another group of friends. She came over to me and said, 'I'm not your friend anymore', and she wasn't. She completely ended our friendship and stopped talking to me. Stopped wanting to hang out with me, forever. I was devastated. I got really depressed and withdrawn. She never came back to our friendship. It just ended. My parents were concerned. I was completely depressed and broken-hearted and in some ways, I think I still feel like no one wants to be my friend."

That was it. We eventually uncovered more subtle wounds, like her father's depression and her mother's tendency to avoid conflict. However, the moment we found her childhood loss of a friend is when the door opened to better understanding. It was also the moment she stopped telling herself, "I should be stronger and have forgotten this little thing already."

How many years had Gina talked herself out of looking at that wound because she was so ashamed of being sensitive and seemingly weak for still feeling the discomfort of it? How many of us are hurting from the quiet, unassuming experiences in life? How many of us have forced ourselves to keep our attention elsewhere—stuffing down the pain and chewing on the idea that we should be tough, numb, and indifferent? That we should be strong enough to handle a little breakup or a rough moment here and there?

A *lot* of us.

Can you remember ever feeling separated or excluded from a relationship, family, or group?

How did it feel?

THE BACKPACK OF SHAME

SHAME IS VERY SIMILAR TO INSECURITY. It's a powerful and uncomfortable form of pain that is a direct response to being wounded.

Unlike insecurity, shame is an oversized, heavy backpack with the word "wrong" written on it in obscenely large letters. It is a response to the moments in our lives where we feel we have made unwise decisions and should do things differently in the future, but it keeps us weighed down in a state of sorrow, humiliation, and regret about those things. Through the influence of our parents, culture, profession, and/or religious belief systems, a lot of us learn to wear the heavy burden of shameful self-annihilation day after day.

Both shame and insecurity stem from fear, and both bring up feelings of disconnection and exclusion from others. The difference with shame is that it's directly associated with feeling *personally responsible* and at fault. When we are ashamed, we feel foolish, embarrassed and insecure. We feel that we need to apologize for being bad, broken, wrong, and unworthy. As if the wounded wolf blamed itself for the incident and felt responsible for being attacked, then eventually excluded itself from others because of it.

Shame is unique in that it's a pain response to a wound and also a more aggressive form of self-abuse (which we'll talk more about when we get to forms of defense in Chapter 6.)

- Maybe it's the shape of your body, or the way nothing seems to ease the pain as much as alcohol?
- Maybe you aren't able to provide for your family as much as they need?
- Maybe you just feel nervous and out of place being around people?
- Maybe it's all of the painful words said to you by others, or the hurtful things you said to someone else?

Whatever it is, if there's an element of feeling responsible and (unfairly) blaming yourself, then it's likely that you are wearing the heavy backpack of shame.

Some of the things you might hear yourself saying are:

"It's my fault."
"I should have done better."
"I'm a bad person."
"There's something wrong with me."
"I'm not good enough."
"I'm the reason for the pain."

Sadly, when we see ourselves as the problem, we end up excluding ourselves from the pack and forcing ourselves to remain in a constant state of exclusion and survival. In doing so, we silence our voices, our dreams, and our bodies. We succumb to a state of suffering that we somehow feel we deserve.

Taking a life

A very tender and heartfelt experience that I've heard from numerous people, mostly males, is the shame of injuring and killing animals. Many of us were raised in environments and families that don't honor the consciousness of animals and instead encourage hunting or slaughter. However, these seemingly innocent and meaningless acts of killing for pleasure or food can fester in the heart, especially for younger people.

My husband Kurt recalls numerous memories from his childhood growing up in Texas where he was too young to understand the full spectrum of what shooting an animal meant. As a sincere animal lover from a young age, it was a profound shock and trauma for him to see the lifeless body of the bunny rabbit or squirrel, knowing he was the one who did it. He was the killer.

In moments like these, the natural reaction of crying is often discouraged by family members, and the wounded person may be told to "be a man" and swallow it down. Unfortunately, this is detrimental to anyone who needs to process and understand a traumatic event, and the long-term effect can be a deep sense of shame.

For decades, somewhere inside, Kurt felt guilty and ashamed of himself, like a villain who had taken the lives of innocent victims and later realized the error of their ways. It took many years for him to talk about the traumatizing events of hunting, and to eventually forgive himself to be freed from the shame.

(In Chapter 14, we'll talk about the importance of forgiveness and self-forgiveness.)

SADNESS & THE UNDERCURRENT

SADNESS IS ONE OF THE MOST COMMON responses to being emotionally injured. It's as if our open and loving hearts retract inward, deflated from the painful impact of the wound. When we're hurt, especially if it was intentionally by someone else, we feel as though we're not cared for and not included. And the longer we go without receiving the support and connection we need to overcome this pain, the more our feeling of sadness intensifies.

When I think back to childhood and how it felt for me, my mom, and my sisters to be separated from my dad, we were sad. We were hurting and we were grieving the loss of our family. We felt the break of our familial connection and the break within ourselves. And as much as we developed an understanding that we were "better off without him," it felt very uncomfortable not having him in our lives.

Then, I try to imagine the regret, sadness, and abandonment that *he* must have felt after losing his wife and daughters when his internal wounds became external ones. When he was sentenced to endure the deepest sorrow of his life, losing his family to his unhealed wounds and pain, he was also sentenced to be with himself each day. He had to look in the mirror and *be* with the sadness, shame, anger, and loss inside himself.

I think about how many of us have experienced even one of the thousand wounds of the human life experience, and I realize the strong and collective undercurrent of sadness running beneath the surface of our beings. Without the constructive support, connections, and tools needed to transform our pain, many of us find ourselves caught in the current of pain for years after the wound occurs. This mournful place is somewhere that each of us deserves to be freed from.

Yet, as common as sadness is, it's frequently avoided and covered up. From fear of being judged, called a "downer," or seen as the one raining on everyone's parade, we often distract others from seeing our sadness and distract ourselves from feeling it. Ironically, when someone openly and honestly shows their sadness, they're closer to understanding their pain and closer to freeing themselves from it.

GRIEF & THE HEAVY BUCKET

WHEN WE REALLY LOVE SOMEONE, our hearts open wide and we give and receive the nourishment of love. Our love is nutrient-rich affection, and we use it to water our shared garden with our loved ones.

When we lose those loved ones, it's not just the loss of hearing their voice and the lack of feeling their hugs—it's that our affection has nowhere to go. We get so used to visiting the well each day, filling the bucket, and watering the flowers that when our loved ones depart, we are carrying the bucket of love with nowhere to pour it. We not only ache from not receiving their care, we become weighed down by the heavy bucket of unexpressed love. We carry the burden of grief for not being able to *give* our care.

Sadly, each of us has to walk this path of grief again and again because death happens again and again. Even though it's a natural and inevitable occurrence, as certain as night and day, it can feel so unnatural and unnecessary when it occurs. As if there was a mistake and somehow the angels picked the wrong dog, the wrong child, the wrong husband.

Why?

We find ourselves pleading with the sky.

Why him? Why her? Why now?

We are baffled, shocked, and sideswiped, as if nothing and no one could have prepared us; as if we knew it could happen and yet never believed it would.

At times, the pain of grief can be so severe that it's like drowning, lost in tears and gasping for air. With no option but to just ride it out, we can easily become too much and too heavy for others to be around. If the tears haven't dried up after a couple of weeks, we become a problem—like our grief is as undesirable as death itself. Like there is no place for someone who is carrying a heavy bucket and a face streaked with tears, as opposed to a smile.

So, we turn away. We swallow our sadness and grief, and we encourage others to do the same. We face the television, the springtime, and the merry news of the newly born. We focus on anything that distracts us from the deep ache of sorrow within us.

The different forms of grief

Though we often grieve for losses that involve a death, not all grief relates to death. We can feel variations of grief at the loss of a friendship or a job. We can feel grief from a breakup or from witnessing the suffering of someone else. And if we feel a sense of connection to both of our parents, we may experience grief when they are separated through divorce.

Unfortunately, there is a lack of constructive and welcoming spaces within our society for those who are grieving. There are few places to properly process, understand, and express the pain. As a result, grief is an emotion that is often masked, overlooked, and transmuted into avoidance. It is pushed below the surface.

We can see this in the way that the majority of humans process our sorrow for what's happening to the Earth. We don't. Because our lives and lifestyles require us to stay active, busy, and focused on our personal agenda, we turn away and avoid looking at the sad reality of what's happening to our planet.

Trees are the lungs of our planet, but an estimated 3.5–7 billion of them are being deforested each year, and over 40,000 species of plants and animals are currently on the IUCN endangered list. Each year, around 8 million metric tons of plastic are dumped into the ocean, and that's as well as the 150 million tons *already* circulating in marine environments.

How do you feel when you read these statistics?
Do you feel sad?
Do you feel concerned?
Do you feel grief?

Really acknowledging the destruction of the environment is both traumatically wounding and deeply painful, which is why so many of us *don't* stop to look at it or feel it. We're afraid to experience more pain, because most of us are already drowning in our struggles and grasping for safety, so we don't feel we can handle any more sorrow. Instead, we focus on dinner plans, our upcoming vacation, and what's happening on the latest episodes of our favorite television program.

In reality, our hearts are aching and we are grieving inside.

While I don't imagine that healing our relationship with the planet is an easy task or one that can happen swiftly, I do believe that when we overcome our fear of pain enough to look at the truth, we can better understand and process our grief. And each time we do, we become stronger, more confident, and closer to being healed. And we naturally become more capable of applying that same level of courage, awareness, and healing to the world around us.

I'm guessing you've heard the phrase "when you heal yourself, you heal the world"? This has much, if not everything, to do with this work we're doing together right now.

Do you ever avoid processing and expressing your grief because it's too painful?

*I imagine a world
where we are comfortable and confident
enough in ourselves to not be afraid or ashamed of
our aching hearts.*

*Where we are fearless, confident, and honest
with the truth inside ourselves, and
welcoming of the truth in one another.*

*Wherever your heart hurts,
may you know you're not alone.*

4.
NEED

The state of requiring support, safety, and healing.

"Help!!!" I hollered out from my room, where I was lying face down in bed with my leg hanging off the side. "I need help!" There, on the white-painted wood floor, was a quickly expanding pool of blood. I pulled myself over to get a better look at my ankle and saw the cut that blood was spurting out from and yelled again, "Hurry! Someone! Help me!"

Back then, before we grew old enough for our own individual rooms, my twin sister and I had twin beds that were basically mattresses plopped onto very simple, low bed frames. The bed frames had very, very sharp edges, which is how the incident occurred.

If something like that happened to me now, I would probably make a quick dash to the bathroom (after releasing words of profanity), wrap the wound, and clean the mess. But at eight years old, I was scared and intimidated and I didn't know what to do. All I knew to do was yell for help.

Being so young and unabashed at the time, it made sense that if I was injured and in pain, I needed help, so I asked for it. Easy and simple. And because it was a cut on my physical body, I had a stronger awareness of what the wound was, where the pain was coming from, and the urgency of caring for it (just so you know, help came running and the ankle was saved).

Emotional pain is not so clear. While our new life in the small town seemed like a fresh start, the pain was still there. I still felt uncomfortable and confused inside. My dad was still gone and he and my mom would frequently assemble in court for hearings where they battled it out for custody.

This went on for eight years.

Only a few times times during those years did the court grant him permission to see us. Each time, it was supervised at a shopping mall where he poured his love and emotions out to us as we sat in the awkward silence of not knowing how to feel or respond. Eventually, mom gained full custody and dad was sent away defeated, without any future contact with his children.

Gradually, as if the stagnant pain inside me was beginning to ferment, I became increasingly uncomfortable in my body. I began to feel anxiety and had trouble focusing in the classroom. I got poor grades and began failing classes, something that would continue throughout my years of schooling. This brought on more feelings of sadness and shame, and especially when I was alone, I felt horrible.

When I was seven or eight years old, my emotional pain and need for support began transmuting into an anxious and restless *hunger*.

In the morning, during school, after school, after dinner—hungry. Hungry for attention, hungry for new toys, hungry for anything, *especially* food. At the time, I didn't understand that the hunger was actually a deeper need calling out from the pain within me. Just like the cut on my ankle, I was injured and needed help.

When our tender hearts have experienced painful wounds and abrasions, we need to care for ourselves in the same way we would for a physical wound. The pain alerts us that something's wrong, which is followed by a *need* to care and tend to that wound.

Examples of feeling NEED:

- Distress
- Anxiety
- Restlessness
- Fearfulness
- Nervousness
- Emotional hunger
- Sense of urgency
- Desire for attention
- Desire for acceptance
- Desire for control

While there's immediate distress and unease created by the initial impact of the wound, intensified with the experience of pain, it's in the state of need where the fear begins bubbling up like molten rock and spewing out.

It would go:

<u>HEART</u>: *I am here, experiencing life.*
<u>WOUND</u>: *Ouch! That hurts.*
<u>PAIN</u>: *I don't feel good. I'm in pain.*
<u>NEED</u>: *I'm hurting and I'm scared. I need healing.*

In those moments of emotional pain, we *need* relief. We need to experience connection and know that we're not alone; that we belong. We need to open up and release the emotions and feelings of pain deep inside. And just like if we're injured or unwell, we need the medicinal warmth of comfort and love.

Unfortunately, we often associate feeling need with *being needy*, and as a result, we may see it as negative. But like the importance of the pain and fear that precedes it, need is an indicator of being wounded. So, we can think of pain, fear, and need as being friends of ours who have good intentions, but we must be discerning with them because their friendship isn't always healthy for us.

The issue is, if we don't take action and tend to the pain in constructive ways, then the need will potentially spiral into the realm of unconscious fear, leaving us anxious, distressed, and on our way to suffering, which is *not* what we want.

As we travel this path together, we'll go a lot of places and cover a lot of important ground. Each step in the process is important to understand. However, this stage of need is especially important and a pinnacle moment on the journey towards suffering and eventually out of it.

Why? Because the key to our healing lies in understanding what the wound is, how we feel because of it, and what we *need* to feel better. At some point in the not-too-distant future, the focus of our journey will be about understanding our needs and getting them met.

Simply put, when we don't get our needs met, we suffer.

When we get them met, we heal.

THE ECHO OF PAIN

WHEN WE THINK BACK TO THOSE intense moments of wounding when the lightning bolt of trauma struck our tender hearts, the experience came with a sound.

Very similar to an actual lightning strike, this shocking, cataclysmic explosion of force slices into the atmosphere of our beings. It radiates an intensity so great that there is a huge vibration, which ripples outward. Not only does the lightning of the wound create a shocking resonance, so too does the thunder of pain that rumbles after it.

Sadly, because so many of us learned to not acknowledge our wounds or consciously identify our pain, we can still feel the echo of a wound that happened long ago. It's as if that thunder is trapped in a closed space, and so it reverberates for months or years, bouncing and ricocheting throughout our beings and our lives.

This is often what a need feels like—an echo of discomfort reminding us of the painful wound inside that needs our attention. While the lightning storm may have long since passed, the feeling of discomfort and the need to tend to the pain remains.

Maybe you're still feeling the grief from an accident in your youth or a breakup two years ago? Maybe you had an intense argument last week and still feel nervous and unsettled by it?

Regardless of what happened and when, without bringing awareness to the root cause of the wound and receiving the care you need to heal the pain, you will likely still feel the response of discomfort, anxiousness, and restlessness echoing out from it.

Without considering the wound within yourself as the culprit, you feel the vibration of discomfort echoing, though you don't know where it's coming from. Like being lost in an echo chamber, you may instead associate the discomfort as being caused by something outside yourself —like your spouse, your job, your family members, or a random person ahead of you on the highway.

You may find yourself saying:

"It's his fault I feel this way."
"She's the problem."
"They don't love me enough."
"I can't stand being around them."
"I'm not fulfilled by them."

In reality, the pain and need are echoing out from a wound deep within *you*, not them. Those waves of distress, anxiousness, and discomfort will likely remain inside you, echoing and bouncing around all the surfaces of your life until you're ready to look within yourself for the cause.

What does nervousness and tension feel like for you?

Can you think of any experiences where the pain from your past may have been projected onto your current life?

HUNGER & LONGING

WHAT DOES HUNGER FEEL LIKE TO YOU? Is it the gurgling pangs in your belly when you've gone too long without food? Is it the anxiousness and irritability that makes it hard to focus on anything else when all you can think about is eating?

Yes, we hunger for food and we also hunger for more than food. Just like the discomfort in our physical bodies when we need nourishment, we can experience anxiousness, irritability, and discomfort when our hearts haven't received the nurturing and nourishment they need. Like a longing, thirsting, yearning need for fulfillment, we try to fill a deep and ravenous emptiness inside us.

The experience of hunger is intentionally uncomfortable to get our attention and notify us that maintenance is needed. Just like physical hunger notifies us that we need sustenance and physical pain notifies us that something is injured or unwell, emotional hunger is a blinking light telling us that something inside needs our attention.

However, we may confuse the emotional need for attention, nourishment, and care with the *physical* feeling of hunger. Thus, we may find ourselves constantly trying to appease, soothe, and nourish ourselves with anything that takes away that discomfort. Once we latch onto something that provides a sense of relief (such as food, alcohol, social media, orgasms, aggressive venting, etc.), we identify that external substance or action as being relief from the discomfort.

Unfortunately, this painful and innocent journey of trying to soothe the pain as best we can may easily lead us down the path to addiction. And because the hunger is coming from the heart and not the body, it becomes an insatiable and unquenchable yearning. So, not only is emotional hunger unpleasant, but it is also a layered dilemma to solve. Like multiple alarms going off, we have to soothe the feeling of hunger *and* go within to address the wounds beneath it.

However, if we're unwilling or unable to look at the original wound, we may get caught in a cycle of trying to constantly tend to the emotional pain by temporarily appeasing the discomfort of the hunger—without going deeper to understand why the alarm is sounding and what it's trying to communicate. And so, we fail to realize that the pain can't be physically healed or fulfilled until the wounded heart is consciously seen, acknowledged, and cared for.

Do you ever experience a hunger-like need for something?
What are some things (besides food) that you hunger for?

THE INSATIABILITY OF SOCIAL MEDIA

I OFTEN THINK OF HUNGER AND NEED when I think of social media. We need connection, comfort, and love in our moment of feeling insecure, sad, and uncomfortable—and so social media is a sticky and alluring web.

In many ways, social media is a resource that allows people from all over the world to correspond and connect. It also provides news, stimulation, information, and networking, all things that we humans feel reliant on. And it's definitely possible to experience genuine friendship and honest, heartfelt exchanges through social media.

But how many of us actually log in to social media with the genuine intention of accessing news, information, and connection? More likely, we're scrolling in an attempt to ful*fill* an inner sense of emptiness and loneliness. A brief moment checking social media can easily sink from minutes to hours. It can lure us into a seductive, drug-like state that is supposedly calming and relaxing, when in reality, it's the opposite.

Basically, social media is a kitchen. You might be hungry and have the intention to go in and eat something, then be done. But if you go in to graze (without intention) because you're trying to fill an emotional emptiness, you may find yourself mindlessly *snack-scrolling*. Before you know it, you've been in front of the screen-fridge for hours, binging on copious images, stories, egos, and dramas. Perhaps you went in with some inner need for nourishing connection, but you leave feeling stuffed, lonely, and disconnected.

For anyone already feeling insecure and ashamed, it's a dangerous place with the potential to cause intensified feelings of self-doubt and worthlessness. It's a palace of smoke and mirrors, where the truth is often concealed behind walls of false confidence and insincere happiness. In this place, it's easy for us to hide in our protective ego cage and present tales to one another that are not always genuine or honest.

I saw this with Gloria, who I spent months doing counsel with. Each week when we met, our goal was to find the root of her pain and why she was struggling with insecurity and bouts of depression. While she was physically very healthy and had done years of work to heal her childhood traumas, she was still suffering. "Sometimes, I'm fine. I feel great about myself. Other times, I just drop off into an abyss of feeling down on myself."

As if solving a mystery, I asked her to break down what a normal day looks like for her. Suspicious of caffeine or a hidden sugar fixation, I wanted to know why she mysteriously felt good, then dropped into an emotional well. "I start my day with a light breakfast, then usually sit at the table and do some online work."

"Ok, is the online work for your business?" I asked.

"Pretty much. I have to post a bunch of content on social media to get my name out there. Honestly, it really stresses me out and feels like this huge burden I have to uphold in order to succeed."

Suddenly, I sensed we were getting to the source of her discomfort. "You sign on in the morning, then is that it? Are you done for the day?"

"No, once I post something, I check it *constantly*. Like, all day long, which is awful because then I'm seeing masses of other people's posts where they're thriving and succeeding," her voice was both frustrated and deflated.

I replied, "Gloria, I think you might need to use some discernment in how much you engage with social media. I think it might be generating a lot of shame and feelings of entrapment for you."

By working together to create a sacred structure in her daily routines and put in place firm and mindful boundaries around her time spent on social media, she instantly felt less burdened, less trapped, and less inundated by the hundreds of daily reminders that she wasn't good enough or successful enough. Very quickly, she became more balanced and emotionally grounded.

Now, I'm not saying that social media is a bad thing, but it's important to enter with intention so you can exit feeling whole, rather than feeling more disconnected, insecure, and unfulfilled.

When we reach Chapter 11, we'll talk more about connection and ways of creating a constructive and healthy relationship with social media, rather than one that is potentially hazardous to our health and wellbeing.

Are you ever drained or negatively altered after being on social media? What does that feel like?

THE NEED FOR INCLUSION & ATTENTION

WHETHER IT'S OUR PRESENCE ON SOCIAL MEDIA or the way we choose to dress when walking down the street, another common way that our unmet needs for connection, comfort, and love play out is through the need for attention and approval.

Think back to the wild wolf. If we were excluded or disconnected from the pack (our family, peers, partner, or society) at any time, we may have understood it as we aren't important, cared about, or loved.

If we don't get those needs properly healed and tended to, we may have an ongoing sense of insecurity and yearning to be included and reconnected in the circle. This internal feeling of lack in who we are encourages us to seek continual attention, compliments, and reassurance that we are important and included.

This ongoing need for attention also contributes to the "me first" behavior that much of the world displays. If someone is in need, and therefore in a constant state of repair, they may pull the majority of their own and other people's attention inward to continually focus on themselves. As a result, they may appear egocentric, selfish, or narcissistic. However, we have to understand that beneath the layers, they're in pain and trying their best to soothe their insecurity, loss, and internal separation.

In other words, "I didn't get enough so I don't have enough to share. Your needs are important but I don't have enough time, energy, or resources to contribute to you and your needs because I need to focus on me and my needs."

This is also reflected in the way we feel the need to receive approval and acceptance from others. Whether through social media, peer groups, career settings, family gatherings, or community environments, we are often driven to ensure that we are not excluded. We strive to look attractive, be financially successful, and be accepted and respected by others.

While achieving these things may potentially offer a sense of happiness and fulfillment, there's often an underlying intention that stems from fear, need, and a sense of lack. The underlying narrative is: "If you accept me, then I will feel included. When I feel included, I'll feel safe, secure, protected, and important—and this will allow me to feel a sense of belonging."

Another way that this reveals itself is when we succumb to destructive and judgmental camaraderie with peers. It goes like this: someone you love and care about says something judgmental and hurtful about or towards someone else. Inside, you don't agree and your conscience hesitates. However, in honor of the relationship you share with your loved one who is dishing out the negativity, you agree with them. You withhold your feelings and nod along.

Why do you do this?

Because you're afraid. You're seeking love, connection, and inclusion, and you don't want to be left out of the pack. You want to feel secure. By confiding their intimate feelings and judgments to you, that person is displaying what seems to be trust in you, and that feels like a valuable form of connection that you don't want to lose or jeopardize. So… you agree with them.

Regardless of how judgmental or destructive their behavior is, you nod your head to feel included and avoid being outcasted, or worse—the one who is being judged. Essentially, you agree to judge someone else so that you're protected from the judgment and you do this because you need to feel included and secure inside the pack.

There's also a strong likelihood that whoever is initiating the judgment is not genuinely confident or secure in themselves (we'll talk more about this in Chapter 6). Because so many of our wounds result from being ignored, neglected, or abandoned, we often share our destructive and judgmental remarks with others to be seen and heard. Our internal dialogue here is:

"any attention is better than no attention," and this can lead us to being rude, ostentatious, obnoxious, or even destructive to receive any form of attention.

This is something you might notice among people who are argumentative or who contradict others and push buttons to get a reaction. From an outside perspective, it may look like they are comfortable creating negativity and disharmony. However, the underlying reality may be that they're actually very *un*comfortable in themselves. Rather than overly confident as they appear, they're hurting and afraid. They're insecure and need attention to gain a temporary sense of connection and reassurance that they're not being forgotten or abandoned by the pack.

Can you recall any moments in your life when you didn't receive the attention and support you needed?
Did this lack of attention generate any feelings of anxiety for you?

THE NEED FOR CONTROL

ANOTHER WAY THAT WE OFTEN TRY to soothe and tend to the pain inside us is through control. While control carries the qualities of both need and protection, there is often an underlying fear and yearning within it.

For those of us who feel a need to control, it likely has a lot to do with the control we lacked in other, more poignant moments in our life. Whether it was childhood abuse, rape, an overbearing parent, or a controlling partner, there are many experiences where we can lose our sense of empowerment and respect in our bodies and our voices. If our wishes and requests weren't honored and we couldn't constructively protect or defend ourselves, we can be left feeling insecure, sad, and uncomfortable.

It's not just past experiences that have this effect but present ones too. We can be displaced by shocking and unexpected experiences, which make us feel like we've been thrown off-guard, or like the rug has been pulled out from beneath us. A divorce that came out of nowhere or a loved one being suddenly killed can leave us feeling unsafe, on-edge, and frightened by the unexpected occurrences of life.

Even though the underlying needs may be to feel heard (connection), feel safe (comfort) and know that we're respected (love), we may not get those needs met. Because of that, the need may play itself out through a temporary sense of security gained from knowing that we're in charge and have everything in our control. If everything is predictable, organized, and properly in place, we believe we can avoid any more pain from unexpected threats. We may do this by controlling our children, spouses, bodies, diets, lawns, dirty dishes, and so on.

Though our controlling and micromanaging ways may be unbearable to those around us, there is an underlying current of fear and insecurity propelling our actions. Our inner dialogue is: *As long as everything is in order and I'm in control, I can trust that I'm safe and won't be hurt again.*

Within the need for control, we may have a need to keep things incessantly clean and orderly. Because many of our wounds leave us feeling ashamed or embarrassed, it may seem like we're confused, disassembled, and unkempt inside. One way we try to manage our sense of internal disorder is by obsessively tending, regulating, and organizing everything around us. We are trying to compensate for our internal dishevelment and disarray, especially if we lack confidence and understanding of the wholeness of ourselves.

In that sense, the internal dialogue might be: *As long as I appear together, clean, secure and confident on the outside, no one will see what a weak and broken mess I am inside, not even me.*

Now, if you relate to any of these traits or patterns, please release your shame and self-judgement right now. The reality is, if you're presenting yourself in a certain way because you're feeling uncomfortable inside, that's no reason to be hard on yourself. Somewhere inside, your focus on your external appearance stems from your lack of feeling worthy, safe, and secure in who you are—and that's an innocent and understandable response to your pain.

As we'll talk about, especially in Chapters 14 and 15, true confidence and a healthy sense of security in ourselves comes from within us. Regardless of how perfect, clean, or flawless we may appear on the outside, our inner selves are often depleted and very much in need of our own care, respect, and attention. We've forgotten what it feels like to belong or feel at home in our lives and in our bodies.

When we begin offering ourselves the nourishment of self-care and support, we stop needing to control and "fix" everything that appears askew outside ourselves, because we realize the truth: that we're fully balanced, complete, and whole beings *inside*. From this, we find empowerment and fulfillment within, rather than constantly, painfully trying to present a facade of physical perfection to feel worthy and accepted.

A WORLD IN NEED

BECAUSE MOST OF US HAVE BEEN DEEPLY wounded and have unresolved pain inside, we live in a world that is predominantly in a state of desperation and need. Many of us don't know where we belong or who to talk to when we need support, and rather than opening up to one another and experiencing healthy and honest connection, we get lost in our anxiety and fear.

Without a healthy connection to the source of our longing or the noble heart within it, we are constantly and desperately seeking full*fill*ment and emotional connection through material objects and temporary comforts. We have an insatiable hunger for *more* to make up for everything we feel emotionally deprived of. More clothes, more food, more cars, more likes, more sales, more everything. Where there was once an emotional need for healing, it became a hunger, then an insatiable hunger, then an insatiable *wanting*. Sadly, we have turned into a species addicted to that wanting.

In fact, the average American produces around 1.5 tons of trash per year. This means that every 26 years, each person fills a semi-truck worth of unnecessary stuff headed straight into the landfills and oceans. Yes, a lot of that may be necessary food waste, but how much of it is unnecessary clothes, toys, shoes, decorations, gadgets, trinkets, and makeup we chose to purchase because we were seeking fulfillment, comfort, and acceptance?

Why are we doing this?

Because we're hurting and we're afraid. At some point, we lost trust in one another and lost touch with the essence of connection. We began exchanging the warmth of love and family for the cold and sterile reward of personal gain.

What's more, our industrial and capitalistic society often encourages these feelings of insatiable hunger, dependency, and longing. Unless you *buy something*, *do something*, or *change something*, you're made to believe that you're not worthy of being something. The carrot of completion is constantly dangled in front of us, always one inch and a few dollars out of reach.

What can we do about it?

We can awaken deeper levels of connection within ourselves and rejoin the broken pieces of our hearts. By becoming courageously aware of our wounds and where our emotional pain is stemming from, we actively and constructively take action to heal ourselves. Each time, we feel more at ease and satiated, and we want less and less in order to feel whole.

The less we need, the less we want.
The less we want, the less we take.
The less we take, the more we can give.

*Perhaps your mind wanders at times,
thoughts whispering,
reminding you how alone,
unworthy, and lost you are.*

*If so, may you be reminded right now and always—
the pain and hunger that plagues your heart
is not something you created
nor is it yours to carry.*

*The pure and tender essence of your being was born into
a world that was already hurting when you arrived.*

*This pain is an ache that each member of this family is
working through daily
to heal and overcome.*

*May each and every one of us be reminded
that we're not here to continue the story of fear and pain.*

We're here to create a new story:

Love.

5.
PROTECTION

The experience of feeling sheltered and protected; separated from harm.

WHILE I DON'T HAVE A LOT OF MEMORIES of my grandmother, my Daadi Maa, I do have a very clear and distinct recollection of the way she smelled—like warm kitchen spices, sunlight, and silk. The memories I have of her are laden with angelic hues, and each glimpse comes wrapped in fragrance and warmth.

In one memory, we were riding in the car after a day-long outing and she was in the backseat with us little ones. As I began to doze off, she put her arms around me and laid my head on her lap, streaming her fingers through my hair. I didn't speak Hindi and she didn't speak English, but together we spoke the language of love and I remember going into somewhat of a trance before I fell asleep, swept away by her nurturing touch.

Throughout the divorce, my mother's and father's sides separated from one another and it was many years before I was reintroduced to my dad's family. Sadly, by the time I had reconnected with my Indian relatives, both of my grandparents had long since passed away, and those moments of resting on her lap in the car would be the last.

Sometimes, I would think about her and remember fragments of the past. As if trying to recall a dream that was faint and out of reach, I would ask my mom questions to learn more, like "What happened when we were young?" and "Where does papa live?" and "What is India like?"

In response, the door of communication would slam shut. She would get protective and defensive, claiming the importance of not thinking about it and not talking about it. Rather than offering the intricate stories and missing clues I needed, she would close up. It was too much for her. Too many wounds, too much pain.

I imagine that if she had the support she had needed to process her own trauma, maybe she could have talked about the abuse and worked through whatever frequently woke her up in terror at night. Maybe she would've been more equipped to help us process ours. She wasn't, though. She didn't have the counsel or support she needed, and she wasn't able to guide us through those uncomfortable places.

She protected herself from the overwhelming pain by avoiding it and taught us to do the same. "That was then, this is now. Don't think about it, don't talk about it."

It worked. I stopped talking about it. I stopped trying to make sense of the many broken pieces of memory. I learned that thinking and talking about the past brings the pain to the surface, and if I didn't want me or my mom to feel the pain, I had to swallow it down and *forget about it* (which as you'll see, is definitely not the solution).

Unfortunately, without feeling able to address the wounds and process the pain that I desperately needed to understand and release, I didn't get my needs met. I didn't have a network of emotional support or a safe place to understand and heal what was trapped inside me. Instead, I turned away and immersed myself in whatever gave me a temporary sense of relief. For me, that was food.

Food was a way for me to numb the pain and avoid the uncomfortable, undesirable feelings inside. Rather than openly and honestly speaking about what I was feeling and what I needed, I closed up. I distracted myself and disconnected from the truth that I was hurting inside.

From the age of seven to thirteen, I gained over 100 pounds without growing much taller. I was considered overweight and constantly picked on. This brought on a continual cycle of wounding, pain, need, and protection—as I constantly felt hurt, then soothed myself through eating, then gained more weight, then experienced more judgement, more shame, and more eating.

Then, high school happened. I entered the sticky web of peers, popularity, and hormones. No longer was it just the old wounds I was trying to figure out—now, my body was a gaping problem that needed fixing.

At 13, I skipped my first meal and explored the realms of anorexia. While it successfully shrunk my body to the bones, I felt separated from the food that I had become dependent on for comfort and relief. So, at 14, I threw up my first meal and entered the enticing and hollow chambers of bulimia, which allowed me to eat all the food I wanted while not gaining weight or getting judged for being "fat."

Bulimia provided a steady, destructive, and soothing relief. Rather than feeling the aching pain in my heart, I constantly felt distracted and numb, no longer helpless and empty-handed.

Protection has a way of doing that. Even though the pain and needs are still very much alive and calling out from within us, we gain a sense of relief through avoiding and desensitizing ourselves.

When we're wounded and in pain, we need to tend to it. We need to care for our aching hearts and heal them with the sacred acts of connection, release, comfort, and love. However, if we don't get our needs met, we do what feels like the next best thing: we protect ourselves. We close up and tuck our aching hearts away where they feel safer and less exposed. We dissociate from the pain and essentially, that's how protection works.

Examples of PROTECTION:
- Distraction
- Avoidance
- Detachment
- Desensitization
- Lack of caring
- Protectiveness
- Secrecy
- Dishonesty

These are some of the ways that we learn to tend to our aching hearts when our need for healing has not been met. We resort to building a cage around our hearts to protect ourselves from the feelings of discomfort.

Basically, we're saying, "I don't have what I need to feel better. I'll protect myself by trying not to feel the pain."

In sequence, the stages would go:

<u>HEART</u>: *I am here, experiencing life.*
<u>WOUND</u>: *Ouch! That hurts.*
<u>PAIN</u>: *I don't feel good. I'm in pain.*
<u>NEED</u>: *I'm hurting and I'm scared. I need healing.*
<u>PROTECTION</u>: *I don't have what I need to feel better. I'll protect myself by trying not to feel the pain.*

Of course, not everyone chooses food. Some of us disconnect from the pain by soothing ourselves with alcohol, caffeine, or cigarettes. For others, it's games, social media, or anything that takes our attention *away* from our wounds.

Unfortunately, as we'll see, it doesn't really work. While avoiding the pain may seem to reduce it, it doesn't go away. Avoidance just separates us from our true feelings and places our hearts in a cage. Eventually, we feel alone, lost, and in survival mode, which can also be described as *suffering* or the realms of *unconsciousness*.

Since suffering is not our destination (though a very important stop along the way), let's continue into protection and learn more about what happens when we don't get our needs met. That way, we can have the awareness and the tools we need to eventually get them met.

EGO: THE GREAT DIVIDE

NOW, I IMAGINE YOU MAY BE VISUALIZING an actual cage when we talk about this *cage* of protection. While yes, it's much like a cage, it's also an invisible layer that shields our tender hearts from experiencing more pain. While it doesn't heal the wound or fix the pain, it allows us to *cope* with the pain.

When our needs for healing aren't met, we go through life with a broken, aching heart. This is painful, uncomfortable, and not sustainable, so we shift our internal gears from sensitive to more dense and less pliable.

It's as if we are saying, "I'm not safe. I need to come up with something to ensure protection," and we replace our consciousness and presence with perspectives, stories, and patterns that separate us from the truth—and the pain that comes with it.

Basically, we go from having open hearts to having closed hearts.

I tend to think of this stage as *the Great Divide*. It's where deep internal separation is initiated. Like a cellular device moving out of range, our hearts move and the reception is cut off. We lose service. We disconnect from the network of consciousness and communication inside ourselves.

Another way to imagine this is like a shield or wall between the conscious and the unconscious self. Because we experience pain most intensely when we're conscious and present, this barrier allows us to step back from presence and be immersed in a state of numbing unconsciousness where we become less sensitive and care*less*. We convince ourselves that we're fine and that we don't care, which isn't true and doesn't honor our deeper needs and feelings. Indeed, it only leads us deeper into the realms of unconsciousness.

What is unconsciousness?

Simply, it's the opposite of consciousness. It's when we're separated from presence and disengaged from the crisp clarity of the moment. As if our bodies are here, but the radiant aliveness of our hearts is deep asleep. While the conscious state is one of presence and awareness, the unconscious state is one of avoidance and unawareness.

Is unconsciousness bad, then? If consciousness is seemingly benevolent, is unconsciousness malicious?

No—unconsciousness is not a malevolent force and doesn't have an intention to cause ill-will to you or anyone else. Unconsciousness doesn't *want* to do anything; it can't want because it's not conscious. It's nothingness. It's what remains in the space where there is no consciousness. It's a blank space of lifelessness.

Because we aren't consciously aware of what we're doing when we begin acting unconsciously, it's in this place of disconnection from ourselves that we begin losing sight of reality. We separate ourselves from the awareness of our thoughts, feelings, and actions and enter the realms of unawareness. In other words, we disconnect and dissociate from our hearts without being aware we're doing it, and as a result, we lose touch with where the pain is really coming from (ourselves). This makes it much more challenging to understand the pain and take the necessary and constructive action required to heal it.

THE ILLUSION OF AVOIDANCE

MUCH LIKE THE PAIN ANNOUNCING THAT something hurts inside and the need that motivates us to do something, protection is something initiated in honor of our wellbeing. By building a cage around our broken hearts, we're genuinely acting out of the intention for self-preservation and safety. We're shielding and safeguarding what's important to us: our hearts.

It's just like how we might hold our children's hands to protect them from cars or cover our ears when we hear a loud siren. We do these things because we care. We care about our kids; we care about our bodies; we care about our wellbeing. We *consciously* engage in acts of protection with the desire and intention to preserve what we value and love.

With that, we may think that by closing our hearts to protect them, we're preventing ourselves from feeling hurt and tending to our wellbeing. And that makes sense. If we discover a way to not feel pain, what's the problem?

Well, as I've mentioned before (and will again), by not feeling something, we don't actually empower ourselves or eliminate the danger. We just turn away from the feeling and prolong the uncomfortable experience. We don't overcome it; we just avoid it. In a sense, the *fear of being hurt* takes the reins from the part of us consciously seeking support. It aligns us with a false sense of support, power, and confidence—one that's created from fear rather than trust.

When we actively avoid discomfort, we might hear ourselves say something like:

"It doesn't matter."
"I'll just focus on something else."
"I'm not going to think about it anymore."
"I'm not upset."

"I'm just going to forget about it."
"What's done is done."
"Their loss, not mine."
"I'm over it."
"I don't care... whatever."

Is it true? Do we genuinely not care?

No, of course we care. We are genuine, loving, and caring creatures to the core. However, being caring comes with an open and tender heart that can be wounded, so we choose not to care, not to feel the tenderness.

Is this choice not to feel something we do intentionally?

Perhaps sometimes, but more often than not, no. Likely, we're dissociating from the *heart* of our pain and doing so without intention. Yes, if we cover our ears to protect them from a loud sound, we are consciously taking action for self preservation. However, when we actively *avoid* discomfort because we're afraid of it, we're not fully in touch and attuned to what we're doing. We're not doing it with conscious intention to preserve what we love; we're doing it unconsciously to escape what we fear.

Because so many of us are uncomfortable with feeling our undesirable emotions, we can be equally resistant to being intimately honest with others about what we're truly feeling. By acting strong, looking "normal," and keeping the conversation limited to small talk, we feel safer and less exposed.

Unfortunately, most of us live like this every single day. Rather than opening up and confidently speaking the truth like, "My heart is really aching right now and I'm in a vulnerable place. I'm feeling a lot of grief and uncertainty," we present an illusion day after day. We do everything we can to not disturb the *facade of fine* and to pretend that we're ok. But doing so only perpetuates the problem. The longer we turn away from the wounds and ignore or deny the discomfort of the situation, the more the pain thrives and the worse our problems become.

While it was originally the wound that caused us so much pain, this burying of our true feelings can eventually create so much pain that it's ultimately far more destructive than the original wound.

THE FACADE OF FINE

MANY OF US HAVE SPENT SO MANY years avoiding the pain and pretending we're "fine" that we are genuinely unaware of the pain we're in. In a sense, we become professional forgetters and don't know how to talk about what's really going on because we don't really know.

This is something that came up when I worked with a woman named Adriane who was seeking counsel to get her life organized. At first, she talked about her career goals and areas in her life where she wanted to be "stronger," "more successful," and "more confident." Because she associated financial security with her self-esteem and confidence, she was driven to feel empowered and secure in her business.

As I invited her to talk more about her apprehensions, she spoke about regrets from her past and areas of her life that made her feel insecure and weak. With tears pouring out, she shared her experience of being sexually abused by a pastor when she was a child and the subsequent drug addictions that she had shamefully struggled with. She talked about how she lacked a sense of security and self-worth, and her troubled relationship with her body, saying "If I don't get a bunch of stuff accomplished each day, I feel like I don't deserve to sleep at night."

By the end of our first session, she had a refreshing glow of relief and I could see that an emotional weight had been lifted when she said, "Wow, I honestly thought I was coming to talk about my career. I didn't realize how much I needed to talk about all of that old stuff."

How much had her continual performance of pretending everything was fine contributed to her not understanding what was really going on inside and getting to the root of her pain? How much was she overachieving in her life to compensate for what she felt she lacked within? How much was her deep discomfort playing itself out through feeling unhappy with her job? In reality, her career success was just a front for the deeper security, connection, and confidence she yearned to feel inside.

Over time, through confronting her fear of being vulnerable and building a more authentic and honest relationship with herself, she made her way through the rose-colored avoidance. She became a more loving, accepting, and nurturing friend to herself, which ultimately brought her the reward of fulfillment, which she was seeking all along.

Do you ever find yourself saying that you're "fine" or "good" even when you're not?

THE LULLABY OF DISTRACTION

THERE ARE LOTS OF WAYS THAT WE can actively avoid feeling, dealing with, and talking about the pain we're in, and distraction is a very common way. Similar to a drug, it can be persuasive and seductive, drawing us into a state of unconsciousness and disconnecting us from our true feelings and pain. We also use distraction in an attempt to calm the anxiety we feel as a result of our unmet need for relief from the original pain and discomfort.

Some examples of **distraction** are:
- Fixation with cellphone
- Watching television or movies
- Shopping
- Social media
- Caffeine
- Eating food
- Drinking alcohol
- Sexual stimulation
- Drugs

We tend to distract ourselves when we're uncomfortable (sad, anxious, stressed, grieving, exhausted) and our needs haven't been met. Because the unresolved need may be to receive comfort, connection, and care, we distract ourselves but we still seek a sense of comfort and connection. Like many of our other tendencies, there's an underlying attempt to mend what feels so broken and disconnected inside.

Unfortunately, distraction is sneaky. It leads us to believe that by opening the fridge, pouring a drink, turning on the TV, or scrolling through online stores, we're being supported and lullabied back to feeling whole and connected. In reality, it's pulling us further away from presence, our true selves, and a genuine feeling of wholeness.

I think of distraction like caffeine. If we're tired and exhausted, we may choose to drink caffeine to get a temporary burst of energy, rather than looking at the real cause (needing more sleep or other health factors). In doing so, we don't create sustainable solutions to our problems. Instead, we turn to a false fuel that gives us a temporary sensation of energy. Sure, we may be able to get through the day, but unless we stop to understand *why* we're tired or not inspired, we avoid the underlying cause. And, in the long term, caffeine can be detrimental to our overall health.

Likewise, our protective cage can only keep us safe for so long. Although we become consumed with feeling happy, capable, and "fine," at some point, we either burn out, get sick, or get hurt. We might end up in a traumatic situation that forces us to stop and look at the truth, like an accident or injury, which can be a *very* uncomfortable, startling way to wake up.

If we don't closely monitor and observe ourselves when we're engaging in an act of distraction, we can easily drift further and further away from ourselves and eventually end up in a state of addiction, which we'll talk more about in Chapter 7.

That said, not all acts of avoidance and distraction are destructive. Especially if you've dealt with severe trauma and intense emotional upheaval, the act of allowing yourself to retreat into a space of comfort and ease can be very healing. There are times when our minds are caught in a cyclical pattern and our bodies are experiencing severe stress, which is not healthy or sustainable. In those moments, it may be most productive to stop *doing* and just curl up and relax with a movie. Like a turtle going into its shell, we sometimes need to actively remove ourselves from what is overwhelming, stressful, or incapacitating.

The key is to ask ourselves whether our actions are consciously working towards how we want to feel (intention) or unconsciously working away from what we don't want to feel (avoidance). We'll talk about healthy forms of connection and comfort when we get to Chapters 12 and 13.

In what ways do you tend to distract yourself when you feel uncomfortable?

THE LURE OF SCREENS

ONE OF THE MOST COMMON WAYS THAT we humans avoid feeling discomfort is through staring at screens. Billions of us devote hours of our day to interacting with technology. In fact, statistics show that the average person spends 11 hours a day interacting with technology and screens (be it cellphones, computers, television, or video games).

We have quickly become a species that has adapted to accessing connection, comfort, and relaxation through screens, whether it's a video call or a favorite TV series. While this may be necessary for education and careers, it's also likely that we are in a state of avoidance and searching for something to do, something to see, something to *distract* and *soothe* ourselves.

When you watch a screen, your body begins releasing dopamine and your brain enters a pleasurable, meditative, alpha state. While this zoned-out, relaxed state allows your brain to be seemingly still and do nothing, it's also in receiving mode, which means your subconscious is taking in and absorbing what it witnesses. This is not a bad thing if you're watching something that expands your awareness and stimulates your curiosity. But what happens when you're absorbing a vast, dramatic array of conflicts, struggles, and turmoil?

While watching TV or scrolling through social media may feel soothing, it's important to stop and ask yourself: *exactly how much of my life do I spend staring at a screen and encouraging my mind to do nothing?*

If you spend 2.7 hours a day watching TV shows like the average person, that's almost 19 hours a week, which is 76 hours a month, which is 900+ hours a year. How does it feel to spend so much time sitting in the audience watching other people experience life? Are you gaining something from it, or is it slowly draining the consciousness and inspiration from *your* life?

Perhaps watching TV or interacting on social media is a way for you to feel a sense of unity and connection with your fellow humans? However, it's also possible that you're tuning into someone else's story so that you can forget about your own. Ideally, you should love your life so much that you don't want to spend one minute forgetting about it—you want to live it. I'm not saying that those of us who watch TV every day or engage with social media don't love our lives, but it's important to decipher whether our actions are consciously moving *towards* the experience of living life or unconsciously trying to *escape* it.

900 hours is a lot of time and a lot of very valuable life energy that could be fueled into the creation of a project or the manifestation of a dream. Have you ever wanted to learn a new language? What about astronomy? Wouldn't it be fun to learn how to play an instrument? Maybe you'd like to write a book? It's up to you.

You've got over 900 hours to work with; what do you want to do with them?

THE WALL OF DESENSITIZATION

WHILE AVOIDING OUR PAIN BY WATCHING TV, drinking alcohol, or being absorbed on our phones might temporarily lessen the discomfort inside us, it actually weakens and drains our sensations all together. Another way to say this is that we become *desensitized*.

What does it mean to be desensitized? It means we've figured out ways to numb our pain and be separated from our senses to be less impacted by the experiences of wounding and pain. We may think we're able to filter and avoid only the uncomfortable feelings like sadness, shame, regret, and grief, though it doesn't really work like that. A wall is a wall and a cage is a cage; nothing comes in and nothing goes out, including true love, empathy, intuition, and compassion.

Because the core essence of your true self is all of those things, when you're disconnected from your heart, you're separated from the lifeline that unites you with the true nature of your being, behind a wall. Rather than living in expansive wonder and curiosity as you once did, you're influenced by the contractive forces of fear. These fears encourage you to be guarded, withheld, and removed from presence, in a place where you aren't able to feel the crisp aliveness of life.

When you're desensitized, you might think this means you don't feel any emotions. But as we'll talk more about in Chapter 10, emotions and feelings are different. Just because you're trying to avoid the undesirable emotions of pain and discomfort, it doesn't mean you're completely numb to emotions. It just means that you're choosing not to feel certain ones (like grief, sorrow, and shame).

Over time, as we become more skilled in desensitizing ourselves and blocking out our feelings, we gradually train ourselves not to feel. For that reason, we can still be emotional (angry, jealous, excited) while remaining desensitized and disconnected from the deeper, more sensitive feelings, like love, compassion, and intuition.

A global problem

It's tempting to think that desensitization is something that only addicts or people who have been through severe trauma experience, but I honestly feel that most humans are somewhat desensitized. Because we have all experienced wounds, we all know what pain feels like. Without an accepted, effective approach to consciously addressing and healing our pain (individually and collectively), most of us have learned to cope with our pain by disconnecting and dissociating ourselves from it. Rather than being sensitive and feeling it all, we desensitize ourselves and choose not to feel it.

In fact, when you look around and realize how expansive the problem really is, it begins to make sense why our world is filled with so much suffering and ignorance. We're not able to sense or feel what our own selves are going through, so we're not likely to sense what others are going through. And if we can't feel what others are going through, we're less likely to feel compassion for them or a desire to help.

Sometimes, it's only when the state of protection is lifted that we're able to really understand how deafening, diluting, and desensitizing it is inside the cage. This is why there are so many accounts of people having a heartfelt awakening when they experienced something very traumatic and humbling, like an accident or a near death experience. It's as if the incident was so jarring that it rattled the cage open.

When something serious happens, people are suddenly overwhelmed with feelings of gratitude, presence, and awareness for how valuable life is. They realize how much they appreciate their loved ones; they "see the light" and return to presence. Rather than living in a constant state of distraction and avoidance, they feel a newfound sense of connection and a desire to be more caring or serve others.

This "light" is consciousness. It's the bright, beaming radiance of awareness that allows us to feel connected, engaged, and united with all life on this planet and beyond. It's this light that gets blocked when we enter a state of protection and hide within the cage. As we move into the second part of the book, we'll talk much more about opening our hearts and constructively removing the cage from around us to let the healing light of consciousness into our lives.

THE LOSS OF INTUITION

WHEN WE BECOME EMOTIONALLY DESENSITIZED, we also lose the ability to sense, feel, and hear the subtle inner workings of our bodies and beings. This is similar to when the physical body goes numb if an area receives poor circulation. When we're not connected to our hearts, we break away from the powerful, guiding strength of our intuition—our ability to sense through an instinctual *knowing*.

Without our intuitive awareness, we're more prone to feel self-doubt and insecurity. This lack of trust in ourselves nudges us to seek answers, guidance, and insights from outside ourselves. When we seek answers outside ourselves, we lose touch with our internal compass of awareness, and we drift further away from our sense of purpose and direction in life.

Oddly enough, some of us may find a strange and satisfying sense of fulfillment in being disconnected from the heart of our true selves and intuition. Why? Because when we're connected and empowered to make conscious decisions for ourselves, we're the ones held responsible for our actions and decisions. For some people, it can feel intimidating to be held accountable for our own state of being. What happens if we don't succeed? What happens if we pursue what feels right and it turns out to be wrong?

Feeling deflated and disempowered is a feeling we already know very well, so the last thing we want to do is set ourselves up to feel even more ashamed and let down. This is why it can feel less burdensome to place the accountability for our decisions on something or someone else. If the problem (and the solution) is outside ourselves, we can relax in the passenger seat, focusing our attention away from ourselves. We can avoid taking the wheel and directing the course of our own lives.

Unfortunately, this dampening down of our intuition is largely a learned behavior and is highly encouraged by our culture and environment. From a very young age, we are often led to believe that we need to look outside ourselves for the answers and the truth. We are trained to listen to parents, teachers, advertisements, and pharmaceutical companies. We are given a constant spew of rules and directions from other people in order to consider ourselves worthy humans.

While these systems and industries may have our overall wellbeing in mind, we put a lot of energetic and financial power in the hands of others, and we trust them with our minds, bodies, and futures. And rather than hearing our own intuitive voice, we learn to do as we're told and devotedly follow what others are doing.

Of course, it's important to have civil order and organization within our culture and species. It's important to work together and honor each other's guidance and expertise. However, it's also *essential* to have a direct and pure connection to the wise, clear knowing within our own hearts. This is what connects and guides us toward a healthy and fulfilled purpose in life, rather than being led by others. When we talk about feeling in Chapter 10, we'll look more at honoring and strengthening our own senses and intuition.

Do you ever feel separated from your intuition?

Can you recall having a stronger sense of intuition when you were a child?

THE DISCONNECTION OF DISHONESTY

DISHONESTY IS A COMMON WAY THAT MANY of us intentionally disconnect from our hearts (and from one another) in an attempt to preserve ourselves. When we don't trust the truth or ourselves to keep us safe, we create a story that we imagine will keep us safer. We lie out of fear, insecurity, and distrust, which is damaging to any relationship.

Unfortunately, there are numerous reasons why lying is detrimental to you and others. If you lie to someone else, you create a barrier that divides you from them and weakens the connection. If or when the lie is revealed, it damages or eliminates trust, which creates pain and grief. The revelation also brings on a sense of internal shame and embarrassment, which feeds your insecurity and self-doubt—not what you want.

What if it's just a little secret? Just a white lie that won't hurt anyone? It doesn't matter. Each time you say to yourself, "I have to keep this a secret because I can't be honest," you tell yourself that you're not strong enough. You tell yourself a story that you're weak, which isn't true or supportive. You also make a choice and commitment to hold the heavy weight of secrecy on your back, and over time, that weight can drag you down. Each time you lie, your backpack of shame gets heavier and further weighs you down.

We may also deeply damage others when we lie to them. As it's important for each of us to be tethered to our intuition as our compass in life, when we tell a convincing lie, we encourage others to contradict their intuitive knowing. This impairs their relationship with themselves and leads them astray.

In fact, this is something I've heard countless times from people who were in committed relationships and discovered that their partner was seeing someone else.

My friend Chris shared the grief of his marital breakup after it turned out that his wife had been secretly engaging with lovers over their 12-year marriage. Chris said, "There were so many times when I sensed something. I knew something was off. I was constantly asking questions and trying to find out if she was seeing other men. Always, she would say NO. Then she'd go on and on about how insecure, paranoid, and wrong I was until I was so ashamed that I stopped saying anything. I've honestly spent years thinking something was severely wrong with me and that I was crazy."

While it's possible that his wife may not have understood the full extent of the destructive dishonesty, she was not only separating herself from Chris but also encouraging Chris to be separated from himself.

Each time he felt an intuitive message, he dishonored his internal voice by contradicting it and telling himself he was wrong. Over time, his sense of self-trust and intuition was diminished. By lying, his wife put him in a position to either choose his intuition or choose her words, and by continually choosing her, he repeatedly felt confusion, uncertainty, and self-doubt. He intentionally stopped listening to his intuition, and eventually became disconnected and desensitized from himself.

In the moment, while you may find yourself being dishonest from a place of fear and protection, it's important to remember that you may be unknowingly creating a lot of unnecessary pain and disconnection within yourself and others. Regardless of whether you believe in karma or a religious or spiritual belief system, lying isn't good. It's not beneficial to you or anyone else. Unless the lie is consciously being told to save someone's life, it's not worth it.

Can you recall a time where you bent the truth, made up a story, or lied to someone?
How did that lie separate you from them?
How might it have separated them from themselves?

DISHONESTY WITH THE SELF

THOUGH DISHONESTY WITH OTHERS IS detrimental and has major implications, when we lie to ourselves, we unknowingly cause the most severe damage. If we think of our relationship with ourselves as a friendship (which we'll do often in our time together), we can see ourselves as the giver and the receiver; the speaker and the listener. When one part of you lies to another part of you, no matter how small or seemingly insignificant the tale, you *know* you are being lied to. You obviously know the truth, so you begin to lose trust in yourself.

Say your life has become stressful and you notice you're drinking a bit more than usual. It used to be once a week, and now it's one or two glasses a day. Over time, your stress level rises and nothing takes the edge off like alcohol does. You know it's not good for you and you feel ashamed of drinking, but you have trouble stopping. You become dependent on it. As the shame is so uncomfortable to feel, you tell yourself things to avoid looking at the truth. You say, "It's not so bad. It's just alcohol. I don't have a problem. In fact, I'll stop tomorrow. This will be my last drink."

And for the moment, the statement is relieving for you to hear. It gives you a little ray of hope that perhaps this will be the last drink. But what happens the next day when you say and when you hear, "Just one more, I'll stop tomorrow?"

Distrust.

At this point, you've been dishonest with yourself. You've told yourself a lie to avoid feeling the discomfort of the truth. Just like lying in any other relationship with a friend or loved one, you've damaged the bridge of trust. You've impaired the belief and confidence in your own strength, willpower, and word. This lack of trust weakens your sense of security within yourself and eventually translates into insecurity, shame, and contempt for yourself.

When we lie to ourselves, we are essentially lying to our best friends. We're widening the gap of disconnection and division, making it more difficult to believe in ourselves, love ourselves, and find our confidence and purpose. And the more we lie to ourselves and lie to others and are lied to, the thicker the wall of our cage becomes because we feel that the outside world is not safe. The distrust encourages us to stay nestled within our cage of protection.

Though it may be overwhelming and uncomfortable to look at the truth and be honest with yourself, it's a necessary part of building a healthy, strong relationship with yourself. As you'll continue to learn throughout the book, trust and connection are two of the most vital elements in any healthy relationship. Without trust, we can only go so far in experiencing true love with others and with ourselves.

Can you think of a time in your life when you lied to yourself? How did that lie affect your trust and confidence in yourself?

I imagine what it's like to be a bird.
To be born of a species that persevered through eons of fear
to arrive to a place
where the giant and infinite leap
is the nature of being and
no longer the hurdle to overcome.

What it must be like
to fly.

To look up at the sky and feel at home
rather than daunted by all that is unknown and not yet understood.

At some point, we must lean into the wind
with trust that we will be carried.

With knowing,
that we did not come here to cling to the rock.

We came here to fly.

6.
DEFENSE

The act of defending that which needs protecting.

"Is everything ok with you?" my mom asked as we were putting dishes away one evening. My heart began to race and my eyes peered out from beneath my furrowed brow. "Me? I'm fine. Why do you ask?"

"Well," her voice trembled as she continued, "you've definitely been losing a lot of weight and I'm getting concerned about you." Her eyes were heavy and I could see it was hard for her to find the courage to say something. She was never very comfortable with confrontation or sensitive conversations.

At that moment, I wasn't sensitive to her struggles as a mother trying to raise teenage daughters. I was too consumed by my own pain and fear to open up and be honest about what I was going through. Rather than allowing myself to cry and reach out for a hug, I did everything I could to cover it up and make the uncomfortable conversation go away as quickly as possible. Like anyone trying desperately and unconsciously to guard their pain, I was armed and ready with sharp words.

"Why does everyone think something's wrong with me? I TOLD you, I'm FINE!! Now leave me alone," I scoffed, then left the room.

Unfortunately, at that time, I reacted strongly to people asking me personal questions, trying to make their way into my well-protected cage, even my mom. It also made me very uncomfortable to see her so worried about me. I just wanted her and everyone else to forget about me and focus on something else.

Plus, I was ready to fight. Even though we'd plucked the destructive behavior out of my family, by escaping my dad, it was still there. Maybe he was gone, but the wounding was still very much a part of our lives and played itself out through the way me and my sisters treated one another. My older sister had experienced more trauma than I had, and with no constructive way to process her discomfort and pain, she released a lot of it on me. In response, I defended and deflected, became fully trained in the art of sibling combat, and was ready to jump into action and swing at any moment, even towards someone who was innocently and compassionately asking if I was ok.

That's often how defense works. We're hurting, we're afraid, and we haven't had our needs met. But instead of reaching out and being honest about our wounds and our pain, we do whatever it takes to further avoid and separate ourselves from the discomfort, even if it means using aggression.

While protection is often an internal experience, defense is the progressed, externalized form of protection—one that often involves others.

Unfortunately, when we're defensive, we're even more disconnected from our true feelings and understanding our needs than when we're protective. We're still inside the cage, but now we're actively defending it. When we're in situations that bring up fear and pain, we react unconsciously, defending our very lives, regardless of the situation or whether our wellbeing is genuinely being threatened or not.

Also, because our emotions, fears, and unwept tears are building up inside the cage, we often find ourselves being irrationally aggressive and defensive in harmless situations, simply because we need to let go of some of the built-up energy within us (we'll talk a lot about constructive forms of release in Chapter 12).

For a while, I referred to this entire stage of suffering as *anger*, but after going deeper into understanding defense, it became clear that not everyone reveals and releases themselves in outward expressions of anger when they're actively defending themselves. Some of us get competitive, some become judgmental, others become silent or passive aggressive.

In the heat of the moment, when we're aggressively protecting our cage, it's so easy to blame and focus on others. This is why it's important to use the term "defense" so we can tether back to our own pain, our own actions, and our own growth. It inspires us to question "defending what?" This takes us instantly to the place we need to go to heal: the wounded heart.

Examples of being in a state of DEFENSE:
- Angry
- Irritated
- Judgmental
- Aggressive
- Passive aggressive
- Envious
- Competitive
- Pompous
- Enraged

Like a scared, hurt, and angry tiger, we will guard and defend ourselves from anything we see as a threat. We will scowl, scream, hiss, bite, and claw to keep the cage (and our endangered heart inside) safe from harm. We will defend all of the perspectives, stories, and identities that are woven into the cage walls as well.

Together, the stages go like this:

HEART: *I am here, experiencing life.*
WOUND: *Ouch! That hurts.*
PAIN: *I don't feel good. I'm in pain.*
NEED: *I'm hurting and I'm scared. I need healing.*
PROTECTION: *My needs aren't met. I'll protect myself by trying not to feel the pain.*
DEFENSE: *To avoid feeling more pain, I'll fight to protect myself.*

Now, I'll let you in on a secret: the defensive and angry tiger isn't real. Just like your ego isn't who you really are and the cage isn't your true home, your anger and defensiveness is not who you really are. It's a mask that disguises the pain and fear within you, and it's designed to keep your tenderness safe and hidden. Even though the anger and defense can be very believable and intimidating, and cause sincere harm and wounding, it's merely a front. Though it may appear loud, strong, powerful and confident, it's hiding an internal fear and need for protection.

So, it's important to remind ourselves when confronted by defense that *within the fear, there's pain and within the pain, there's a wound.*

While the ability to defend ourselves can at times be constructive and useful, when we're in a place of disconnection and unconscious protection, defense can be very destructive to ourselves and others, causing more wounds and more pain. We don't need more wounds. We need to feel better, not worse.

So, let's learn more about defense and inch our way closer to change.

A FIST IN SLOW MOTION

TO BETTER UNDERSTAND THE PROGRESSION of the wound, pain, need, protection, and defense in action, imagine a fist fight in slow motion:

- The first thing we notice is fear. Assuming the person had been hurt before, we would see a look of apprehension, surprise, and fear as the fist came toward them.

- Then, we would see the wound being placed. We would see the skin being stretched and the impact of the pressure and the injury.

- Next, we will see the wince of pain and discomfort at having received the wound.

- If we could freeze the frame here, we'd see that the wound is in need of care. But in the pace of the fight, the need would be bypassed and the fight would continue.

- We would watch as the person's facial expression slowly changed from receiving pain to going into protection mode.
We would see the protector emerge and the look of fear slowly dropping from their face.

- Lastly, their facial expression would transition to anger as the protector is in a state of defense, and the fist would swing back in retaliation.

Defense is the *swinging back*. It's the response to being hurt and trying to defend oneself. While it can easily feel like a productive action, defense is not an action; it's a reaction. To what? The pain and fear.

We know that verbal and emotional assaults can be just as damaging as physical ones, so we can imagine what happens when words are thrown back and forth instead of fists. As the words strike against the steel of our cages, we defiantly (and often unconsciously) swing back. We spew destructive venom to protect and defend what we love and care about: our wounded hearts within.

FIERCE MOTHER INSTINCT

MUCH LIKE THE STAGES BEFORE, THERE IS a valid reason and purpose for defending ourselves. Like a reserve of super strength and adrenaline that we can tap into when needed, it has the power to destroy in order to save.

In fact, it's often said, "The most powerful force in nature is a mother protecting her young." If her cubs, pups, fledglings, or toddlers are in danger, she will not think twice. Like a cord that connects her heart to each of theirs, she will reach beyond time to protect and *defend* them at all costs, even if it means she has to kill.

Personally, I don't think of myself as being capable of killing anything, then someone will blindside me with the question, "What if you were alone and someone pulled a gun on you? Would you defend yourself and fight back, potentially killing them before they killed you?"

I respond, "Nope. I wouldn't. I would figure out some other way of solving the situation."

Then the questioning increases, "What if you had children with you? What if someone was about to hurt those children and you had to do something to save them?"

I pause. That changes things. I try to imagine what it would take for me to get to a place of knowingly hurting something, and it's not easy. However, if it was to protect and defend something or someone that I deeply cared about, it's possible I would do anything, finding the strength of my hands and the fierce nature inside me.

I think of my own mother who was often timid and insecure, and I wonder how that powerful fire awoke in her to realize her children's lives were in danger. She took action, even though it meant doing something intimidating and bold. Where did that fearlessness come from, giving her the courage to leave to save herself and her children from continued abuse?

The reality is, we all have within us this powerful strength and deep instinct to protect what we love and care about. Chances are, you know this fire well. You've likely tapped into it before, and been fierce, aggressive, and angry. While a lot of those times, you may have reacted with unnecessary aggression, you were driven by an impulse to protect what you love and care about: your hurting heart. Like caring for a vulnerable and small child, you were concerned about the safety and wellbeing of your tender self and did what you could to protect it when it was in danger.

We can all awaken this force inside us that makes us courageous and strong. But, here's the twist: we don't always need to. Yes, there are times when you need to constructively save lives but chances are, you don't actually need to utilize this fiery force every time life presents a frustrating obstacle or challenging person to deal with. The only reason you may react aggressively and defensively is because you're actually disconnected from what you are trying to protect (your heart) and reacting *unconsciously* because of it.

Let's imagine someone says something hurtful or unkind to you. Unless you're in a conscious and present state, you might impulsively react with a flood of automatic emotions and begin defending yourself by saying or doing something loud, aggressive, and hurtful. Because you feel in danger and under threat, you respond by quickly reacting. Even though you're much safer than you think you are, you'll feel triggered and overwhelmed, reacting as though you need to defend your life. In reality, the stress, pain, and discomfort already reside within you.

Alternatively, if you allow yourself to reconnect with your heart and tend to the internal pain within to heal those wounds, you'll likely be in a lot less pain. You'll also be more able to remain present and connected to your genuine feelings when you're in a troubling, dangerous, or challenging situation. Then, you can utilize this force constructively to take action (rather than reacting) to protect what you love when needed.

Let's say you're walking down the street and an aggressive-looking dog is running towards you. Suddenly, you're scared, flustered, and overcome with emotion. You begin reacting defensively and screaming uncontrollably at the dog. What would happen? It's hard to say, but potentially the dog would not react well to your emotional display and might react defensively by attacking you to retain its own safety.

Instead, if you remain present and in your conscious state, you can think quickly and either get yourself to a safe place or reach for something to use as constructive defense, such as your intelligence to consciously strategize a solution to the potential threat. This is harder to access when you're reactive, unconscious, and overcome with emotion.

It's important to understand the difference between when we're actually under threat and need to take conscious action and when we're caught in a cycle of our own internal pain and unconscious reactions. When we get to Chapter 14, we'll talk about self-respect and healthy actions towards self-protection.

THE HARSHNESS OF JUDGMENT

SO, WHEN WE HURT INSIDE, WE MIGHT ACT aggressively, destructively, and unconstructively. As we're in a desensitized, unconscious state, our mind isn't clear and our actions often reflect that unconsciousness. One way that we tend to do this is through *judgment*.

> Judgment: an opinion or conclusion; a misfortune or calamity viewed as a divine punishment.
>
> Calamity: an event causing great and often sudden damage or distress; a disaster.
>
> Punishment: the infliction or imposition of a penalty as retribution for an offense; rough treatment or handling inflicted on or suffered by a person or thing.

When you break it down, judgment is a form of abuse, and it's deeply destructive. Because it often happens behind the closed doors of our thoughts, it can be as hidden as the wounds within us. And because there is a strong current of pain and fear within us when we're in a defensive state, we can easily feel like a victim whose judgmental actions are justified by our pain, regardless of whether the person or thing we're judging has anything to do with that pain.

For example, how many times have you casually voiced a strong opinion or conclusion about someone else? Was it the way they spoke or the way they were dressed? Did they invest their beliefs and hopes in a leader that you disagreed with? Maybe it was the color of their skin? What triggered you to feel protective, defensive, and aggressive enough that they deserved punishment?

Chances are, your feelings of defensiveness have less to do with the other person and more to do with you. Likely, what's really going on is that your needs aren't being met and you're hurting. So, your judgmental reaction comes from your own state of unconsciousness, protection, and defense. In thinking or venting judgments toward someone else, you are serving nothing except your own need for relief from your pent-up pain. Causing pain to someone else provides a strangely satisfying, though dysfunctional, sense of release.

Maybe you're thinking, "Well, I sometimes have judgmental thoughts about people but I rarely say anything aloud. I keep my thoughts to myself so no one will be affected by them."

Yes, I used to think that too. I remember sitting with a friend on the subway, waiting for the train to depart. We were looking out the window and my friend casually poked fun at a man standing on the platform with his back to us. She made a remark about his pants not fitting.

She was "making fun" of someone else to spark a connection with me. While her intention was to make me laugh, it was an unconscious and destructive way to accomplish that. She was also revealing her own insecurity, lack of confidence, and need for attention. Because I loved her and also dealt with insecurity myself, I didn't speak up and say, "Hey, that's not cool. Leave that guy alone. We can find other things to laugh about." Instead, I chuckled along with her and gained a temporary sense of inclusion. I honored our connection more than what I knew was right in my heart, even though it meant being harmful to someone else.

Despite being 50 feet away, in a crowd, with a thick layer of glass between us, the man quickly pulled his jacket down over his hips. He turned around, and with a look of concern, sadness, and insecurity in his eyes, he stared across the station directly at us. Even though there was no way that he heard us, he sensed us.

"Whoa," I said, "he felt that." The two of us sat for a moment in apologetic silence and awe.

The problem is that even when we can't hear each other, we can feel one another. We can intuitively sense what others think about us and feel each other's cruel thoughts. If we were all separate androids that didn't have the ability to feel, then this wouldn't be the case. However, we're not robots (thankfully)—we're tender, breathing, feeling, sensitive, caring creatures. Our thoughts, words, and actions are felt by one another through intuition, perceptivity, and awareness. Although many of us are desensitized, it is never entirely. As long as we're alive, we can feel and that's a *good* thing. It's something we want to nurture in ourselves and one another, not destroy.

Have you ever felt or said something judgmental about someone? Can you imagine how that judgment may have been damaging to them?

SELF-JUDGMENT

WHAT HAPPENS WHEN IT'S *you* JUDGING YOU? The same thing: damage, distress, and harm.

When we put ourselves down, make negative comments, shame ourselves, and create unrealistic standards to live up to, we create pain, fear, and distrust inside. We create the internal dialogue of, "I'm not good enough and I deserve to struggle and suffer." This generates feelings of fear, insecurity, and confusion.

We engage in self-abuse and in return, we feel defensive and protective. We create self-inflicted emotional abrasions, becoming both the aggressive wolf who is attacking *and* the wounded wolf who is being attacked. As a result, we experience division of the self. We break and divide our wounded hearts, all the while justified through the filter of "I deserve to suffer."

Why would we ever want or choose to cause ourselves more pain and harm?

Well, what's so interesting and unfortunate about being in an unconscious state is that we're not really thinking or acting with intention. We're just wandering through life, overwhelmed by the pain echoing within us, unconsciously associating that pain with what is around us, and continually reacting to it. We're hurting, scared, and swinging fists in every direction, even at ourselves. We repeat a cycle of feeling hurt, then creating more hurt inside.

For example, we might say, "I'm so stupid. I feel ashamed of myself." Maybe within those words, there is a ray of encouragement to stop and observe our actions to become a better person in the future. However, more likely, we're aggressively attacking ourselves.

This place of being the abuser and the receiver is very troubling and confusing. We become knotted in a tangle of insecurity, frustration, anger, shame, uncertainty, and apprehension. We very easily feel uncertain of who we are or how we feel. With that, we distrust ourselves and are afraid of being alone in the presence of ourselves. This is why so many of us feel antsy and uncomfortable in still, quiet, and meditative environments. Not because we don't appreciate it, but because we're left alone with the abuser and feel under threat from hurtful words, thoughts, and judgments.

Sure, you genuinely want to relax and appreciate the stillness, but then someone says to you, "Why are your thighs spilling out so far onto this chair? Have you gained weight? You look awful," or, "You think you have the time to just sit here doing nothing? What about your bills that need to be paid? When are you going to make something of yourself and have a career that allows you to sit around doing nothing?"

Who would say such hurtful and destructive things to you?

You.

It's you saying those things to yourself. Rather than allowing you to receive the quiet relaxation that you need to soothe your discomfort, you fall into a destructive, abusive dialogue with yourself that prevents you from getting your needs met.

Sadly, this self-judgment and verbal abuse can make the journey of healing very challenging. The state of suffering is a deep hole that requires every ounce of our beings to climb our way out of. If we're forcing ourselves to crouch down and wear the heavy backpack of shame, it's that much harder to pull up and out of the suffering. Every day, we push ourselves down while whispering, "I've done wrong and I should struggle my way through this. I deserve to suffer." This isn't true or constructive.

Will judging and shaming ourselves really help us become better people?

No. In order to feel inspired and ready to start healing ourselves, it's essential that we feel safe and confident. If we're constantly attacking ourselves and kicking ourselves down, how will we ever get up again?

We have to break the cycle of abuse and recognize our participation in it. We have to infuse our unconsciousness with awareness of the unnecessary destruction and give ourselves permission to lift back up to the light of our true nature.

Do you ever judge yourself?
What kind of things do you say to yourself?
How does it make you feel?

THE SURVIVALISM OF COMPETITION

COMPETITION IS SOMETHING THAT MANY BEINGS naturally experience and partake in. Whether it's a sibling rivalry for the attention of a parent, two dogs battling for food, or a plant competing with the forest for sunlight, competition derives from the need to ensure life, safety, and security.

If it's such a natural and normal experience, why do we need to talk about it in the context of defense? Well, within the instinctual drive of competition, there's often a sense of insecurity and scarcity: *not enough* food, *not enough* water, *not enough* light, *not enough*. From that space of need, we may become protective and defensive to guard our resources.

Rather than competing for the necessities of food and light, most of us will find ourselves entering that same level of defensive survivalism for things like money, career goals, lovers, attention, affection, notoriety, etc. We compete, strive, and even fight for success and achievement as though our lives depend on it.

What are we competing for? Usually, we're striving to fulfill our unmet needs for attention, respect, acknowledgement, and the sense of safety acquired through those things. For the wolf who was discarded from the pack, they might feel that if they can win and gain a sense of notoriety, they'll be welcomed back into the pack and become included and accepted again.

Whether we're competing with others or with ourselves, there's often an underlying message within our competitive nature that says, "I long to feel accepted, included, and safe. If I succeed, then I will feel respected and worthy, which will help me to feel safe, secure, and content."

It's also possible that what drives the need to succeed is a wound from the past. Maybe a parent or relative who said or implied that "you'll never amount to anything," or "you don't have what it takes." Maybe you were raised with little money so your competitive drive is influenced by insecurity or inadequacy at not having enough.

If you can relate to this internal competition that feels like survivalism, it's understandable. We've been trained by our culture through sports, talent shows, TV shows, school tests, clubs, universities, career promotions, and highly competitive industries to be in a constant state of competition and survival. We've been indoctrinated to think that who we are and what we have isn't enough; that there's always something outside ourselves that we need to feel whole and successful—a thing, a person, a social status, an achievement.

What happens when we're striving to achieve that thing, then we perceive that someone else has more or is seemingly ahead of us?

Jealousy.

> Jealousy: feeling or showing <u>envy</u> of someone or their achievements and advantages; fiercely protective or vigilant of one's rights or possessions.
>
> Envy: a resentful longing for someone else's possessions and qualities.

But how does someone else's bank account have anything to do with our pain? If we're in a place of need and feel that we don't have enough (financial success, beauty, attention), then we are protective to safeguard what we believe we don't have enough of. And if we see or perceive someone having what we feel we lack, we become defensive to ensure that we get enough.

Often, what we feel jealous of (money, beauty, attention, a lover) are symbols of safety and security. If we have money, we can afford whatever we want, including healthcare, a roof over our heads, and the soothing relief of luxury. We feel taken care of; we feel safe. If we obtain physical beauty, we're more admired and assured that we're valuable; we feel secure. If we have a lover who appreciates us, we feel seen, important, and loved.

So, what happens if our lover is on the other side of the room at the party, talking to someone else? We feel scared! We feel protective. We feel the need to defend and conserve our lifeline to security and safety, the things we so desperately need to feel whole and content.

We might start being defensive—aggressive, passive aggressive, or competitive, all because we don't feel secure, safe, or confident enough within. We're scared, hurting, and reaching outside ourselves for something or someone to provide a temporary ease and soothing relief from the pain within.

The issue is, a sense of security won't come from outside you; it comes from within. It comes from the heartfelt work of being courageously honest with yourself and building a strong relationship of trust and connection inside yourself.

To admire something of beauty and to observe someone else's achievements is a natural and ordinary part of being alive. However, when our admiration turns into jealousy, that longing speaks through unconsciousness, pain, and insecurity. In those moments, we're reacting from fear, not love.

Have you ever felt jealousy towards someone else?

Do you remember feeling an underlying fear of losing something or not having enough?

What did you feel you lacked?

What were you afraid of losing?

THE FIRE OF ANGER

LIKE OTHER FORMS OF DEFENSE, ANGER IS a natural response to defend and protect what we love. For some, it can feel mysterious, foreign, and undesirable, so we do everything in our power to deny it. While someone can feel angry (annoyed or displeased) without being actively aggressive, it can still be a feeling and state that we avoid.

With that said, many of us find ourselves feeling angry, *a lot*. Even though pain and fear are at the root of the anger, it's often more comfortable (and culturally accepted) to be angry rather than feel the vulnerable expressions hidden within it, like sadness and grief. For that reason, anger is something we may frequently use to disguise and avoid our deeper, more intimate pain. And because it often occurs when we're disconnected from our hearts, it's likely that we won't even feel the underlying grief and pain because we're so swept away in the unconscious experience of it.

When we are angry, we are filled with a fire that can easily injure others and damage ourselves. Anger flourishes in the realm of unconsciousness, so it can quickly take over our entire body in ways we're not able to control. If we continually get angry throughout our lives, the stress weakens our body's immune system and increases the risk of stroke, heart attack, and heart disease. Essentially, anger burns us from the inside.

For example (almost *identical* to a fear response), the adrenal glands flood the body with stress hormones (adrenaline and cortisol), which increase both our heart rate and our breathing rate, sending us into *fight or flight* mode. Pulled from presence and clear thought, we go from feeling grounded to feeling ungrounded; from settled to feeling unsettled.

Because so much anger takes place without our conscious awareness, it can easily lead to destructive words and actions that later we feel shame and regret about. This comes up again and again when I work with people. While they may have the sincere desire to work on their anger, I often help them free themselves from the shame and self-judgment they feel *afterward*, the humbling mess after they lose their temper and say or do something regretful.

They might ask themselves, with a look of confusion, "What was I thinking? I don't know what came over me. Why did I act like that?"

The reality is, when we react with anger, we aren't acting, we're *reacting*. In the moment, we may feel empowered and in control, but we're not. Without the ability to think clearly, we lose the ability to act mindfully. Rather than taking conscious action, we respond and react unconsciously. Because true strength comes from being fully present in our bodies and in our hearts, anger often disempowers us rather than strengthens us.

Unfortunately, because the feelings stem from internal pain and fear, we may feel justified in our (re)actions, like we're doing what we have to do to protect ourselves, even if it means causing wounds to another.

Can you recall an experience in your life when you were desensitized and reacted with anger?
How did you feel about the episode when you returned to your senses?

THE SLOW BURN OF PASSIVE AGGRESSION

WHILE SOME PEOPLE ARE OUTWARDLY AGGRESSIVE and have a tendency to fight, others shut down emotionally and go further into avoidance and flight. Maybe we don't feel safe speaking up or learned that it's not ok to show anger. Maybe we don't want to lose control or make a scene that would lead to us being feared, judged, or receiving unwanted attention (as it makes us feel exposed and vulnerable). Instead, we silence ourselves and swallow our heated emotions.

Many people fail to realize that we're still capable of being destructive and abusive without showing physical signs of aggression. This hidden defense can be displayed through being irritated, resentful, judgmental, and passive aggressive. Passive aggression is when we feel the same level of upset and pain, but we deflect those feelings through sarcasm, stubbornness, or indirect hostility. Though it may not look like aggression, it is. And, it can cause as much damage as physically aggressive behavior.

Many of us learned to be passive in our outward expression of aggression from a young age. For example, my sisters and I grew up in a home where talking openly about our uncomfortable feelings was not comfortable. As a result, we often protected our vulnerability and released our pent-up emotions through aggression and passive aggression. We didn't have the tools to constructively understand our pain or functionally move through it, so we were caught in a destructive cycle of expelling that pain by abusing one another. Through snide remarks, hurtful put-downs, and full-blown physical battles, we generated a lot of harm and destruction.

Unfortunately, when we release our pain through passive aggression, like my sisters and I did, it can be extremely detrimental to our health, growth, and development. Since many of us learn to discount it as "kids being kids" or "they're just jealous," the wounds generated from the aggression and passive aggression of sibling abuse are often hidden. As a result, the traumatic events that shaped our lives in those formative years can easily slide off the radar of our awareness of what is generating so much of our present-day insecurity and discomfort.

Also, because passive aggressive behavior displays itself through a mask that is potentially smiling or expressionless (rather than looking scary and angry), we might excuse the behavior in ourselves or have trouble identifying it in others. This makes the healing process more challenging because in order to change something, we have to know that it needs changing and in order to know that it needs changing, we have to consciously recognize that it's happening.

Unless we tether ourselves to the awareness of the throbbing wound and aching heart beneath the mask, we may associate ourselves or others with being hurtful, mean, or cruel and not understand the deeper pain and compassion required to forgive.

As we continue on our journey together, we'll address this again and give ourselves permission to go deeper within to understand the pain and fear beneath the outer shell of anger and aggression. It's my hope that you'll eventually feel safe enough to be honest and present with your true feelings, so you don't need to resort to aggressively defending yourself when you're hurting. Instead, you can look at what's really going on, give yourself permission to feel it, and take action to get your needs met to heal it.

Do you ever feel more comfortable being passive aggressive than aggressive?

Do you ever find that you're less likely to be accountable for your actions and behavior when you're passive aggressive, rather than aggressive?

What happens when the fire of your pain becomes the fire of your purpose?

*When you no longer invest hours, months, or years of your life to
defending and surviving
and instead
begin fueling that energy into the movement that becomes
the meaning for being alive?*

You return.

*You begin feeling inspired
and led by what you love
rather than racing away from what you fear
and in that,
You awaken a sense of belonging.*

*You come back to the present moment and know
that you deserve to be here
without needing to change a thing.*

7.
SUFFERING

*To experience continuous pain, sadness, and loss;
to feel trapped, alone or lost.*

When the streamers and confetti settled after discovering what appeared to be the world's best way to eat all the food I loved and remain thin, I was confronted by the suffocating reality of addiction. What started out as a soothing solution to help me cope with the unresolved pain became a cage that I was trapped in for many years.

In fact, 17 years.

Many times, I would think I had found a path out, some solution that could set me free. I would see books or practices with the promise of guidance and support, but I couldn't get through the wall of resistance enough to talk about my suffering and addiction with anyone, not even myself. I was too embarrassed and buried too deep.

When I mustered the courage to try a new diet or routine, I would get my hopes up, then inevitably fail. In doing so, I fell deeper into the maze of shadows, back to the very place I started, only with more wounds and more doubt each time.

By this point, my suffering was invisible to most people. The days of loved ones asking if I was ok were long gone. Over the years, I had become so talented in hiding and protecting my secrets that anyone who knew about eating disorders in my youth just figured that I had outgrown it all. Plus, I looked normal and healthy on the outside. I was outgoing, energetic, and seemingly happy, so no one suspected that I was secretly depressed. To successfully hide secrets from everyone is a very desolate and lonely place to be.

In many ways, I was in worse shape than in my teens. Through years of forcing my body to throw up, the patterns and impulses were ingrained in my bodily responses and had become part of my everyday routine. Because I couldn't seem to stop, I got used to it—as if my mind and body accepted that I was bulimic and it became part of who I was.

I also got used to feeling lost and completely disconnected from myself. When I was little, I remember feeling confused and at times, out of place. When I was growing up, I spent a lot of time feeling sad and uncomfortable in myself. This was different; more intense. As if I was genuinely lost and untethered from myself. My wounds were so carefully buried inside me that I lost all awareness for where the pain was coming from. It felt like my whole reality was getting tossed and swirled around, and I was the pathetic mess tumbling inside it.

That's what suffering can feel like. It's like being lost in a vast, dark forest where there are no maps or signs guiding the way—just endless, disconcerting walls of blinding brush and briars on all sides.

In this stage of suffering, our need to defend is combined with the haze of unconsciousness and our anger has the ability to spiral and descend into realms of hate. Before, we might have found ourselves in the heat of anger from time to time, but when we get so lost and disconnected from ourselves, we carry that torch of fire in our hand, ready to burn anything down. We are resentful and unable to forgive.

While not everyone deals with depression, addiction, or the deep ache of hatred, most of us can relate to feeling trapped in a state of suffering. We know what it's like to be so disconnected from ourselves that we can't hear or feel what's really going on inside, yet our bodies keep breathing.

Examples of feeling SUFFERING:
- Lost
- Stuck or trapped
- Depressed
- Regretful
- Compulsive
- Lack of self-control
- Uncontrollable anger
- Inability to forgive
- Resentful and blameful
- Victimization

- Helpless
- Denial
- Inability to relax without distraction or substances
- Addicted and dependent
- Hatred towards self or others
- Lack of purpose
- Suicidal thoughts
- Apathy

If we look back at the list of wounds, many of those experiences create suffering. When our loved ones die, we're instantly shattered and immersed in a state of deep pain and suffering. When a relationship ends where our hearts are open and trusting, we're often completely miserable and destroyed by the separation.

In that sense, suffering is something we might experience from the moment the wound is placed throughout the progression of pain. But how is this place of suffering different? Why is the final stage labeled "suffering" when we could have been suffering the whole time?

Well, this final stage occurs when we enter a prolonged state of suffering. It's where the doors of the cage have become rusty and it's harder for us to break out. We become stuck in the cage.

Instead of being present and connected to the consciousness and love inside, we become disconnected and overpowered by fear. Rather than fully being ourselves (the sacred, conscious, light-filled being), we become the story of who we think we are: the ego, the person suffering.

The painful song of our beings becomes "I feel lost, lonely, and stuck."

The narrative would sound like:

<u>HEART</u>: *I am here, experiencing life.*
<u>WOUND</u>: *Ouch! That hurts.*
<u>PAIN</u>: *I don't feel good. I'm in pain.*
<u>NEED</u>: *I'm hurting and I'm scared. I need healing.*
<u>PROTECTION</u>: *My needs aren't met. I'll protect myself by trying not to feel the pain.*
<u>DEFENSE</u>: *To avoid feeling more pain, I will fight to protect myself.*
<u>SUFFERING</u>: *I feel lost, lonely, and stuck.*

Very soon, we're going to turn things around and get you back to your true self. We'll leave this realm of unconsciousness and suffering to get you back home, where you belong. But first, let's complete our mission through the stages of suffering to understand why we suffer so we can stop struggling and start living.

STUCK IN A PATTERN OF AVOIDANCE

FOR MANY OF US, FEELING *lost* AND *stuck* is our normal experience of life. Sure, we might be able to sustain a job or uphold a relationship (or not), but underneath the surface of our day-to-day routines are deep and sustained feelings of disconnection, uncertainty, insecurity, and entrapment. As we've been untethered from our true selves for so long and uncertain how to get back, we are suffering. And, because we've been doing it for so long, we might not even realize how disconnected we are.

These feelings of deep disconnection and suffering are often the direct outcome of *prolonged avoidance*. What is that? It's what happens when we've spent months, years, or even decades dissociating from the memories, wounds, pain, and true feelings within us.

By avoiding the things you don't want to look at and only focusing on the things you do, you create a very narrow mental pathway filled with blockages, barriers, and "do not enter" signs. This can also be described as "denial," and it leaves you with very narrow visibility and limited thinking capabilities. If you've trained yourself to not go *over there, through there,* or *behind here,* you don't have much space to work with and you can easily feel constricted and trapped. Essentially, you become trapped in a habitual pattern of turning away and your life feels stuck as a result.

Because we're resistant (and avoidant) to looking within ourselves at our own wounds and pain, we may associate the feelings of limitation and entrapment with our relationships, jobs, passions, and so on. While it may feel more comfortable to focus the problem outside ourselves, it only separates us from experiencing healthy connection with others, which slows down the process of healing.

When you avoid something, you turn away and hide from it. In a way, you're telling yourself that it's more powerful than you and that you're not strong enough to handle it or overcome it. This inner dialogue generates a feeling of weakness and fear, which emphasizes your insecurity and lack of self-esteem. Also, when you feel the need to hide from something, you nurture secrecy and protectiveness. This leads to heightened feelings of shame, as though you're not worthy of being honest or fully exposed.

While avoidance is something we initially began doing to protect ourselves, it gradually blooms and blossoms into a toxic overgrowth that becomes challenging to tend to. Like a garden left untouched for years, it can get unruly and out of hand, taking over our psyche and leaving us in a state of suffering.

The good news is that whatever discomfort you feel in your life right now may be drastically decreased by simply confronting and overcoming the avoidance. Sure, you may have initially felt insecurity and shame from the experiences you originally withstood, but how much of that has increased from the prolonged state of avoidance?

You may be pleasantly surprised and relieved when you finally look at the truth. This is something we'll talk more about when we get to Chapter 9.

Can you think of any feelings, emotions, or needs that you may be avoiding looking at and feeling?

THE WAVE OF COMPULSION

IT'S OFTEN WITHIN THE SUFFERING STATE OF unconsciousness that we become engulfed in compulsive behavior.

Compulsive: to act from a place of irresistible urge and need without conscious awareness; to act without thinking.

While we may associate compulsive behavior with someone who is addicted or not psychologically sound, the reality is that many of us are living in a compulsive, urgent state of being. We compulsively check our phones, emails, and text messages. We compulsively put something in our mouths when we're hungry. We compulsively react with emotions and words to what others do and say.

We're also compulsive thinkers. We're constantly bombarded by a steady stream of automatic concerns, worries, thoughts, and narratives of need, distraction, and defense. These thoughts circulate in our minds continually, without us consciously deciding if those thoughts are genuinely desired or are serving us.

Perhaps being a constant thinker doesn't sound like a bad thing? Thinking is good, right? Well, there's a big difference between constructive, conscious thinking and compulsive, *unconscious* thinking.

Say you're lying awake at night staring at the ceiling. You're trying to get back to sleep but you can't stop thinking. Your mind is a blizzard of thoughts:

Wait, what day of the month is it? Oh shoot, I need to mail rent out. What did I do with that envelope that came in the mail? Maybe I put it on my desk. I need to clean my desk. I need to clean the bathroom too. Oh yeah, we need more toilet paper, I should grab that tomorrow. What else do we need? I need to make a list. Unless, did I leave the mail in the car? Oh, the car, shoot, did I lock it?! Yeah. I think I did. I hope I did. I need to get the check engine light looked at. I wonder how much that's gonna cost? Last time it was over $500. How much will it be this time? I can't afford that right now. Why is everything so expensive? What can't we all just live happily and barter everything? Why do we even need money? Who created money anyway? Those guys are banking in big time and meanwhile, I can't even get any rest. What time is it? What?? My alarm is going off in two hours? This is awful. I can't sleep.

Even though sleep is probably what you need more than anything, you can't sleep because your mind can't stop thinking. You are automatically doing something without being able to stop. You are compulsively thinking. Even though all of the thoughts are valid and important to look at, they are happening on their own, without your conscious intention, consent, or control.

It's in this place of compulsivity that we're no longer living our lives. Instead, life and everything else is happening to us. We're a bystander to the life experience, being washed along on the waves. Rather than being strong and deciding what we want to think and say and how we want to feel, we're powerless. We don't have control of our thoughts or our emotions. We simply get washed along in the stream of what's happening and wait to find out what will happen next.

THE CYCLE OF ADDICTION

IF YOU CAN RELATE TO COMPULSION, you may be able to relate to addiction. We could have covered addiction in each chapter because it relates to our entire journey from wounds to pain to not getting our needs met to protecting ourselves.

I believe that addiction is one of the most challenging hurdles for humans to overcome. Perhaps we start out wanting whatever provides a sense of relief, though very quickly that *want* turns into a *need* and before we know it, we lose our willpower and our consciousness. We become increasingly compulsive and dependent on the thing that offers temporary relief from the deeper layers of pain, which we're not comfortable looking at. What originally appeared as a savior can gradually turn us into slaves.

When we become addicted to something, we become so disconnected from ourselves that we become reliant on whatever seems to calm the pain and ease the insatiable hunger within us. The thing supplying a sense of comfort and connection becomes somewhat of a friend, or the family pack that we long to feel connected to and safe inside.

But because our actions come from a place of fear and avoidance, our hearts are closed. We can't actually access the genuine experience of connection and comfort that we need because we're desensitized by the cage. So, what we gain from the experience is only a temporary stimulation and leads us to feeling more empty, hungry, alone, and in need.

This is the case whether you're addicted to alcohol, food, social media, orgasms, money, work, or opiates. While each of these comes with its own unique challenges to chemically ease your body off, each carries a similar frequency of need and longing. We're seeking some form of soothing comfort to put the broken pieces back together—to feel loved, accepted, cared for, safe, satiated, included, and whole.

While emotional hunger is the uncomfortable sensation of hunger and the original pain from the wound, addiction adds another layer of complexity. Before, you were in pain and needed support, but now you're in pain, needing support, and actively transferring that need (for comfort, safety, security, or connection) onto whatever you're addicted to.

And because we are so connected to the sacred display of patterns and cycles (sleep, digestion, menstruation, etc.), we can easily get stuck in these cycles. We get into a habitual pattern of experiencing pain and tending to it unconsciously, and we get tightly hooked into that cycle until we become comfortable with it. Once that happens, we're stuck.

The **progression of addiction** often goes something like this:

1. We experience a wound.
2. We feel the pain and discomfort of the wound.
3. We don't receive proper care and comfort for the pain.
4. Our internal feelings of hunger, longing, and anxiety intensify.
5. We don't deal with the wound, so the pain continues and the longing increases.
6. We discover an external substance or engagement that provides relief and distraction from the pain.
7. We develop a sense of dependency on the substance that continues providing relief.
8. The dependency becomes an unconscious, overpowering behavior.
9. The cycle continues and we become trapped.

Unfortunately, in none of these steps do we look at the wound to understand where the pain stems from or access constructive forms of connection, release, comfort, and love to get our needs met and to be healed.

While addiction causes a lot of pain, it is actually the *effect* of deeper pain. If we don't understand the "why"—the wounds, pain, and unmet needs—then we might work resolutely to heal our relationship with the addiction only to discover that it transforms. An insatiable hunger can become an insatiable thirst, so instead of compulsively eating, we compulsively drink.

Sure, opiates, ice cream, and cigarettes may temporarily bring a sense of relief, but they won't heal the real wounds that need healing. In fact, they only distract us from where the true healing lies: within us.

If you're suffering from addiction, know that you're not alone. Somewhere inside you is an innocent and powerful being who deserves to be held, forgiven, and loved unconditionally. As you'll come to learn, beneath the layers of shame, struggle, and wrongness that you feel about yourself, there is a radiant and pure light of your true self. Hidden beneath the pain and the wound is the real you, and I hold a strong and sincere vision that our time together will help you see the truth and rediscover the incredible, powerful being that is you.

Have you ever dealt with an addiction?

Do you currently feel a compulsive need or dependency on anything in your life?

THE CLOUD OF DEPRESSION

WHILE SADNESS IS SOMETHING WE NATURALLY feel after a wound, depression is a prolonged state of sadness, melancholy, and despondency. It often goes hand in hand with addiction, but you don't have to be addicted to something to experience depression. In fact, it's said that around 264 million people worldwide suffer from depression.

For some, depression is influenced by long-lasting pain from a particular situation such as a death or a loss. It may bring on the storm clouds of depression, which hover for days, weeks, or even years. For others, it can be summoned by years of wounding and unmet needs that have gradually accumulated over time, and the cloud lingers for long periods without a clear start or a finish. At times, our senses may become so blocked that we no longer feel sadness—because we no longer feel—we're just suspended in a state of apathy and nothingness.

For me, depression was like a thick, heavy blanket that covered my thoughts, hopes, and desires. While my eyes were able to see, my heart couldn't reach out and feel. As a result of being so heavily weighed down, I would be completely exhausted. Depression didn't just make my body exhausted; it made every part of me exhausted. My mind was too tired to think and my spirit was too tired to try. Sometimes, I would lose my interest in caring and just become indifferent and numb.

One of the most challenging things about the cloud of depression is that when we're under it, we often feel very alone and alienated. Because that heavy blanket or storm cloud is invisible, we may look and act seemingly fine, but inside we're struggling and in pain.

Unless there is someone you feel really comfortable being honest with, and who really understands what it's like, your depression can easily be misunderstood and disregarded as something that you should be able to fix. People might say "just switch your frown around," or "don't be such a downer," or "cheer up." When you're dealing with depression, those words can easily add to the weight of feeling alone and disconnected.

The reality is, if we're in a state of depression, it's likely that there are unresolved wounds and hidden emotions that don't have a safe and proper outlet to be constructively understood, supported, and released. Unfortunately, because our culture has such an aversion to the expression of sadness (*everyone, smile and look happy!*) depression is often overlooked, avoided, and neglected.

If you are experiencing depression in your life, my heart goes out to you right now. I hold you in my heart and look forward to continuing on this journey together with the intention and vision that our work together may somehow help you see the light through the clouds.

*Have you ever struggled with depression?
What does depression feel like for you?*

THE STORY OF ROSE

FOR SOME TIME IN MY 20S, I WORKED as a waitress in a small, family-owned restaurant. As the job was my main source of income at the time, I worked a lot of shifts and spent a lot of time taking orders, delivering meals, and cleaning tables with my fellow waiters and waitresses. I developed some close and heartfelt friendships. I often worked with a woman named Rose. She was somewhat mysterious, and while she was kind, I had trouble reading her and understanding her.

On the outside, she was blond, beautiful, and no more than 20 years old. However, she carried a heavy look of intensity and often distanced herself from others. She would smile then immediately look away. I couldn't tell whether she was frustrated, anxious, or ready for a new job. Knowing that she needed to work to pay the bills, I assumed she did the job solely for the money.

One day, a fellow waitress let me know that Rose was "going through it and could use some help." They were roommates, and I agreed to come to their house that night and offer whatever support I could. Upon entering the apartment, I instantly felt uneasy. The space was very dimly lit and it felt like I was entering a cell.

We sat in a circle on her floor and I invited Rose to know that the circle was strong and secure; that she could open up and share what was going on. After meandering around various topics and struggling to push past the resistance, she finally said, "I have a problem. I'm an addict."

Struggling with addiction myself at that time, I had no judgment towards her. I asked, "What is it? What are you dealing with?"

"Heroin." As soon as she said it, she broke into shame-filled tears and finally showed the emotion she had been burying deep inside. She described how disconnected and separate from herself she had become, and how depressed, numb and lost she felt each day.

She explained that the heroin was something she did with her boyfriend, and how much she loved him. Filled with regret, fear, and enthusiasm to get better, she exclaimed that she was ready for change. She wanted to get clean, but it seemed she had to choose between him or recovery. Almost unable to speak complete sentences, it was as if she was literally pulled between two worlds before my eyes; she was clearly struggling between the force of consciousness and unconsciousness, struggling between healing herself and honoring a relationship that meant everything to her.

I explained how incredible it was that she had finally reached out and opened up, how it was such a huge first step, and how she was going to get through it. I shared inspiration for us finding a nearby recovery center and helping her with some life changes.

With hope and concern, I went home that night and collected whatever information I could to help her. The next day, I brought her a bag with a journal, books, teas, and information about local centers and recovery programs. I offered her whatever I could offer at the time, which sadly was far less than I could offer her now.

Each time we worked together, I checked in to see how she was doing. With an exhausted and insincere smile, she would say something along the lines of "fine" and I would hold a moment of space for the fact that she wasn't fine.

Not long after, she quit the job and I moved to another state. We lost touch with one another. I was completely devastated, then, to find out that both her and her boyfriend had died only months later in a drug overdose.

I've thought about her a lot over the years and worked through my regret at not doing more to help her. I've also reflected on how separated she was from the tether to herself and how hollow her life had become through addiction. I think about the pain she must have felt having disconnected from her intuition and her sense of purpose.

So often, we read people for how they appear on the outside. We look at our coworkers, classmates, grocery clerks, and people in line beside us, but we are unaware of the deep suffering they may be dealing with inside. So easily, we project a story onto them and don't imagine that they may be dealing with severe depression or addiction, and may only be inches away from the border between life and death.

I hold Rose in my heart, like a shining jewel of remembrance and connection to all those who have forgotten the importance of life and become separate from their heart.

May this work that we are doing together somehow bring healing to those of us who are lost and hurting right now.

THE BROKEN BRANCH

WHEN WE FEEL DEPRESSED, JUDGED, LET DOWN, and abandoned enough times in our lives, we can easily lose an appreciation for our individual value. Many of us feel unloved, untalented, and unworthy, like we don't have anything of importance to offer others or contribute to the world. Like a branch broken from its tree, we lose our life force, and we forget our necessary place within the expansive community of life on earth.

In this situation, people naturally say "you're not alone," but with over 7.8 *billion* people in the world right now, I imagine you're fully aware that you're not alone. Yet, somehow, even with a mass of humans surrounding you in every direction, you may still feel extremely isolated and lonely, like no one understands and no one cares.

The truth is, even though everyone has been through trauma and everyone has experienced pain, people probably don't know what you're going through or that you need help. *Why?* Because most of us are so caught up in the constant battle of life that we're not present. We're too absorbed in our own stories, our own problems, and our own affairs to really feel, understand, and care what someone else is going through. We're hurting and desperately trying to survive as best we can. Deep inside, we do care, but because we're so unconscious, we've forgotten how to access our tenderness and we have become care*less*.

It's also possible that you haven't ever felt safe enough to genuinely, honestly communicate the depths of what you're going through. It's hard enough to know what's going on inside you, let alone find a way to describe it in words to others. It's also possible that in those moments when you mustered the courage to talk openly to someone, they may not have had the skills, desire, or presence to support you.

So, when you're feeling lost and alone, when you're questioning life, you may not receive the care and support you need, and so you may feel unimportant and unloved.

This is something I've witnessed in a lot of people over the years, including myself. Even though someone can be surrounded by family and friends, or be in a committed relationship, they may still feel deeply alone inside.

Karina is someone who was working to overcome a dependency on alcohol. At the time, she was dealing with anxiety, uncontrollable emotional outbursts, and marital issues. When she was alone, she felt a sense of hollowness in her being. Continually feeling more and more displaced, she began to question her purpose for being alive, which scared both her and her family. She was often defensive and aggressive, constantly taking her pain out on her husband, who was like an emotional punching bag for her.

To find the root of the emptiness, I asked about her ambitions and her fears of following them. For the most part, she didn't know. She just felt "stuck" and "empty inside." Over time, as we retraced steps from her past and sorted through piles of memories, we unraveled some very distinct experiences where she was teased and chastised, where she was ingrained with the belief that she was "useless," "unimportant," and "not good enough." Since childhood, that tale had echoed again and again until she lost touch with herself and the importance of being alive. Her separation from her heart turned into the senseless treatment of her husband.

While the relationship with her husband did need work and while she was ready for a career change, something deeper needed to shift. Karina needed to know that she was important and necessary, that she had a role in this world. She needed to know that she was worthy of receiving love, and that was something beyond what her husband could provide. It was an awareness that required her to look within herself, find the hidden wounds, and heal them. Then, she could reconnect to that tree of life, love herself, and form loving relationships with others.

Have you ever felt lost and unable to understand your purpose in being alive?

Can you remember any painful experiences throughout your life that may have contributed to this feeling of unworthiness or lack of belonging?

ONE BILLION RISING

IF WE SPEND LONG ENOUGH FEELING EMPTY, LOST, and depressed—without a deep connection to the consciousness and love within ourselves—our senselessness can become destructive and eventually violent, as it did with Karina.

Unconsciousness turning into violence is something I learned about during my work with the One Billion Rising (OBR) movement in India. I had always imagined my return to India being a light-filled walk of fragrant spices, marigolds, and family reunions but it was something much different and much more than that. What pulled me back to my blood's home soil was an invitation from the incredible activist leader Eve Ensler to join her tour and speak out against the abuse and violence of women. It was a powerful invitation to return to the land where so many of my wounds derived from and an opportunity to look directly into the eyes of the big, masked tiger that caused them.

If you've ever been to India, you might easily say it's one of the most magical, beautiful, and sacred places you've ever experienced. Indeed, it is otherworldly and radiant, with a light that is uniquely its own. Indians are masters of meditation and astral travel—like mystics, wizards, and walkers between worlds. For a long time, they have been leading our species forward into deeper understandings of consciousness and spiritual awakening.

Then, reality sets in—like any picture that appears perfect, there is another side that is less beautiful. Sworn into an old and outdated system, arranged marriages are still prominent, gender inequality is a way of life, and the abuse of women and girls is at times *supported*, meaning: there are some places in India where you will be arrested for reporting a rape. In fact, studies show that at least one in three women in India will experience domestic abuse in her lifetime and only one in ten of those will seek help. I imagine that fear of punishment and backlash at speaking out means girls and women have learned to silence themselves to avoid further abuse.

Together, the global director of One Billion Rising (Monique Wilson), a filmmaker, and a small team of coordinators stepped forward and confronted this painful problem. In solidarity with the Indian women activists who had organized events and activities, we spent weeks traveling the country, participating in marches, and tending to the topic of abuse and violence towards women. We called with our voices "Rise! Resist! Unite!" Together, we encouraged women to confront their fears and un-silence themselves.

As inspiring and compelling as our work was, it was equally daunting and appalling to hear women in their 70s speak out for the first time about the hundreds of rapes they had endured, and to hear the mothers who had never forgiven themselves for their baby girls being killed at birth for simply being female.

The reality of abuse and violence towards women in India was heartbreaking to witness, and it was also overwhelming to realize that almost every one of those acts came from men.

THE STORM OF VIOLENCE

WHILE IT MAY SEEM THAT INDIA IS UNIQUE IN THIS lineage of abuse towards women, it's not. Violence and abuse towards women is a problem happening across the globe in every country. In fact, it's not just India where one in three women are abused in her lifetime, it's happening *worldwide*.

How is this possible? Why is this happening?

There's strong evidence and research that reveals it's not just learned behavior—men have a different hormonal makeup and are more aggressive by nature. However, there's also strong evidence and research that shows how violence also has a lot to do with how someone is raised and nurtured (or not).

If a boy is taught and trained not to cry or show his emotions, how many walls does he build within himself that prevent him from hearing his heart and the conscience that speaks from it? If he is continually taught to express those blocked emotions through anger and hatred, how much more likely is he to go into an unconscious state when he's hurting and release that withheld tenderness through violence and rage?

Very likely.

Are men bad people? Are they the cause of all the violence and abuse in this world?

No. Certainly not.

There are plenty of women in the world who are abusive, violent, and destructive with their anger. It's definitely not just men. In fact, many of us need support in working through our mother issues, not our father issues, and it was the females in our lives that caused the wounds, not the males. The truth is men are wounded too.

While my time with OBR helped me see the importance of empowering women, it also helped me understand the *essence* of hatred and violence. For so long, I thought that my dad was uniquely violent and destructive. But as I grew older, I realized that most women have dealt with some form of abuse; it wasn't just my dad or my family—the problem was *bigger* than that. I saw that it wasn't just India—the problem was *bigger* than that. Then, I started seeing that it wasn't just men abusing women—the problem was *bigger* than that.

The destruction caused by violence happens to people of *all* ages, *all* genders, and *all* races. It happens in every country across the globe and has been happening for a very, very long time. Violence and hatred is a worldwide, *systemic* problem.

Have you ever felt hatred for someone or something?
Did that hatred lead you to do or say something violent or destructive?
How did you feel afterwards?

A SUFFERING WORLD

AS HEARTBREAKING AND TRAGIC AS IT IS, almost all of us play a part in these unconscious and destructive ways of life. With closed eyes and covered ears, we hurt our bodies, we hurt animals, we hurt trees, we hurt bees, we hurt the earth, and we hurt one another. Because we've been caught in this cycle of experiencing pain, closing our hearts, and causing more pain, we've become comfortable understanding this as a way of life. And we've been doing it for hundreds and *thousands* of years.

It's here, in this space of severe unconsciousness, that we become part of the collective unconsciousness. We become part of the bigger problem of suffering. You may not be actively involved in physically injuring someone, but how many times have your unhealed wounds led you to be so distracted, so self-absorbed, and so defensive that you carelessly caused more pain, more shame, and more suffering in the world?

I can tell you right now, the answer is: *a lot.*

How does that feel? How does it feel to know that you, me, and billions of others are so lost in our pain that we're actively contributing to the painful mess our world is in right now?

Sad?
Depressing?
Humbling?

I feel it too. It's heartbreaking and daunting to think about.

However, we *have* to think about it. We have to courageously confront our avoidance and look at where our closed hearts are contributing to the bigger pain. We have to *consciously* look at where our own *unconsciousness* is part of the bigger problem.

Otherwise, we will remain lost and trapped inside the cage, adding to the suffering of the world, and we don't deserve that. We don't deserve to suffer and neither do any of the animals, trees, plants, and insects who are suffering because of our unconsciousness. Each of us deserves better. We all deserve to feel safe, cared for, and at peace inside. We all deserve to be empowered in our hearts and free from this suffering.

Though you have been broken,
you are not destroyed.

Those cracks in your heart are the openings
where the light of your love speaks.

Those cracks are where you have been broken
open.

You are not lost
floating through space.

You are the Sun.

Let the light of your love awaken the entire sky,
reminding us all to come home.

A MOMENT OF PAUSE.

This has been quite a journey, with some intense, mountainous terrain.
How are you feeling?

It takes a lot of courage and personal determination to do this work and explore the cavernous spaces of your being. You could easily choose to distract yourself and carry on with your daily routines right now, but you're not. Instead, you're reading this book. You're devoting your time and your focus to healing yourself.

Thank you.

I hope you're able to witness that with each moment of your dedication to self-healing, you are healing the world.

◆

Now, as we depart the land of understanding *why* we separated away from ourselves, let's turn things around and enter the realm of *how* to return home to ourselves.

8.
REALIZATION

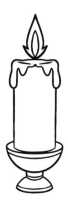

To become fully aware of something.

Like an *ah-ha* moment, when I met my husband Kurt for the first time, I felt it. It was a spark, as if something inside me was ignited. I felt a sense of intrigue, intimidation, and alertness. While it all felt unfamiliar and fresh, there was also something natural and faintly nostalgic about it.

At the time, I associated this mysterious feeling with Kurt. As he is genuinely remarkable, magical, and unique, I assumed he was the reason for the colorful bouquet of sparks and strange new feelings inside. However, as time passed and months turned into years, it became clear that the sensations I felt when we first met were less to do with him and more about what was happening inside me.

While our love was, and still is, glowing with rays of beauty and mysticism, what began culminating during those early moments of our relationship together wasn't fireworks of infatuation and jitterbugs. It was the bizarre and sacred siren sounding the alarm that *I needed to change my life*. With that, I was both intrigued and terrified.

Am I about to die? I would think to myself.

Really, that's how it felt. I felt like something transformational, sacred, and scary was about to happen. Something as profoundly transformative as what I imagined to be my own death, which wasn't an entirely new thought to me. I had imagined my own death many times. I suppose anyone who undergoes years and years of a destructive addiction at some point has to consider the fact that they are indeed killing themselves. However, this experience felt different. While the breeze seeping through the cracks of my being felt like the spirit of death, it also felt like the anticipation of birth. The birth of change.

After so many years of bulimia, my body was beginning to shut down. My teeth were crumbling and my organs weren't able to digest food. There was only so much more my body could handle. I was in trouble and needed to make a huge change if I wanted to live, especially if I wanted to walk alongside a healthy, strong partner like Kurt. In order to do this, I knew I would have to confront my fears. Rather than running away from my pain, I would need to stop, *turn around*, and face it.

In the past, I was intimidated and resistant to doing anything that brought me in contact with silence and stillness, but now, driven by a desire and palpable urge to heal, I was ready to try new things. Gradually, I began exploring shamanic plant medicine, lucid dreaming, journal writing, spending time alone in nature, and speaking openly with people about what I was going through—all of which were very necessary for my eventual recovery. However, to even get to the point of being willing to try those things, I had to realize that I was ready. Instead of constantly keeping myself stimulated, distracted, and focused on anything but the truth of what was really going on, I was ready to do things differently. I was ready for change.

This is often how realization enters our lives. The light of awareness breaks through the clouds, and suddenly we understand something we didn't previously get. We experience a gust of realization that changes the course of our understanding, welcoming us into new perspectives and new possibilities. We finally realize that we're done suffering and are ready to stop and turn around. We're ready to heal and we're ready to do whatever it takes to get there.

Examples of experiencing REALIZATION:
- The birth of a new idea
- A shift in perspective
- The awareness of something previously unknown
- Being open to fresh feelings and understandings
- An expansion of understanding
- Discovering and recognizing a new aspect of reality
- Fully comprehending something

Whether it comes as a subtle and faint whisper in the night, a loud and belting laugh, or a deep and wailing cry—the moment of recognizing "I'm ready" will be different for everyone. You may feel so stressed and stretched to the far reaches of your capacity that this insightful readiness will come as a last resort. If so, it's possible you've sunk so far to the bottom that there's nowhere to go but up. Or it might not be the suffering that inspires you to change but the pure desire to experience the freedom of being alive without suffering.

Regardless of how the realization comes into our lives—and how many months, years, or decades we have been struggling—when we fully understand that we're done suffering, it's as if we're saying, "I'm ready for change and I'm going to do something about it."

Now, having a realization is not new to you. It's something you've already experienced.

How do I know this? Because you're reading this book. You wouldn't be here right now if you hadn't come to the realization that something in your life isn't working and that you're ready for change. While there are a lot of important steps on the path to healing, I see this as one of the most important. If we don't recognize that we're ready for change, we won't take the initiative required to make it happen.

Let's imagine that your home has a hole in the roof. For years, it was something you were aware of but didn't put much attention into. "So what? It's a little hole. It's not going to hurt anything." The weather is fine and you go on pretending it's not there. You put up with it. Until, suddenly, the weather changes. When it rains, the water comes into the hole and splashes everywhere. You ask yourself, "Is it really a big deal? Do I actually need to stop and put energy into fixing it? It's such a bother to gather the materials, find a ladder, and crawl all the way up onto the roof to patch up the hole."

Motivated by your lack of inspiration and tendency to avoid, you come up with a plan. You get a bucket and place it in the house on the floor beneath the hole. "Perfect," you say to yourself. "Now I can go on about my life, not deal with the hassle of fixing the hole, and pretend like it's not there."

Until, of course, the hole gets bigger and the bucket fills up. Eventually, you find yourself living in a wet, musty pile of mold. Your carpet is soaked, your clothes are damp, and you begin showing signs of asthma.

"Why? Why is this happening to me?" You plead and curse to the sky.

Because you were avoiding fixing the actual problem. You were avoiding the work and it created a whole mess of other problems.

Where is the realization in this? The realization is the moment when you look around you and say "Enough is enough. I can't live like this anymore. I'm done avoiding this and I'm ready to deal with the problem. I'm ready to heal my life."

We often see the depiction of a light turning on when someone has a realization, and in many ways, that's what it's like to have the realization that you're done suffering. As if you've been sitting in that dark and musty room-like cage for long enough, the light of awareness is like a candle ignited inside of you. At that moment, you realize, *I don't have to do this anymore. I don't have to suffer. Either I can stay stuck inside this cramped cage and let death take my life or death can take my suffering so I can get out of here and start living.*

So, let's do it. Let's learn about realization and take the first steps to free ourselves from the cage so we can start living life again!

THE HIDDEN BENEFITS OF SUFFERING

AS WE TRANSFORM OUR LIVES FROM SUFFERING to empowerment, there is an important key hidden here. It's the bittersweet realization that we are in many ways *benefiting* from our suffering. While the struggles you've endured for months, years, and even decades were never anything you would have knowingly desired or chosen—somewhere inside, you may actually enjoy and appreciate the safety, convenience, and relief provided by the struggle.

Does this mean you should be *grateful* for your suffering?

Like a teacher telling you to say "thank you" to the kid who started the fight, punched you in the gut, and held your head under water until you couldn't breathe, you should now be *thankful*?!

No, and also yes.

Maybe you feel relaxed and get more sleep when you're depressed? If you're intimidated by receiving attention, then maybe staying silent and hidden in the shadows of your shame and suffering feels comfortable and safe? Maybe seeing yourself as the victim means you don't have to acknowledge where you're also being hurtful and destructive to others?

What about anger? Maybe it feels good to completely lose your cool and scream at the top of your lungs? There are probably times when those jagged blades of your defensiveness make you feel stronger and more confident?

What about drinking? Maybe you struggle with insecurity and confidence, so you really appreciate the attention and sense of freedom provided by alcohol?

As much as compulsive eating and bulimia were my biggest, most painful hurdles to overcome, there was a part of me that enjoyed it. I *loved* binging and getting lost in the sedation of sugar. I *appreciated* being able to eat tasty, unhealthy food and not worry about gaining weight. I *wanted* to hide from my life and enter a quiet, secluded kitchen of comfort.

Does my acknowledgement of these benefits justify my suffering or encourage my habits? No. By acknowledging the truth, I can build a more solid foundation of honesty and trust within myself and:

- Empower myself to be more consciously aware of why I'm stuck
- Place the power of change into my own hands
- Strengthen my friendship with myself

By realizing the hidden joys of my suffering, I also have a better understanding of what my needs are and what I'm seeking—in my case, relief, joy, adventure, comfort, and solitude.

While it may feel counterintuitive to intentionally acknowledge where we have benefited from our suffering, it's essential to have a transparent understanding of where we *choose* to knot ourselves into the pain. That way, we are more aware of how to get ourselves out.

In what ways have you benefited from your habits, struggles, and suffering?

LEARNING FROM OUR STRUGGLES

IT TOOK ME QUITE A FEW YEARS TO LOOK BACK at my so-called "mistakes" and rather than shrivel in shame, appreciate what a significant, necessary, and enriching experience it was. If I hadn't endured that entire journey of addiction, shame, insecurity, depression, and suffering, you and I wouldn't be here right now. I wouldn't be who I am, nor would I have the confidence, strength, and wisdom to be here helping you. Who knows if I would even be alive right now?

Life is mysterious, and had I not taken the exact path I have taken, I might have gotten into an accident years ago and not lived through it. Who is to say that what we consider the short end of the stick isn't actually the long end in disguise?

Though it may not feel like it when you're going through it, when you finally make it through the storm of your suffering, you may look back and realize how strong, perceptive, intuitive, compassionate, and resilient you are after that long, arduous journey. Every choice, decision, and regretful mistake you have made has been serving some strangely divine and unseen purpose, offering you eventual wisdom, knowledge, and growth.

When we see our suffering as the enemy—something that controls us, holds us down, and tortures us, we run the risk of disempowering ourselves and seeing the suffering as a malevolent force to be feared. We tell ourselves the convincing tale that we're helpless and have no control, that someone else is forever to blame, that it was the cage's fault for locking us in. If we fear something that we think is potentially stronger than us, we're apt to feel insecure, protective, and nervous, which holds us hostage in a state of immobilizing fear and continually drains our power.

You don't need to be afraid and you don't need to blame yourself or your past. There are no enemies here. Your suffering is not who you are and it's not anything that has power over you. Your struggles are simply the layers of protection and defense that were built up around your heart to guard your tenderness within.

Are those layers serving you?

Maybe.

Are they serving you enough to continue being separate from your heart and living a life of struggle?

No. They're not.

It's up to you to make the choice to live differently.

What have you learned about life through your experiences of struggling?

LETTING GO OF THE PAST

SOMETIMES, WE HAVE A BETTER IDEA OF WHAT we *don't* want long before we know what we *do* want. People might ask you what you want and the first thing that comes from your mouth is "I'm so sick and tired of ____." Maybe you've tried marching up the mountain of transformation so many times and fallen so often that you can't handle getting your hopes up?

Maybe what you want is *freedom* from suffering? But that sounds like winning the lottery, and what are the chances of that? Especially for someone who has felt caged and stuck inside themselves for a very long time?

Yes, the past may be filled with thousands of experiences that are stacked up high into towering piles labeled "the way things are." And yes, the future may have nothing to show for itself—no promises or guarantees. However, because the future is unwritten, it doesn't mean that it's weak or empty; it just means that it's a mysterious blank canvas of possibility; it's a living, breathing herd of potential.

Even if you've been doing the same thing for 20 years, it doesn't mean you'll be doing it for the next 20; it just means you did it in the past. That's all. Whether you're comfortable with it or not, the past is gone now so you can relax and *let it go*.

While a big part of our work together includes looking at the past, our intention isn't to get caught in it. In fact, a big part of enabling ourselves to be free of the past is to witness it without identifying with our old perspectives and stories. Anytime you retell an old story and project a fearful vision of it onto what you think will happen in the future, you start to make it happen. Remember—you're *powerful*.

When we focus on what's not right, it often encourages more of what doesn't work, so let your future self be like a child who you don't want to brainwash with your fears and thoughts. Allow yourself to be humble and inquisitive, right here in this moment, without all of the answers and assumptions—and without the need to tell the future what to look like, what to think, and how to be.

Just let your future self be themselves: perfectly *unknown*.

THE DECISION

THERE WILL BE TIMES WHEN YOU OPEN YOUR heart to love, then experience the deep heartbreak of loss. When you believe in something and nurture it with all of your time, only to watch it turn to dust. You will rise up to the highest of your potential and at some point fall. Life is unavoidably filled with hardships and challenges that break us open and break us apart. It's a full package deal, and there's really no getting around it.

While we can't change that, we can change how we respond and evolve through those experiences. We have the power to decide and choose how we want to feel, act, and be in each moment.

Does that feel intimidating or irritating? Sometimes, hearing that we're in charge of our own emotions, reactions, and perspectives can feel overwhelming, especially if we're already exhausted and uncertain. It can also be challenging to envision ourselves as being free from suffering when our lives are so deeply interwoven with people and situations that are beyond our control.

Sure, we can studiously work on shifting and bettering ourselves, but what about our parents, spouses, children, friends, employees, siblings, and caregivers? What if we grow into more honest, communicative, and grounded people and they don't? How can we choose to feel better in life when we're surrounded by annoying, needy, hurting, lying, competitive people?

Well, being *done with suffering* doesn't mean that you're suddenly immune to pain, challenges, and loss for the rest of your life. It means that you're making the choice to change the way you show up, handle, and respond to those uncomfortable encounters *when* they happen. It means that rather than turning away or avoiding life, you make the decision to show up and courageously turn *towards* it, confront it, and understand it. In doing so, you awaken the clarity, courage, and insight necessary to choose different actions, and this affects your entire life. It also nurtures a sense of empowerment within you.

Mahatma Gandhi is a great example of this. He was a civil rights leader and humanitarian, and his individual practice and devotion to walking the path of conscious action (rather than unconscious reaction) led him to accomplish great feats. Again and again, he was confronted with conflict, resistance, and aggression. He was given the opportunity to fight, but he didn't.

Instead, he made the choice each time to continue on the path his heart knew was right—the path of peace, integrity, compassion, and healing. He could so easily have been detoured by the resistance. He could have given up. He didn't. He stayed true to working on his own behavior, actions, and mindset. With that, he created profound change, which included bringing independence to the entire country of India, over 350 million people at the time.

Gandhi's dedication to living a peaceful life didn't mean he would *never* encounter challenge or struggle. It meant that he was stronger and more capable of handling the challenges *when* he encountered them. His seemingly small choices to work on one individual human (himself) had profound effects that were 350,000,000 times bigger.

There is a lot we can't change in life, including other people. However, when we make the decision to change our own behavior and actions, it inevitably affects the entire world.

COMMITMENT

Imagine you and I seated together right now, reflecting on where this journey has led us so far, and you say, "I'm ready for change. I'm done suffering. I see how I got here and I want to do things differently."

I might then ask, "Are you committed?"

You might say, "To healing? Yes!"

I would reply, "Yes to healing, though more so, to yourself. Are you committed to yourself? Are you ready to be more fully present and available for yourself in new ways?"

Yes, we're about to delve into some really incredible and awesome insights, perspectives and opportunities for change, however, unless you're committed to being more fully available to be a better listener, friend and teammate for *yourself*, it won't work. We'll get part way there and your old patterns of resistance, shame, judgment and separation from yourself will slow us *way* down.

This is something that took many years for me to understand. Committing myself to anything felt challenging. It meant foolishly allowing my hopes to rise only for them to come crashing to the ground. It meant inevitable failure accompanied by the letdown of overwhelming sadness.

While I knew my intention was to heal and my goal was to end my relationship with suffering, I didn't realize how *not* committed to myself I was. I would set goals for what I wanted to achieve and lists of what I wanted to stop doing, but with each one, I was loading more pressure, stress, and shame onto myself. I didn't realize that ending my relationship with suffering meant strengthening my relationship with myself.

The reality is, commitment doesn't require attachment and it doesn't thrive on expectation. This journey doesn't involve winning or losing. When you're ready to devote yourself to healing your wounds, overcoming your fears, and opening yourself to deeper levels of love and trust, it means you're ready to *try*. You're unconditionally devoted to not giving up and not turning your back on yourself anymore. You're committed to the journey, not the destination.

At some point, later down the road, you may look back and realize how far you've come. How the journey was more enjoyable than you thought it would be and how the self-love you achieved along the way was really what you were seeking all along.

What does commitment mean to you?

Are you willing to commit yourself to trying a new way of being with yourself?

INTENTION: THE DIRECTION HOME

FOR A LONG TIME, I ASSOCIATED MYSELF WITH being the problem. I resented my annoying habits and felt that I was weak. I drew the line between myself and the green grass of what I wasn't, and I genuinely felt that I had to change myself (my annoying, problematic self) to become the better, stronger person I longed to be.

In doing that, *change* came with a constant desire to leave. Leave what? Anything. Anything that would separate me further from myself, the one who was so hard to be around. I left jobs. I left careers. I left towns. I left friends. I left relationships. I left my family. I kept searching for a place that was cleaner, lighter, and more inspiring; free from the memories and the stagnant pain that was nauseating and too much to be with.

For so long, I was trying to separate from myself, not realizing that it was actually the separation from myself that was the problem. I could no longer stand the shame, depression, regret, and constant suffering.

Thankfully, that's not who I was. I wasn't the pain, the addiction, or the suffering; I was the sensitive, tender, hurting, and deserving being *hidden* inside it. I was the one who I needed to walk *towards*, not away from.

What's so powerful about being ready to really create change and be devoted to healing is that you find the direction you're finally ready to face, and it's towards yourself. Rather than constantly looking for some*thing*, some*one*, some *place* that holds the answers to your happiness, you realize you're finally ready to stop and turn towards *you*.

You, the one you've been avoiding.
You, the one who needs your attention.
You, the one who's done suffering and longs to be loved.

This is something that revealed itself to me when I finally broke through the layers of my pain and began overcoming the addiction. Although I didn't expect innocence to be something I would experience through my healing, it seemed that with each week, month, and year of being more present and empowered, I felt newly born.

It was as if all the painful, messy, and shameful stories built up around me began disintegrating. I realized the place I was trying to get to wasn't somewhere else—it was right there inside me. It was a small, sacred room that had been closed off and protected for so long, and in my healing, I was gaining access to that treasured place within me: my true self.

At times, you may think that you're a weak, anxious mess but you're not. That's not who you are. Even though the pain and suffering may have become comfortable or feel natural at times, it's not who you are, nor is it who you were ever intended to be.

Who you are is the clear, calm stillness gently and patiently waiting underneath the layers of pain and suffering. You are something so much deeper, greater, and infinitely more powerful than the stories of struggles that surround you. Who you are meant to be is who you have always been deep inside, before the pain and suffering. Essentially, it's where we're trying to get you home to—back into the loving arms of yourself.

At the start of our time together, we talked about intention...
Has your intention changed as we've been on our journey together?
Do you have any new intentions that are emerging?

ooooo

*I stand alone.
Lost.*

*A foreigner.
Disconnected
from my body.
Untethered.*

*Aware
I am there.
For how long?
Too long.*

*There.
Standing.
Floating.
Lost.*

For too long.

*I am done
being there.*

I am ready

To be here.

ooooo

A SHORTCUT THROUGH THE FOREST

Reflecting back on our time together, we've taken a very distinct path to get from the heart to suffering. Through each of the stages, we've gradually progressed from having an open heart to closing ourselves off in a state of protection and defense.

I imagine that throughout our journey thus far, you've already been getting sparks of insight and curiosity, wondering *why we have to go through all of that unnecessary suffering? Is it really so scary to have an open heart? Why do we have to close ourselves off and hide away in a musty old cage of unconsciousness? There must be a better way, right?*

Yes. There is a better way.

While the experience of suffering offers much knowledge and wisdom, we don't need to always close our hearts off when we're uncomfortable. Rather than continually going through the cycles and stages of suffering, and eventually finding ourselves locked in a cage of despair over and over again, there's a shortcut.

If you think back to the places we've been and retrace the path we took, you'll recall a very prominent moment in our exploration, a significant place where everything went awry. I imagine you already know when and I don't need to say it, but I will—it was when the Great Divide happened. It was the moment you left presence, stepped through the veil of ego, and entered into unconsciousness within the state of protection. That was when the walls went up, the shields were lifted, and the feelings were buried. That's when you disconnected from your heart, numbed your feelings, and began traveling away from yourself.

If you want to hop on a new path that's easier and healthier, you need to go back to that place and undo what was done. You need to find the junction and take a new route, guiding yourself inward, instead of outward.

A *SHORTCUT* TO
THE EMPOWERED HEART
–Understanding the needs and getting them met–

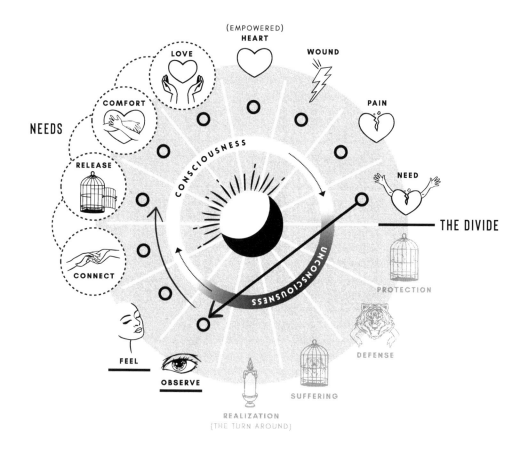

While wounds are something we will inevitably experience in life and pain is the natural response to those uncomfortable occurrences, we don't have to move into the cage of unconsciousness, protection, and suffering if we can better understand the pain and get our needs met. By leaning in closer to ourselves, rather than further away, we can remain open, present, and conscious. We can actively navigate the pain and heal the wounds. We can break the pattern by returning to consciousness and create a healthy support network to aid ourselves back to presence and wellness.

We do this by:
- Finding the wound and understanding the needs (**observe** and **feel**)
- Getting those needs met (**connect**, **release**, **comfort**, and **love**)
- Returning home to the heart (**empowered**)

A new journey

Because the journey is circular, it's here at this midway point that you will enter a new space and move in a completely different direction. Instead of moving away from your heart, you'll move towards it. In some ways, the first part of the journey taught you what you need to know to be prepared for the true journey of healing, which begins now. Like opening a new book, a fresh new experience awaits.

Mapping the steps

While we'll move from **observe** into **feel**, there are no set rules or standards for which comes first. Sometimes, you'll benefit by looking around at what's going on, then asking yourself how you're feeling as a result. Other times, you'll feel inspired to take a better look around at what's going on based on how you're feeling. So, while you'll learn a particular framework on the path I take you on, please adapt the steps to what works best for your own personal process.

The same goes for getting your needs met. While we'll move from **connect** into **release** into **comfort** and then into **love**, you may find yourself going from **feel** into **release** and then into **connect**. Go with it. I will offer you various tools of support and it's completely up to you how you want to use them.

Destination: Home

Through these pages and this journey we're on, it's my intention to help you return home to your heart. Rather than feeling lost, I want you to feel found. Rather than alone, I want you to know that you are completely surrounded by immense support and a plethora of opportunities to experience healing.

I want to set you up and send you off with so many great tips, tools, and insights that you don't need me or anyone else to help you through the challenges of life because *you* will know how to do it. You will be able to hear yourself, understand yourself, and love yourself the way you *need* it. You deserve to experience life without the burden of pain and fear and I'm honored to be here beside you.

*So, without further ado, let's get started
on the path to empowerment!*

Part Two
THE PATH TO EMPOWERMENT

9.
OBSERVE

To gain knowledge and understanding through observation.

STILL NEW TO OUR RELATIONSHIP AND INSPIRED by a mutual desire to be in nature together, Kurt and I decided to spend the afternoon hiking. The temperature was in the 90s and due to the intense heat and the sun beaming down, he suggested I bring lots of drinking water.

The path would lead us 10 miles up a mountain face and through various valleys, ideally lasting the entire day. "You'll probably want to pack a hat too," he reminded me. However, due to the ignorance I had gained through years of not honoring my body or my intuition, I casually embarked on the hike with about 8 oz of water and no hat.

For the first couple of miles, I marched as defiantly as I had been doing for most of my life. Leadership being no problem for me, I boldly led us up the wise, sleeping mountain, carrying on about this and that. But as our climb ascended and the scorching heat of the afternoon increased, I began to feel cold. As if a brisk, invisible snow was moving in, I started shivering and questioned whether I'd brought enough layers of clothes. That was the startling clue for my patient, watchful new lover to abruptly realize and say, "I think you need to drink some water, right now. That sounds like dehydration."

Around that time, the edge of the mountain slope began dancing together with the vista and I felt as if gravity was relieving me of all burden and contact. Quickly, I sat down before I fell down and drank all 8 oz of water I brought with me (which took about 5 seconds), and instantly realized it wasn't enough. Then, I pulled out the scarf I had tied to my bag and wrapped it around my head for protection from the sun.

If you'd passed us on that trail, you probably wouldn't have assumed anything abnormal. However, what was happening inside me was debilitating and humbling. It was at that moment that I observed myself. I sat down and took in the spectacle of ego and unpreparedness I had become. I wasn't stronger than nature. The toughness of my spirit couldn't *outdo* the vulnerability of my body. I can't go all day without water. Who was I kidding? What was I doing to myself?

How long would I force myself to march across deserts and up mountains, without water, without care, without listening to the drowned-out voice of the gentle vulnerability inside me whispering "Help!?"

I felt the blisters on my lips and my heart racing. I looked at my bony, dry hands and the hunch of my back that quickly transformed from superhero into old, feeble woman. I was hurting inside and at that moment, I was no longer *tough* enough to pretend I wasn't. I was killing myself and for the first time ever, I looked at that.

I suddenly opened my eyes in shock at what I was seeing. It was like a spiral of images flowing from my childhood through the years and years of suffering. I began recalling the countless times when I had been hurt and where my dedication to remaining protected silenced the voice of my true needs. I watched where my tender heart ached within and when my stubborn, rock-hard layers suffocated the gentle, vulnerable, precious nature of my being.

Genuinely concerned about my health, we moved very slowly down the mountain, seeking out any form of shade we could find, like a cluster of trees and boulders tucked into a valley.

Once there, within the refuge of the shadows, I crumpled to the ground and let myself stop.

Stop pretending.
Stop denying.
Stop avoiding.

Overwhelmed and in tears, I broke down, and for the first time in many, many years, I allowed myself to be present with it all. I allowed myself to look at the truth and in many ways, that was the thing I had been avoiding for so long: the truth.

That's what observation is like for a lot of us. It's the first, necessary step that follows the experience of realization. Once we realize we're done suffering and ready to try something new, the next step is to actually look at the *truth* and the reality of what's going on.

Examples of ways to OBSERVE:

- Acknowledge the truth
- Witness your environment
- Study your personal behavior and habits
- Inspect your internal thought processing
- Look at your personal tendencies and reactions
- Acknowledge your past experiences
- Watch for patterns and similarities

While you don't necessarily need to hike miles and miles up a remote, waterless mountain in the desert to do the important work of looking at the truth, you may find that wherever and however you decide to do it, it will be a humbling experience.

Witnessing the truth tends to instantly transform your life and your understanding of it. One minute, everything is seemingly fine. The next minute, you're looking through a whole new lens of reality that reveals a lot of wounds and discomfort. It's as if everything you believed to be the structure of your life suddenly crumbles to the ground.

The good news is that while the collapsing cage may have felt like home for a long time, it wasn't ever your home. It was an illusion built to protect you from feeling the true essence of your tender, wounded heart. If you want to get you back to your true home of being yourself, that illusion of safety has to crumble. You'll have to consciously look at the truth about:

- What's happening in your life right now?
- What happened in the past?

So, how do we do this?

1. If we were having this conversation in person, I would begin by asking you questions about the struggles you're currently dealing with. You would give me an overview of what's going on.

2. As you know, if you're hurting right now, then something happened to cause that pain, so we would go on an explorative mission to understand why. I would ask you some very tender, prompting questions about your past, and look for patterns and clues to help us understand more about what's happening right now as a result of the past with the very specific intention to find the wounds.

3. Once we had tracked down the wounds and the needs, our journey into the past would be complete. We would return to the present and focus on finding constructive ways to get your needs met so that your aching heart can be soothed and you can feel safe being present again.

In our time together, you've already been exploring the past by asking yourself questions and reflecting on your personal life experiences. The first part of the book was essentially a journey into the past where you gained insight about why you're hurting and what some of your unmet needs are. While it's still important for us to step into the past to find the wound, we need to get really good at returning to the present moment to address what you're going through right now.

It's actually crucial that we don't spend too long roaming around the past because we can easily begin telling and retelling stories that pull us into the web of identifying and defending. At some point, after uncovering all of the wounds, you still have to come back and deal with you and your current situation, which is right here in the present moment.

For this reason, when we enter the land of observation, we'll halt looking so intently on one story, problem, or perspective and see ourselves from a larger, more expansive understanding. We'll look at *what's happening* and *what happened*, then start piecing together the clues to gain a better understanding of what you need to feel better.

CONFRONTING FEAR & AVOIDANCE

WHEN IT COMES TO LOOKING AT THE TRUTH AND observing the wounds, we are courageously contradicting what we've become so comfortable doing for so long—*avoiding*. For that reason, observation is the opposition to avoidance. Because we know there are layers of pain and fear within the protective walls of desensitization and defense, we know that the act of avoidance is done out of fear and self-protection. In a sense, avoidance equals fear.

Fear of what?

Fear of anything that will potentially lead us to more pain and discomfort.

It's likely that in those moments where we were honest and present as children, friends, or lovers, our hearts were exposed and became deeply wounded. As a result, we're afraid to be present. We're scared to open up and be in the moment without a layer of numbing protection separating us from potential wounding. Whether consciously or unconsciously, we're *choosing* not to be present.

And because our distant past is where so much of our greatest hurt and suffering comes from, we don't want to look there either. We don't want to think about the sad, frightening, traumatic, embarrassing moments of our childhoods or earlier lives.

That's the conundrum. We avoid being in the present moment and we avoid thinking about the challenging (and very important) areas of our past experiences. So where do we live? Well, if you can call it living (?), we're in an altered state where we're neither here nor there. Like having one foot in and one foot out of life, we're floating in between reality (consciousness) and the uncomfortably cozy cage (unconsciousness).

This avoidance is something we need to acknowledge. We need to acknowledge how our avoidance is pulling us away from the present moment and where that separation from presence is contributing to our suffering. And we need to understand where the decision to avoid, rather than observe, is a choice we're making. Whether consciously or unconsciously, we are *choosing* not to be present, honest, and directly connected to the truth of what happened in the past and what's happening right now.

So, ask yourself this question: *Why do I choose to avoid looking at the truth of what I have been through and what I am experiencing right now?*

As you ponder, here are some common examples to consider:

- I feel intimidated by being present, so it feels better to always have something to do.
- I don't want to relive the past, so I try not to think about it.
- I feel bored when I don't have anything to do, so it's better to stay busy.
- I don't want to feel depressed, so I focus on things that make me happy.
- I feel nervous when things get "serious," so it's better to keep things light and easy.

These reasons make a lot of sense. You have every reason to subscribe to them and honor them as they justify and bring purpose to your avoidance. However, as you've seen, there are many reasons why avoidance is destructive and detrimental to your health and wellbeing.

Even though you may be trying to avoid undesirable experiences, realities, and feelings in the present, that's also where the best and most memorable experiences happen. By not being present, honest, and open, you miss out on all of those experiences. If you genuinely want to get to the heart of yourself and the life experience, you have to get to the heart of what's holding you back. And to do that, you need to get present with the truth of what you've been through and what you're going through right now.

THE GIFT OF LEARNING

MAYBE YOU ALREADY KNOW WHAT'S GOING ON and you don't need to take an honest look at your reality? Maybe you have a very clear understanding of what happened in the past and why you're struggling right now? Well, even though you may feel certain about the lineage of your suffering, if you're inadvertently avoiding something from the past, there are still a lot of valuable and necessary clues to uncover.

Observing the self requires us to study and learn about ourselves. It means being curious and courageous enough to *not know* everything. That way, there is enough space to learn something new.

Let's imagine you're dealing with frustration and anxiety. To help you understand and transform it, I ask you some questions:

Katie: Can you describe your experience with anxiety?
You: Yeah, it's like I'm stressed out all the time.
K: Do you recall when you first started experiencing it?
Y: Yeah, when I moved into a new apartment and got a roommate.
K: When was that?
Y: Right after my partner broke up with me.
K: What was the breakup like for you?
Y: It was fine. I'm better off without them. I don't really care.
K: You don't care about the breakup?
Y: No, my anxiety's coming from my new roommate. She's really annoying and I can't stand her. She stresses me out.
K: Is it possible you might be experiencing anxiety from unacknowledged grief around the breakup?
Y: No, definitely not. My problem is my roommate. The breakup didn't affect me.
K: Are you certain?
Y: Yeah. Certain.

Whether you realize it or not, your certainty is creating a very small space for you to exist. By not allowing yourself to go deeper into the possibilities of the unknown, you're preventing yourself from getting to the root of what's really going on.

But why would any of us do that? Why are we so insistent on knowing everything and staying attached to our perspectives?

Well, for many of us, *not knowing* is very uncomfortable. It takes us to a vulnerable place that brings up feelings of insecurity and uncertainty. If we don't have the answer, the seemingly stable ground of knowing, we're left to lean into trust and that's understandably hard for us.

There's often also residual trauma from the many weeks, months, and years of schooling. Whether we wanted to or not, going to school each day and "learning" was something we *had* to do. Because of that, we might have a strong aversion and resistance to trying to learn something new because it triggers uncomfortable feelings of being controlled, inadequate, and not respected. Especially if you were stressed and struggling to get good grades, you might still be throwing yourself a "school's out" party and celebrating your freedom from having to study or learn anything ever again.

If you look around, you'll notice that many adults are resistant to being curious and learning something new. We don't want to go through the draining act of having to learn something or memorize something (or even read the directions). We don't want to question; we just want to *know*. We want to *know* what we like and what we don't like. We want to *know* who we get along with and who we don't. We want to *know* what the weather will be like and when it's going to rain. We want to *know* what our retirement plans are and where we're headed after we die. We don't want to hang out in the vulnerable space of the unknown; we just want to *know, know, know*.

Unfortunately (and fortunately), we don't know the answers to everything. In order to reach higher levels of intelligence and broader thinking, we have to re-enter a state of humble curiosity and embrace the journey of learning. We have to allow ourselves to be courageously open and inquisitive, like we were when we were babies, rather than the tough, puffed-chested know-it-alls we've gradually mutated into over the years.

This means *un*learning what we've learned to do throughout our lives and creating space for something new. What does unlearning include? The fear-driven stories, perspectives, and false understandings of who we are and what's going on.

In all honesty, almost everything I share in this book evolved from giving myself permission to be inquisitive and curious about myself and others. I allowed myself to be open, intrigued, and welcoming of the insights that generously accompany presence. Rather than sleepwalking through addiction and suffering, I kept myself awake enough to pay attention to my environment, reactions, interactions, conversations, and dreams. That way, I could better understand what was really going on. I didn't just want to get better; I wanted to dissect my pain and understand the inner workings of *why* I was suffering and how to be free from it.

To do that, I had to be a curious, present, and engaging student of life. I had to ask a lot of questions, then be open—listening to and witnessing what revealed itself in return.

Let's imagine that when I asked you the questions about your anxiety, you instead said "My roommate is really challenging for me, but there may be something else going on that I'm not aware of. I'm not sure but I'm open to looking deeper within myself to learn more about where this anxiety and frustration is coming from." You would instantly unlock yourself from your perspective and open yourself to look deeply, more expansively into the entire situation. You might also open yourself up to seeing patterns and coincidences you previously didn't notice.

By giving yourself permission to receive the gift of learning, you gain access to worlds unknown and infinite possibilities. You re-engage with the magic and pristine beauty of being alive and allow yourself to be a part of it. Doesn't that sound a lot more fascinating and fulfilling than spending your life hiding inside a musty little cage, constantly distracted and defending yourself?

Do you ever find yourself coming up with answers because it feels uncomfortable to not know?
What does curiosity feel like to you?

OPENING THE DOORS

WHEN OFFERING COUNSEL TO PEOPLE WHO are hurting, I've seen again and again how freeing and empowering it is when someone finally looks at what they've been avoiding for so long. With immense relief, they have the sudden realization that looking within themselves isn't as bad as they thought.

I spent time helping Charlie work through her emotional hurdles of shame and insecurity. Each time she entered our shared space, she was hesitant to open up and share what she was really going through. Her painful habits and memories were embalmed with secrecy, so she would hold back and find clever ways to not speak the truth about the present or the past.

It's as if she was always anticipating something coming up that was too heavy, too dirty, or too embarrassing to talk about. I addressed this by asking her, "Are you concerned about there being something revealed that's too much for me to handle? Or are you concerned we're going to talk about something that's too much for *you* to handle? Because I'm good. I'm not worried or put off by anything you've been through."

The truth is, she didn't really know why she was so intimidated to acknowledge the truth. She originally feared judgment and shock from other people, but really, she was just stuck in a pattern of avoidance. As it turned out, all of the hidden places she felt too embarrassed to look at weren't too much for either of us. In fact, what revealed itself was far more manageable and less dramatic than what her fears had built up.

As we lovingly opened doors to the rooms of her past, she had the opportunity to shine a light onto the truth inside her. Each time, she became aware that there was no part of her deserving of being kept secret. Gradually, she began feeling lighter, less ashamed, and more trusting of herself.

Sometimes, facing the truth is a lot less stressful than we imagine it to be and the more we do it, the more we realize how capable and powerful we really are.

Do you have secrets or memories that feel like "too much" to share with anyone?

How would it feel to not hide from the truth or bury it inside you any longer?

THE CLEANSING LIGHT OF AWARENESS

A HELPFUL WAY TO IMAGINE THIS PROCESS is to visualize a house within you. When you were born, this spacious house had a fresh breeze and sunlight streaming in each of its windows. With your sincere presence and attentive nature, it was filled with consciousness and wonder. Each day brought a gust of new experiences.

However, as you began experiencing the wounds of life, your inner house began converting from a peaceful to a fearful one. Each wound was like a damp patch, and where you didn't address it, mold began growing. The more you avoided looking at them, the more they festered, multiplying and taking over. And for every part of your sensitive being that was shut off, a window in your inner house was boarded up, so the light of consciousness could no longer get in. You were left with a dimly lit space with no fresh air.

Unfortunately, mold thrives where there is no light; unconsciousness thrives where there is no consciousness. On the flipside, when you allow yourself to acknowledge the truth and shine the cleansing light of awareness inside, the house begins to change. You take down the boards and fill it with light. You scrub off the mold with honesty and truth. The warm sunlight beams through the windows, drying the damp. Before you know it, the entire space is transformed.

This act of honest observation not only brings awareness to the painful areas of the past that need our attention, but it also creates a healthier, cleaner environment where pain is less likely to thrive in the future. We change the entire ecosystem of our internal selves. Sure, we can bring our scrub brushes and sanitizer to address the pain, but unless we completely transform the environment where the pain is thriving, it's only a matter of time until it takes over again. We don't want to just wipe a little bit of the fear and pain away—we want to uproot it and completely clear it out of our beings.

FINDING THE PATTERNS

NOW WE'VE TALKED ABOUT THE IMPORTANCE OF observing the truth, let's learn how to do it. One very helpful tool is *finding patterns*, much like a childhood game of matching colors, shapes, and numbers. There is an entryway into our past that can be found by observing where our present experiences are strikingly similar to something we've already experienced in life.

This act of becoming aware of patterns is something I often do when helping people unravel from their struggles. Regardless of what they are currently dealing with, I remain present and listen closely to everything they say. I take notes to map out the storyline of their life, and track where the echo of pain was sent from an earlier wound. Eventually, we find out where the pain is coming from and where their very important needs for support and healing weren't met.

I did this with Sally, who was struggling to work through some marital issues. She was frustrated and ready to file for divorce. Fortunately, she allowed herself to talk to someone as a last hopeful resort before dissolving the marriage. As soon as we began speaking, I wrote down any keywords that showed signs of pain, need, protection, or defense. Even though she was dealing with a painful situation in the present, I wanted to discover the painful situations *before* this one to see whether there were any similarities or patterns.

"My husband is a slob," she said. "We have two kids and they're enough to clean up after. He's constantly creating a mess for me to take care of and I feel like he's just a third kid. I feel like I spend most of my life cleaning up after everyone else and honestly, I'm over it. I'm sick of feeling like this."

"What is the 'this' that you're feeling in those moments, Sally?" I asked.

"I feel invisible. I feel taken for granted. I feel like I'm a servant and have no freedom to do what I want to do in life because I'm too busy taking care of everyone else. I feel stuck and it pisses me off."

Knowing that Sally was sharing some important clues, I wrote them down. Invisible. Taken for granted. A servant. No freedom. Stuck.

And because she was very reactive, emotional, and defensive about this, it felt like a deeper wound was hiding beneath the surface. Perhaps one she'd been protecting for a long time. So, I questioned: *Was there a time in Sally's past when her freedom was taken from her? When she felt unsupported, unacknowledged, or taken for granted?* My intention was to find the pattern to reveal the deeper wound. Then, through witnessing where history had repeated itself, I could follow the path inward and get to the root of what was really going on.

Knowing that so many wounds and patterns begin in our youth, I gently and gradually asked prompting questions to find out what happened: *When did Sally first feel these things? When had she been stuck serving and not honoring her own needs? Where and when was she potentially ignored or underappreciated?*

By remaining curious, open to learning more, and watching for patterns, we quickly uncovered that Sally's mom had died when she was a teenager. As the eldest of five kids, she had to take on the role of mother figure. She had to care for the younger children more so than for herself. With that, her needs weren't met. Her needs for freedom, expansion, and pursuing her dreams. She never had a safe place to crumble and be vulnerable to process her mother's death, and so she didn't. She was too busy making sure everyone else had their needs met.

By the time she grew older, she'd perfected the art of taking care of others and found herself in a household that mimicked the same pattern of her childhood, all the while still needing to process her own grief and pain.

Would it always be this way? Had she chosen poorly and ended up with a husband who was a useless continuation of her childhood wounds?

No, not necessarily. Everyone is capable of changing, and when Sally went deeper within to understand where the pain was coming from, she was able to transform her reactions of defense and helplessness to conscious action to get her needs met. Through learning to honor, respect, and accept herself, she gave herself permission to cry and voice her needs. As a result, her husband had the opportunity and encouragement to look at his own unconscious patterns. That way, he could work towards being more respectful and mindful of his actions that affected others, especially his wife.

THE INVESTIGATOR & THE WITNESS

Now, what if you don't have a teammate, friend, or counselor to take notes and track down the clues and patterns to uncover what's really going on?

Well, you can learn to do it with and for *yourself!* Basically, you become both the inquirer and the provider of information to constructively understand the truth about what's happening right now and what happened in the past.

The key to doing this successfully is to look clearly at the truth and tell the honest truth without being biased or persuaded by personal opinion. We have to pull away from our sincere and constant need to favor or disfavor and simply see it like it is and say it like it is. You can do this through a very helpful exercise I like to call "the investigator and the witness."

First, we have *the investigator.*

The investigator

As an investigator, you're hired by the divine forces of consciousness to beam down and study the physical, mental, and emotional behavior of your human self. You're granted the skill of studying your humanness to learn more about where the pain is coming from and what you need to heal it.

Your job consists of a few simple tasks:

- Study the situation
- Look for clues and patterns
- Collect information

The investigator is curious and inquisitive. You are on a mission to gather as much information as possible, to ask questions, and to learn something new.

As the investigator, your job description does *not* include taking sides, proving points, favoring verdicts, or manipulating the story with opinions or conclusions. Though there may be injustice happening, it's not your job to identify or proclaim who is the victim and who is the villain. The moment you begin judging and squeezing your opinion into the experience, you inevitably take sides and get sucked into the overwhelming haze of emotion, ego, and old stories, and this haze separates you from presence and solutions. Tether yourself to *unbiased neutrality* and stick to the facts.

You also need to give yourself permission to ask for very detailed information. You can ask *who, what, when, where,* and *why?* Really get into it. Ask what happened throughout the day and throughout the week. Retrace memories and ask about family members, friends, and coworkers.

If you ask a question and the response seems vague or unclear, dig in to get more information. If it's helpful, imagine that you've walked into a room and a young child is crying. Without knowing the reason for the tears, you are devoted to simply finding out *what's going on? What happened?*

The witness

As a witness, you're here to answer questions. You're the one who is experiencing being human and you're the one who holds the knowledge and the clues. You're here to provide information, descriptions, details, and facts.

Your job description is to:

- Answer questions
- Provide details
- Speak the truth

You are *not* here to exaggerate, judge, fib, get swept away in long stories, or share emotionally charged perspectives. Even though you may feel passionate about certain things that happened in the past, the investigator doesn't need those extra bits of biased opinion. That's too much information. The investigator just needs to know the facts about what's going on and what happened.

The goal

Together, your investigative self and your witnessing self are a team that provides very important information. You'll be working together to lead internal interviews and find out where the painful wounds are and how to heal them.

You'll do this by accessing information like:

- **What's happening?** ~ What's the honest truth of the current situation?
- **What happened?** ~ What past experiences were wounding and painful?

As we go deeper into understanding your needs and getting them met in the next chapters, we'll incorporate more questions like:

How am I feeling?
Where am I hurting?
Where am I afraid?
What do I need right now?

The vibe

It's important to mention that these two internal conversationalists are not roaming around your head wearing costumes and actually portraying characters. By all means, you're welcome to visualize your internal investigator in a trench coat and carrying a pipe, but it's definitely not necessary. A "witness" may bring up images of a scared, trembling person at the scene of a crime, but again, this isn't necessary.

The intention is for you to begin strengthening your ability to honestly and openly communicate with yourself. You're having a conversation with yourself—you and you—through the filter of the *question seeker* and the *answer provider* personas.

THE HIGHER SELF

PERSONALLY, MY INVESTIGATIVE SELF IS A NURTURING, patient, older version of me who is very calm and understanding. Essentially, she's my "higher self," my *true self*. She's strong, unbiased, and absolutely dedicated to the truth. She brings that out in me and allows no space for judgment, exaggeration, or lying. I feel safe in her presence and I trust her wholeheartedly. I know she's here to help and I know she loves me unconditionally.

When she asks me a question, I want nothing more than to tell her the truth and give her as much information as possible. Over time, she has become a guiding force of wisdom who asks very heartfelt and prompting questions that have served me again and again.

It's my hope that this practice will evolve into a clearer, healthier relationship with yourself. Over time, as you get more comfortable with self-inquiry and honest response, you won't need to play out the role of your investigative and witnessing self. Gradually, you'll just become more communicative, honest, transparent, and connected to your higher, true self.

If you were to connect with a wise, curious, and non-judging version of yourself, what might it be like?

How would it feel to be completely honest, without holding anything back from yourself?

JUDGMENT AWARENESS

ANOTHER INCREDIBLY USEFUL TOOL TO KEEP in your back pocket as you become a better observer is "judgment awareness." It is exactly as it sounds: becoming aware of judgmental behavior. In those moments of observation, if you begin declaring anything as *good, bad, acceptable,* or *unacceptable*, take note. That is judgment.

Each time you judge yourself, you intensify the need to defend yourself, which continually stimulates your ego and holds you hostage in a sleepy state of unawareness (and suffering). You wouldn't feel the need to abuse yourself unless you were already in pain, so the self-judgment is an indicator that you're hurting and that there is a wound lingering somewhere close by. You're the investigator and the witness, *not* the judge.

One way to ensure you don't judge yourself is through the response of "interesting." When you're engaging in this internal dialogue with yourself and a clue reveals itself, recognize it and rather than deeming it positive or negative, let it be *intriguing*. Allowing yourself to be *interested* means you're giving yourself permission to be curious and not have defined opinions or conclusions. *Interesting* offers space for the next piece to reveal itself, rather than a harsh judgment, which leaves us nowhere to go.

Say you're reflecting on an incident from your past and it comes with feelings of regret, resentment, or upset toward yourself. Pause for a moment and observe the experience. Hover over it as if you're not identified with any role or part in the story. Rather than telling yourself a story of how wrong or bad you are, return to a space of unbiased neutrality. As if the investigator has found an important clue, take note and say, "Interesting, I'm shaming myself right now." Shine a light in and become aware that you are being judgmental. If it's helpful to say it out loud (I do), you can casually call yourself out by saying "Judgment awareness."

You may discover that these tools are useful in bringing awareness to how you're treating those around you and when it's you who is generating wounds. If you catch yourself thinking negative or cruel thoughts, call yourself out! As soon as you observe yourself thinking or saying something destructive, stop and feel the judgment awareness inside you, only without judging yourself for being judgmental.

This has become very evident through the workshops and retreats I've been a part of. When everyone enters the space, it's natural and common for people to look around and make assessments, assumptions, and judgments about one another. Most of us do it, and we believe it to be harmless.

However, after arriving at the topic of judgment and seeing the reality that we're all wounded and hurting, the energy of the room instantly shifts and softens. People realize they are continually creating more wounds with judgment, and the group feels a bit safer and more at ease because the judgment has been verbally, consciously addressed. With that, each person is more accountable for their thoughts and actions, making them less likely to project it and less likely to receive it.

Every time we catch ourselves being judgmental, the better we get at spotting it. Gradually, our unconscious tendencies begin to lose their power. Like the cleansing light of awareness on the moldy room, we become cleaner and brighter inside.

SELF-AWARENESS

IT MAY APPEAR THAT I'M ENCOURAGING YOU to hang out with and talk to yourself, and it's true. That's exactly what I'm doing. I'm encouraging you to start connecting with yourself and creating a channel of communication that allows you to speak, listen, and be honest with yourself. The goal is to become more self-aware, and there's nothing crazy or abnormal about that. I believe that everyone would be a lot less crazy if we could all *consciously* connect and communicate with ourselves, rather than being caught in a constant flow of unconscious dialogue with ourselves.

Self-awareness is really an underlying goal in all of the work we're doing together. Every moment you become more self-aware, you move away from identifying with your suffering and empower yourself to choose not to suffer. You begin to see beyond the walls of self-preservation. You realize how deeply wounded you are inside, which awakens compassion and the desire to free the innocent being stuck inside the cage—you.

In every session and workshop I lead, I do everything I can to help people feel safe and comfortable enough to be honest with themselves. Why? Because when you stop hiding from yourself and let the conscious light of truth and awareness in, there's no space left for avoidance or unconsciousness.

This is perhaps the most monumental key to overcoming unconscious habits and addiction. As so many of our attempts to fulfill our aching needs happen through the filter of protection and fear, when we finally stand up to the fear and look truth in the eyes, we gain control and confidence. We begin to feel more comfortable and natural looking at ourselves objectively, and less attached to constantly protecting and defending.

Instead of feeling out of control, we enter the driver's seat. Instead of feeling stuck, we feel emancipated. Instead of feeling like the victim, we realize we are the creators of our reality. We are the heroes who have the power to save ourselves. With that, no fear, memory, or bad mood can hold us hostage again.

FOLLOWING THE TRAIL OF PAIN
Self-exploration exercise

Ok. Now that we have a better idea about the importance of looking at the truth, it's time for our first exercise! As there is a very specific direction we traveled in to enter suffering, we want to follow that same path in (and out) to go deeper, to find the wound and the unmet need.

As we move through these questions and examples, try your best to come from a neutral and investigative space. Remember, you're the investigator and the witness, not the judge. If at any point you judge yourself or talk yourself out of acknowledging something, pause, be aware of the judgment, find it interesting, and continue. This exercise will give you a feel for the kinds of questions you'll want to ask yourself to prompt self-awareness.

Anytime you're answering questions and begin to feel your mood and emotions shift (fear, sadness, shame, anger)—take note! These are very important clues that will help us better understand what's going on inside.

As we move into the next chapter, we'll talk more about these subtle shifts in sensation. To help you keep track of where you're at, should you decide to close your eyes throughout the exercise, each question/step is numbered.

ooooo

Also, it's important to keep in mind right now (and always) that as you go into the realms of the past and come in contact with old wounds, you're coming in contact with old trauma. These painful memories may be hidden within internal chambers of your heart and if you hid them well, you did that because the original experience was sad, scary, and uncomfortable. Now, as we re-enter those guarded and internal spaces, please be gentle with yourself and only go at the pace that feels natural and comfortable for you.

If the past wounds feel like too much, that's ok. Skip over what feels like too much and continue to the next section. As we enter Chapter 11, we'll talk about the importance of having a network of support. You may not feel ready to do this deep and internal explorative work until you have that support in place. By reading this book, you'll have a clear overview of the importance of doing this work, whether you're ready to do it right now or not.

ooooo

1. First, we need to identify what's going on.
   Do any of these descriptions align with your life right now...?
   - Feeling stuck/trapped in your life
   - Feeling lost
   - Depressed
   - Compulsive
   - Numb
   - Unable to relax without distraction or substances
   - Unable to forgive

   If so, it means you've been hurting for some time. You're not just suffering; you're experiencing a prolonged state of suffering. You've learned to protect and defend yourself and it's been happening for so long that you feel stuck.

   Of the examples listed, does one stand out to you?

2. Let's move further inward to understand how you've learned to defend yourself.

   Do you ever find yourself being...?
   - Judgmental
   - Angry
   - Envious
   - Irritated
   - Malicious
   - Resentful
   - Competitive

   If so, it means you've been hurt and learned to protect yourself through actively defending yourself.

   Can you think of a recent time in your life when you were actively expressing one or more of these forms of defense? What was that like?

3. Let's move further inward to understand the ways you may be trying to protect yourself.

   Do you ever find yourself feeling...?
   - Distracted
   - Desensitized
   - Protective
   - Guarded
   - Detached
   - Distrusting
   - Dishonest

   If so, it means you've been wounded and needed help, but didn't receive the support you needed. Because of that, you learned to protect your tenderness and your pain through avoidance and creating separation from yourself and from others.

   From the examples listed, which form(s) of protection do you relate to feeling and embodying?

4. Let's move further inward to understand what those unmet needs are.

Do you ever find yourself feeling...?
- Distressed
- Nervous
- Anxious
- Lonely
- Hungry for something
- Longing
- A need for attention

If so, it means you've been hurt, experienced pain, and needed help but didn't receive the support you needed. Because of this, you've been internally and externally reaching out for something to provide comfort and relief from the pain.

When you're feeling that way, what do you do to satisfy that need?

5. Let's move further inward to understand the pain.

   Have you ever found yourself in a state of...?
   - Fear
   - Sadness
   - Discomfort
   - Shame
   - Insecurity
   - Disappointment
   - Grief

   If so, it means you've experienced something that created a painful wound and it made a crack in your heart. There are endless ways that this could've happened.

   <u>What happened?</u>

   You don't have to turn away from it or pretend it didn't happen. Regardless how trivial or unimportant it may seem, we need to acknowledge it.

   If it's helpful, flip back to pages 28 to be reminded of some examples.

   Do any stand out? Do certain examples sound an alarm within you? Maybe it was when you were a small child?

   Maybe it was yesterday? Allow yourself to gravitate toward one example.

Let yourself observe that experience for a moment. You don't have to spend too long pondering if it feels unsafe though. All you need to do is acknowledge it. If you find that you're judging yourself or changing the subject, pause and remind yourself that it's ok to be temporarily uncomfortable.

Your goal isn't to dig up old wounds and relive them until you feel powerless and weak. It's to shine the light of awareness onto the pain and transform the discomfort so you are empowered by conscious awareness.

•

Now, to build a deeper understanding of how that wound is affecting you, let's come back from the past to the present along the path of pain and suffering. While holding the wound in your thoughts, ask yourself these questions:

1. When you experienced this wound, what pain did you experience afterwards?

    Did you feel sad?
    Did you feel scared?
    Did you feel ashamed or insecure?
    Did you feel anything else?

2. When you were in that state of pain, what support did you need?

    Did you need to be comforted and hugged?
    Did you need to know that you weren't alone?
    Did you need to express yourself through tears?
    Did you need anything else?

3. In what ways were those needs not fulfilled?

    Were you neglected?
    Was there no one you could trust or talk to?
    Were you too embarrassed to cry?

4. How did it feel when those needs weren't fulfilled?

    Did you feel alone?
    Did you feel hurt, distrusting, or protective?
    Did you feel unimportant?

5. In what ways have you avoided thinking about or dealing with it?

    Did you try to convince yourself to get over it?
    Did you pretend it didn't happen?
    Did you focus on something else to distract yourself from it?

6. In what ways do you defend yourself when you experience similar pain to this wound?

    Do you get frustrated?
    Do you raise your voice?
    Do you push people away?

7. In what ways do you feel that this wounding experience is still affecting your life?

    Do you feel lonely and unlovable?
    Do you feel uncomfortable being intimate?
    Do you feel depressed and disconnected from yourself?

    To see it all mapped out together, you might say:

    When _____ happened, I felt sad and needed to be comforted and hugged. I didn't receive that. Instead, I was neglected and felt alone. I tried to convince myself to get over it, and now, when I sense that a similar wound might happen again, I get frustrated and push people away. I feel lonely, depressed, and unlovable.

8. Now, let's lean into the area of the need and ask:

    How would it feel to receive care and get those needs met?
    How would it feel to be comforted, hugged, and surrounded by care?
    How would it feel to know that you're cared for, loved, and not alone?
    How freeing would it be to openly express your emotions and cry?

Even if receiving this kind of love and care is something you can't imagine, having never received it, you deserve it. You deserve to be nurtured, comforted, soothed, and loved. It's my goal that you begin experiencing this kind of healing with and for yourself in our time together.

As we enter the chapter of **feel**, you'll learn more about allowing yourself to uncover the hidden feelings inside. The more you're able to understand what happened and where the pain and fear still resides, the more you'll understand what your needs are and how to get them met.

EXAMPLE CONVERSATION

TO BETTER UNDERSTAND THE IMPORTANCE of conversing with and within ourselves, here is an example conversation. These conversations are something you'll continue to see throughout the book, and while each story may not necessarily align with the details of your own life experiences, they will give you a chance to recognize the stages of suffering and see the application of the Empowered Heart tools.

You will notice that the conversations are positioned in second person, as "You" and "I." While it may appear as if from two separate individuals, they are examples of how one can communicate with one's self. Through being both the *investigative* and *witnessing* self, we can ask ourselves questions (as if asking someone else), then answer the questions as openly and honestly as possible. As we continue forward in the book, we'll shift to speaking directly with ourselves in first person so we can explore what it's like to be naturally more open and honest with ourselves.

For this example, let's imagine that you were just fired from your job. While it wasn't your dream job, it definitely paid the bills and was income you relied on. Sadly, the job loss also came at a time when you're emotionally struggling. Now, you feel overwhelmed and buried in stress and self doubt. In order to better understand what's really going on, let's find out more.

What's happening? What happened?

Investigator: Can you describe what's going on right now?
Witness: I was just fired.
I: Why?
W: My boss is a ****.

Judgment awareness. Let's try that again.

I: Why were you fired?
W: Because I've been coming in late for work too many days in a row.
I: Is it true? Have you been late for work?
W: Yeah.
I: How long has this been going on?
W: I'm not sure.

Ok. That's not true. I know how long this has been going on but I'm resistant to looking at it. I'm avoiding it. I guess I should be more honest with myself.

W: For about two months.
I: Did anything significant or wounding happen two months ago?
W: Yeah. The divorce was finalized.

Ouch. I really don't like talking about this, not even with myself. This isn't easy.

I: What was that experience like for you?
W: It's been horrible. I've been a sleepless, stressed out wreck for months.
I: Have you talked to anyone about this?
W: Not really. The whole thing is so depressing and embarrassing I don't want to talk about it. Plus, I've gotta make sure the kid's needs are met so I haven't had the time to process it. On top of all that, I just lost my job.

What a pathetic wreck I am. Oops, judgement awareness.
Judging myself isn't helping anything.

I: Does anyone know what you've been going through?
W: Not really. Just my close family and friends and honestly, I feel

like most of them are let down. Like I messed up a good marriage.
I: Are you open to getting some help? Maybe talking to someone?
W: I'm not great at asking for help but obviously I need to do something. I feel like I'm falling apart and I need to remember that I don't have to struggle through this. *I'm done suffering.*

•

Soon, we'll acquire more tools to help us go deeper into self awareness through internal dialogue, as well as how to take action to receive the support we need when going through something challenging, like in this example.

OBSERVATION TOOLS

When I allow myself to contradict the avoidance and witness the truth, I gain confidence and trust in myself.

◆

Rather than always knowing the answer, I give myself permission to be curious and learn something new.

◆

Even though I may perceive some of my life experiences as too heavy or too much to handle, they are not.

◆

Each time I allow myself to acknowledge the truth, I transform the unconsciousness within me, filling myself with the cleansing light of conscious awareness.

◆

As a means of strengthening self-awareness, I can ask myself honest questions and answer myself honestly. I can do this through the personas of the investigator and the witness.

◆

Each time I become aware of judgmental thoughts towards myself or others, I can catch myself and transform the destructive, unconscious behavior to conscious presence.

⧗

*This moment is where you came from.
It's your home.*

*Though it may feel foreign and unknown,
It's not because you've never been here;
it's because you've been away for so long.*

*Being present isn't a matter of mastering techniques
and strengthening practices.
It's about you allowing yourself to feel safe enough
to come home to your true self.*

Right here, right now,

*in this moment,
where you belong.*

⧗

10.
FEEL

The ability to experience an emotion or sensation.

Not long after the monumental mountain hike, Kurt and I spent the summer in Brighton, England, where he was performing a string of shows with his band. From my newly acquired ability to acknowledge that I was an addict, I began studying myself more closely, trying to figure out my addictive habits, tendencies, and struggles. While I was still actively compulsive and bulimic, I felt a sense of empowerment in being strong enough to look at what (who) I had been avoiding for so long: *myself.*

In Brighton, I had begun having peculiar stomach pains with bouts of cramping and at times, difficulty swallowing. Inside, I knew it had something to do with me gradually keeping more food down and in my eyes, re-training my body to digest. What I couldn't understand is why the food appeared to be stopping in my esophagus for hours. The blockage made it uncomfortable to consume anything, including water. I saw various doctors but no one could determine the cause of the discomfort. As the weeks passed, my weight began dropping from being unable to swallow.

As the summer concluded and we returned home to LA, my wilting and weight loss continued, and I became increasingly dizzy and fatigued. It was clear to us both one night as my symptoms culminated that "this is really serious" and I needed to go to the emergency room. Not long after,

I was hooked up to an IV receiving bags of saline solutions, and having CT scans and tests. Though it took time and a few more doctors to figure out the issue, they discovered that my stomach had become lodged in my diaphragm and was blocking my esophagus, also known as a very severe *hiatal hernia*. Combined with ulcers coating my digestive tract and over 15 years of malnourishment, my body was in severe pain and fragile, and it was unable to eat.

Imagine that. A woman who had spent so many years mindlessly, compulsively eating—now unable to eat, unable to do much of anything except rest. Rather than racing around in a distracting whirlwind of haste and pretend glory, I was in extreme discomfort and left to feel the tender, vulnerable, pain in my body and in my heart.

For so long, I wasn't really feeling; I was coping. When I started to feel sad, I ate. When I started to feel nervous, I ate. When I started to feel frustrated, I ate.

Suddenly, I had to feel. I had to stop and *feel* the pain and fear inside. I had to feel what it was like to not have the distracting vice of food to soothe my every need. When anxiety came up, I had to feel it and its extended family of side effects. When anger arose, I had to stare it in the eyes for days until I finally crumbled into tears. When grief timidly peered its head around the corner, I had to sit in the sad and awkward silence of trying to get to know it, like an absent parent being introduced to their child for the first time. When joy arrived, my mouth would fall agape, because surprisingly, it was like a deep laugh that I hadn't felt since I was a child.

It was all so unfamiliar and at the same time, so deeply, deeply familiar. I thought: *so this is what feeling feels like?*

Like so many of us, I had come to associate any feelings of discomfort as being bad or negative so I avoided them. Because of that, I had become desensitized and disconnected from the truth in my heart and the world around me.

To fully be present in the human life experience, I had to tear down those cage walls. I had to resensitize. I had to *feel*.

Examples of experiencing FEELING:
- Feeling emotions
- Being sensitive
- Having a sensation of the physical body
- Sensing those around you
- Intuiting

Just like observation requires us to confront our avoidance and look at the truth of what's happening and what happened, the act of feeling requires us to *feel* our *true* emotions, without judgment.

Observe: *What's happening right now? What happened in the past?*
Feel: *How am I feeling? Where am I hurting? Where am I afraid?*

Rather than leaning away (and plugging our ears and covering our eyes), we need to lean in and courageously *feel* it—regardless of how unfamiliar, undesirable, or unpleasant the experience may be.

Why? Because once we've successfully observed the truth of where we're wounded and felt the reality of the pain we're in as a result, we have a much better understanding of what we need to feel better, which prepares us to get those needs met.

So, let's do it. Let's gain knowledge and awareness about the importance of feeling and reawaken the parts of ourselves that have been dormant and asleep. Let's move closer to being home in the presence of our true selves.

UNDERSTANDING FEELINGS

FIRST, IT'S IMPORTANT TO UNDERSTAND WHAT feelings and emotions actually are, especially as it can seem that they live in a mysterious world of their own. Like unexpected guests, they can show up out of nowhere and quickly change the atmosphere of our beings. The more we study them and understand them, the more empowered we become when dealing with them.

Examples of **emotions** and **feelings**:
- Sadness
- Fear
- Joy
- Compassion
- Confusion
- Anger
- Contentment
- Relief
- Disappointment
- Worry
- Happiness

For a long time, I didn't know there was a difference between emotions and feelings. I thought of them as being the same thing: "I'm sad" or "I'm angry" or "I'm happy." However, there's a slight yet significant difference between the two.

The definition of **emotion** is: **a complex state of feeling that results in physical and psychological changes that influence thought and behavior.**

Essentially, the experience of a feeling is the same thing, except when we have feelings, we're consciously *aware* of the emotion.

In other words, feelings and emotions can look the same, but they're separated by levels of consciousness. In order to resensitize ourselves and allow it to be a constructive experience, we have to be more present and witness our emotions (like we learned in the previous chapter) to turn them into feelings.

Let's say you're driving and have to stomp on the brakes to avoid hitting another car. It startles you and brings about the uncontrollable emotion of fear and shock. However, once you become consciously aware of the situation and your response: "Whoa, that car pulled out of nowhere and scared me," it becomes a feeling: "I feel nervous now." You initially had the emotion of fear and shock, but with consciousness, it becomes a feeling of nervousness.

What's a great way to consciously *feel* the emotion so you can transform it? By simply asking yourself "How am I feeling right now?," which is something we'll talk more about here shortly.

Each time you consciously recognize what's happening and how you're feeling as a result of it (regardless of how desirable or undesirable it may be), you allow a beam of conscious awareness to enter the inner house of your being. You reclaim your power and shift from being the one trapped in the cage to the one who's outside looking in.

GOING INTO THE UNCOMFORTABLE PLACES

SO, WHY DO SO MANY OF US AVOID FEELING? There are two main reasons why. While I don't need to say it as you already know, I will: *pain* and *fear*. Originally, it was because we felt the painful sensations of sadness, shame, hurt, confusion, insecurity, and discomfort. Then, it was because we feared getting hurt again. We know how uncomfortable emotional pain is and we don't want to go there again. So, we numb and distract ourselves to avoid what we deeply fear.

While I completely understand any fear or resistance you might feel, the act of holistically feeling our feelings is essential on the path to empowering the heart, and it's important to confront the avoidance and distraction preventing us from doing so. Just as we did in previous chapters, we need to *acknowledge* and *witness* where we're making the choice to not feel our feelings so we can be accountable for the power we have to create change.

One way to break through avoidance is to simply ask yourself:

Why do I avoid being sensitive and why do I try not to feel my deeper emotions?

While not all of these may relate to you, here are some common reasons:

- Being sad is sad and I don't want to be sad so I try not to be.
- I like having a lot of energy and don't want to feel weighed down.
- I want to always be happy.
- I don't want to be a downer for others to deal with.
- I'll look weak if I'm sensitive. I'd rather be strong.
- I feel lazy when I'm not motivated and filled with energy.

If you relate to any of these examples, it makes sense. However, just because you've figured out ways to not feel the pain, it doesn't mean there's no pain; it just means you've separated yourself from feeling it. Like a wound that festers under the surface, the pain is still there, desperately needing to be acknowledged and healed.

And remember, the cage doesn't let anything out or anything in. If you numb yourself to pain, you also numb yourself to love, which is reason enough to bring yourself back to your senses—so you can feel true love again.

Will it hurt or be uncomfortable to feel the truth of your pain?

It might, but it's nothing you can't handle.

Why is that?

Because you know pain very well. You've been living in it for a long time. By allowing yourself to feel the deeper truth of your pain, it doesn't mean you're suddenly being introduced to pain; it just means you're allowing yourself to finally be aware of the pain you're already in.

COLLECTIVE DESENSITIZATION

WHILE CONSCIOUSLY FEELING OUR EMOTIONS is something a lot of us tend to naturally avoid, the aversion to feeling is also *learned behavior*. Through programming from our parents, society, the education system, the military, and the collective voice of unconsciousness, we're often encouraged to "toughen up" and "act fine." We're taught by fearful leaders to act strong and be *senseless*, and we follow along in fear of the senses.

This has a lot to do with an overall collective aversion to being vulnerable. Because so many of us consider vulnerability a weakness, we avoid being sensitive. Also, because unresolved trauma is prevalent in so many of us, we avoid being sensitive because we don't want to experience the potential discomfort that might arise if we allow ourselves to really feel and listen to what's going on inside.

Desensitization is something that affects people from all over the world, though it seems that males are more often encouraged and susceptible to this robotic programming. Often, if a man shares his vulnerable feelings, he's judged and chastised with "Aww, don't be a baby. Stop crying. Why are you so sensitive?"

This is definitely gender stereotyping and it's also highly judgmental and traumatic. In those moments when a man allows himself to be open, honest, and vulnerable, if he sees that it's not safe and experiences wounding, then he'll learn not to. Rather than being encouraged, accepted and honored for simply feeling, he'll learn to lie, distract, and pretend. He'll learn that it's safer to deny his feelings and swallow them down until he becomes angry or apathetic, rather than sensitive.

If anything, we should honor those, *especially* males, who are strong and courageous enough to be sensitive and connected to the authenticity of their emotions. These willing warriors of the heart have reached beyond the limitations of fear, the very thing that has been holding so many of us hostage for so long.

Regardless of gender, this is something that reveals itself especially through soldiers returning from war. While I tend to bypass small talk and go deep even with strangers (just ask my family—I can make any family dinner awkward), I once had a very moving conversation with a rideshare driver who had just retired from military service. I asked if he'd been a driver for long and he replied, "No, actually, this is my first day on the job."

I asked, ""What kind of work did you do before this?" He replied, "I've been in the military for the past 25 years, I just recently retired. I got this job to keep myself busy and not get too carried away in my head."

Already having an awareness and compassion for the desensitization that soldiers go through in training and in service, I said, "Wow, I can't even imagine what you've been through and what you've seen. 25 years? That's a long time. It must take a lot of intention and ability to even just feel your emotions." Instantly, the tone of the conversation became very calm and tender. As if he suddenly had permission to drop his shield, he said, "Yes, it does."

He went on to explain some of the challenges he'd been through, and the late-night texts and calls he regularly received from fellow soldiers who can't find reasons to live. He spoke about the shame, sadness, and confusion that he and so many others are weighed down by.

"Are you able to cry?" I asked. His face warmed with a smile and he replied, "Yes, I am. I cry a lot."

"Good," I said, "you're a wise man."

He said he offers himself as counsel to military soldiers in need of support and gives them permission to open up about what they've seen and what they're feeling. "You never know when you've saved a life. It could just be a short phone call and that's all they need. They just need to know they're not alone."

As our heartfelt conversation gently concluded, I looked over at him and said, "I have a feeling you just took this new job because you're here to change lives." With tears in both of our eyes, we shook hands and he said, "I guess you're right. You were my first customer and so far, it's been very powerful."

When you courageously allow yourself to be confidently sensitive, you're standing up to your sergeant, your boss, your school teachers, your spouse, your judgmental family members, and everyone else who is too afraid to feel.

You're also standing up to a force that benefits from you giving up your connection with yourself to be a numb, careless, and senseless spoke in the capitalistic machine of our culture. Rather than burying and hiding your emotions inside, you're making the choice to honor what's natural, right, and healthy for your mind, body, and wellbeing. You're reclaiming your senses and empowering yourself to confront a belief system that's deeply outdated and in need of change.

Do you ever hide, disguise, or withhold your sensitive nature to appear a certain way to others?

How would it feel to be confidently sensitive?

LEARNING TO FEEL

In order to actively *resensitize* ourselves, we have to pay attention to that fork where the road divides between need and protection and choose differently. Rather than unconsciously pulling away from the feeling of discomfort, we have to consciously lean in and intentionally *feel* it.

This can happen by asking yourself three important questions:

1. How am I feeling?
2. Where am I hurting?
3. Where am I afraid?

Now, if "where am I hurting" seems like a confusing inquiry, I understand. It might seem more fitting to ask "why am I hurting?"

The reason we ask *where*, rather than *why*, is that once the wound is discovered, we already know what happened and why we're hurting (as we did in the previous chapter). Now, we need to deepen our understanding and connection to the pain to better understand it and work towards healing it. If you were physically injured and trying to assess the damage, you might be asked, "where does it hurt?" In that same sense, we ask ourselves, "where am I hurting?" to encourage ourselves to find the emotional pain hidden inside.

While it would be very convenient to simply notice when we're showing signs of discomfort and insecurity then ask ourselves *why*, it doesn't always happen that easily. Sometimes, we need to be more creative and patiently ease ourselves into the new territory of self-exploration.

Essentially, we have to peel back the mask, open the cage, and find the *pain* and *fear* within. Why? Because if you don't acknowledge that you're uncomfortable inside, you won't recognize that you have unmet needs. And, if you don't recognize you have unmet needs, you won't take the action required to get them met (in the upcoming chapters). Meaning, you won't heal.

So, this step of digging in deeper to find the pain and fear beneath the outer response is essential. Maybe in the moment, you feel anxious, but when you peer deeper within, you realize you're actually grieving. Maybe all you feel is anger, but when you look deeper, you discover that you're really afraid. Maybe you feel envy, but when you go deeper, you find that you're actually feeling insecure.

Now, there's a big difference between feeling envy or insecurity. If you're envious, you've got a shield up and are somewhat disconnected from your vulnerability. However, if you can acknowledge that what you're really feeling is insecurity, you're much more connected to the true feelings. You're also closer to being able to say, "I feel really uncomfortable. I wonder what I need right now to feel better?"

Over time, the more comfortable you are going into the uncomfortable places, the more comfortable you are with yourself, and this awakens deeper levels of confidence and trust with yourself.

HONORING THE SENSITIVE

WITH THIS SAID, MAYBE SENSITIVITY AND THE ability to feel isn't an issue for you. Maybe rather than building a wall that separates you from your feelings, you're more apt to feel a lot. Perhaps you've even been told that you're *too emotional* or *overly sensitive*.

While the majority of people in the world are to some degree desensitized, not everyone is. In fact, the term "highly sensitive person" exists because some people feel so much, and as a result, they may find themselves in a constant state of anxiousness and overwhelm.

If this is you, you may find that this talk about "resensitizing" doesn't apply to you, and that's ok. My suggestion is to view desensitization as a way to better understand what others are going through. By understanding how hard it is for others to access their feelings, you may be brought closer to awakening the compassion needed to forgive someone whose insensitivity may cause you discomfort and pain.

Regardless of whether you consider yourself sensitive or insensitive, it's likely that if you're dealing with anxiety and feelings of overwhelm, there are deeper levels of pain and fear stemming from unresolved trauma. While you may be connected to certain feelings and emotions, it's possible you're dissociated from others. By allowing yourself to continue exploring your wounds and learning about pain and fear, you may better understand the root cause of your anxiety and lessen it in the process.

Either way, we can all benefit from better understanding what's going on inside us and transforming the unconscious emotions (that may easily control us) into conscious feelings.

THE PHYSICAL FEELING

BECAUSE EMOTIONS ARE ALSO PHYSICALLY FELT, the body and the heart are deeply interwoven and connected. In each wound, ache, fear, and moment of neglect that your heart has endured, your body has also felt it.

Anytime you've been in emotional pain and avoided it by saying to yourself "Whatever, I don't care"—your body was listening. Your body is always listening. It's a devoted and eager friend who is always listening to your words, your thoughts, and your intentions. If you have the desire not to feel, your body also receives that message and is affected by the intention to disconnect.

With your body's dedication and devotion to make sure you *feel* alright, it will do what it can to lessen the burden of your emotional discomfort. It will lovingly take your unsettled, undesirable feelings and memories and store them so you don't have to feel them. It will say "You don't want to feel? Ok. You got it. I'll do what I can to tuck them away. Out of sight, out of mind."

Where do they go? It's different for everyone. Some store the discomfort in the neck muscles and some store in the stomach; for others, the lungs or the joints.

However, just like the heartfelt spirit of your being, your body is tender, sensitive, and caring, and it can't bury the pain and discomfort forever. At some point, it weakens and is worn down, tired, and exhausted. If the withholding has gone on for a long time, the body can eventually become ill from retaining the toxic ooze of stored pain.

What's the solution?

Allowing yourself to *feel* your body. In the same way you're learning to acknowledge the truth of what's really going on in your life and allowing yourself to resensitize in your emotional body, you can bring back feelings and the healing light of awareness into your physical body.

If it's in pain, *acknowledge* it and *feel* it.
If it's stressed, *acknowledge* it and *feel* it.
If it's cold, *acknowledge* it and *feel* it.

Stop avoiding it, and feel it. Reconnect with this sacred vessel that is your home and the only thing that keeps you fully tethered to this life.

A SHIFT IN SENSES

A HELPFUL WAY TO UNDERSTAND OUR FEELINGS and become more connected to our bodies is through becoming more attentive to the subtle frequencies of the body's emotional responses. Like invisible passageways from the outer realms of protection into the deeper feelings, when we're able to shift from desensitized to sensitized, we feel that movement and transformation.

For example, have you ever had pain in your body and rubbed the area to bring relief, then felt a shift of energy when you reached the very specific knot where the pain was coming from? As if you found the pressure point?

When we're searching for the root of our pain and uncovering the wound, we experience a similar pressure point. We might feel a sudden shift in energy, like a sense of relief or an especially tender and uncomfortable point.

Personally, when I'm searching within myself to uncover a wound, and I find it, it feels abruptly sobering, like the music has stopped and suddenly everything is quiet and still.

To understand this, imagine that for weeks, you've been feeling irritable and anxious. Everyone in your life, especially your spouse and your teenage kids, are driving you absolutely crazy. While you try your best not to think about it, you're also dealing with strange pains and discomfort in your stomach. However, to not feed the fear, you haven't brought it up or been talking to anyone about how you're feeling. Instead, you try not to think about it and instead, push forward each day, accomplishing tasks and putting up with your seemingly ungrateful family.

Then, unexpectedly, your spouse says "Sweetheart. I can tell you're not feeling well. I want you to know that I love you and care about you so much. You mean the world to us and I'm just wondering if we can schedule an appointment to go see the doctor? I'll go with you." Suddenly, as if something broke open inside you, your heart feels a gentle tingle. Instead of feeling irritated and resentful, you feel strangely present, tender, and sensitive.

You were avoiding looking at your state of health because it brought up anxiety, and in doing that, your entire life felt anxious. However, when the wound was discovered, it was like finding a pressure point that instantly diffused the built-up pressure and tension.

As if we're able to actually feel the cage walls falling down or sense the tiger's mask coming off, we can feel that shift of energy from desensitized to sensitive; from ego-protected to present; from unconscious to conscious.

Another example is to imagine yourself feeling overwhelmed with jealousy. Let's say your girlfriend hasn't texted you back in a few hours and even though she said she was just going out with friends, you imagine her running into her ex-lover, laughing, drinking, and making careless decisions.

How does that feel? Stressful? Perhaps there's rage coming up?

Now, imagine she comes walking through the door looking exhausted with mud all over her boots. It turns out her car had a flat tire and she had to walk home. The reason she didn't text you back is because she was so flustered that she forgot her phone in the car. Suddenly, the wall of defense drops, your heart opens, and instead of rage, you feel compassion.

Realizing your unnecessary assumption, you say "I was so worried about you. I thought you were out partying. I had no idea you needed help."

Why were you so reactive and filled with anxiety and rage? You were afraid. You were worried and concerned she was going to leave you, and instead of feeling those genuine feelings, you desensitized and hid behind a shield of rage and jealousy. The moment you realized your anger was unnecessary, the shield dropped and the emotional pressure was released.

You went from desensitized to a more sensitive and present place of awareness.

Those subtle and dramatic shifts in feeling and energy are the indications that we're getting closer to the truth and pushing through the protective ego-coating. Each time you become aware of those subtle and energetic shifts, you strengthen your self-awareness, connect more deeply to the feelings of your body, and empower your heart instead of your fear.

Have you ever felt a shift in sensation when moving from one emotion to another?

EVERY FEELING IS WELCOME AT THE TABLE

NOW, THERE IS ANOTHER VERY IMPORTANT KEY in transmuting our emotions into feelings without getting pulled into the seductive haze of unconsciousness: *not judging* them. You can accomplish this by pulling out your trusty "judgment awareness" tool and when you ask yourself *"How am I feeling?"*, do so without judging the feeling as good or bad.

The moment we say, "this feeling is bad", we separate ourselves from it and create two sides: the big, bad villain of a feeling and the helpless victim trying to survive it. Our identification with being the helpless human encourages us to live in fear and unconsciously build a wall to protect ourselves.

One way to remind yourself to welcome feelings holistically—without separation and judgment—is to carry an understanding that "every feeling is welcome at the table." Whether it's anger, sadness, frustration, shame, grief, excitement, embarrassment, or uncertainty (maybe you don't know how you feel?), every feeling is valid and every feeling is important.

Maybe you disagree? Maybe you feel that happiness, joy, and elation are welcome to sit at your table but you'd rather not invite sadness and grief? Unfortunately, it doesn't work like that. If you're feeling something and decide it's not welcome or good enough to join in, you don't get rid of it—you just deny it entry and avoid it. But at some point, it'll turn up again.

Even though certain feelings aren't comfortable or enjoyable, you don't need to live in fear anymore. You don't need to trap yourself in a cage and convince yourself you're not strong enough to handle the truth. *You are strong enough.* You can take an honest look at what's going on and where you're hurting, so you know what you need to feel better.

It's also important to note that however uncomfortable a feeling may be in the moment, it won't last forever. Feelings aren't solid or made of stone; they're fluid, so they move and change course. They float in for a moment, then they float away.

If it's helpful, you can say to yourself:

"What I'm feeling right now is uncomfortable. Though I don't want to be feeling ____ (angry, sad, frustrated, embarrassed, jealous), I do. I acknowledge and accept that I'm feeling this way. I know it's a feeling that will soon change and pass, but right now, it's what I'm feeling."

What if you're not feeling one particular feeling but many? Is it possible to have multiple feelings at once? Including ones that don't necessarily belong or make sense together?

Yes! Absolutely.

Maybe you feel sad *and* inspired? Maybe you feel angry *and* compassionate? Maybe you feel grief *and* enthusiasm? Maybe you feel sadness, inspiration, anger, compassion, grief, and enthusiasm all at once! Yes, *feel* it. The realms of the heart are mysterious at times and won't always make sense or be easy to understand.

In fact, I've often found that in moments where I was the most present, aligned, and united within myself, it wasn't easy to describe to others how I felt. That's because I felt it *all*. Every feeling was welcome in my heart (and at my table), and I could feel the expansiveness of suffering and the expansiveness of love at the same time.

By giving ourselves permission to be sensitive and *feel*, we don't just create a more harmonious space inside ourselves, we also build a healthier connection and friendship with ourselves. We switch the internal narrative from:

"Stop feeling that. You're doing something wrong. Hide it. I don't want to see it here again."

To:

"What you're experiencing is valid and I wholeheartedly accept you and support you in this moment as you experience it."

Essentially, when we make peace with our feelings, we make peace with ourselves.

Is there a feeling you have denied in the past and need to make peace with?

ACKNOWLEDGING ANGER

LET'S IMAGINE YOU'RE READY TO WELCOME your feelings, but *not* the defense-driven feelings like anger? Maybe you even find yourself saying "I don't get mad"? While there are the rare individuals who don't *ever* feel any feelings of aggression, passive aggression or anger, most of us do.

The issue is, because the feeling of anger can be so uncomfortable and lead to additional feelings of shame, regret, and self-judgment, we may not feel comfortable looking at it. Instead, we may be blocking it off, hiding it away, and convincing ourselves it doesn't exist.

This makes sense. If you've been wounded or the recipient of judgment, aggression, violence, or other forms of defense-driven wounding, you don't want to have anything to do with any of those villainous ways.

Whether you're comfortable acknowledging it or not, chances are that at some point (or many) in your life, your actions, thoughts, and words have probably been destructive and harmful to others and yourself. While I imagine you would never wish to intentionally cause pain or harm to anyone, when you're hurting and desensitized in a state of protection and defense, it's easy to say or do things without fully recognizing the negative outcome of your actions.

This was something that came up during a phone call with a dear friend who reached out to process feelings about another friend. While it was clear to me that she was struggling to remain collected, she was under the illusion that her appearance of not being angry was working. But obviously, she was fuming. To break the ice and allow us to go deeper, I said, "Well, you have every reason to feel angry."

"Oh," she said, "I'm not angry, I'm just a little bothered by what she did."

Somewhat confused and intrigued, I said, "You're not angry?"

"No, I feel fine. I'm just a little put off."

The truth is, while she was very upset and angry, she wasn't comfortable acknowledging it. As a result, she was flustered, confused, and uncertain how she felt or what to do about it.

When we don't allow ourselves to acknowledge the reality of what we're feeling, we create a traffic jam of emotions that makes everything harder to understand and eventually heal from. While no one wants to be the bad guy—there are no bad guys; we're all just a bunch of hurt guys—so let's be honest that sometimes we're hurting so much that we get angry. Then, let's look at *why* we're hurting.

As she began to acknowledge her frustrations, a gust of freedom swept through that allowed her to open up more. Eventually, she broke into tears and honestly shared her feelings of being hurt and fearful of losing the friendship. As she welcomed and accepted all of her feelings (to the table) and constructively released them (which we'll get to in Chapter 12), she became much more calm and grounded. She was able to consciously look at the situation and find a healing solution.

As we talked about in Chapter 6, anger is a natural and normal response when we feel the need to defend something we feel protective of. Whether it's our heart, career, spouse, ego, or bank account, it's not a bad thing but it can create a block in the road that separates us from our true feelings (and true healing). And, that's a problem.

In order to really heal and transform our pain, we have to find out what our deeper need is. And to do that, it's essential to recognize what might be standing in the way, like a defensive wall of anger. By remaining present, inquisitive, and courageously open to the more tender feelings within, we exchange the false strength of anger with the true strength of consciousness and take a step closer to the empowered heart.

What would it feel like to openly acknowledge your feelings of anger without shame, judgment, or fear?

REMAINING PRESENT THROUGH THE FEELING

WITH THIS ALL SAID, EMOTIONS ARE EXTREMELY powerful and even when you're able to shift the emotion into a feeling, it can still feel overwhelming. And because our emotions are often anything but subtle, they easily have the power to take over, persuading us to act in a certain way and dominating our lives.

To better understand, imagine the emotional body as a moving body of water. When we've been living in a state of avoidance, we haven't allowed ourselves to fully open, feel, and express our feelings. As a result, they can pool up and become dammed inside us as emotions.

When that body of water starts opening up and moving (like in our work together), it can become a quickly moving current with the potential to flood our senses and completely consume us. Whether we're feeling angry, ashamed, sad, happy, or excited, it can very easily take us to a place of being powerless and without control.

Wait... Back up. Aren't happiness and excitement positive things? How would they ever render us without power or control?

Well, it's important to recognize that we never want to be consumed by any emotion, regardless of what it is. If we're consumed by an emotion, without consciously recognizing that it's happening, we're easily swept away in an unconscious state. Essentially, life is happening to us and we're not empowered. We're not fully present and engaged with each experience in life. With that, we lose touch with the power of presence and the important strength gained from being conscious and fully in control of our bodies and thoughts. Sure, excitement is a wonderful feeling, but if it's pulling us from being present, it's not sustainable.

This is something I learned a lot about through lucid dreaming. If you're not familiar with lucid dreaming, it's essentially being in a dream where you're completely conscious and aware that you're dreaming. Rather than being in a mysterious fog that's hard to recall upon waking, you're very present and able to recognize your thoughts and feelings throughout the experience.

In one very memorable encounter, I was hiking up a mountain where I peered out to the vast mountain range. In the distance, I saw a hooded figure standing far off to my right. His attention was piercingly focused on me. Moved by the discomfort and fear of this mysterious figure, anxiety took over. With a gust of emotion, the unconsciousness glazed over me like a heavy blanket.

Suddenly, I was deeply drowsy and leaving hyper-presence and returning to the normal unconsciousness of dreams. Recognizing what was happening, I whispered to myself "Calm. Relax. This is just a dream; it's not real. Just relax. Come back." As my emotions subsided, I felt the clarity of consciousness summon me back into presence within the dream. In that moment, I realized how persuasive emotions are and how influential they can be in the realms of consciousness and unconsciousness.

With the feeling of confidence and accomplishment, I fiercely called out to the figure, "I'm not afraid of you. This is just a dream. I'm not afraid."

Then, as if I needed every rock on the mountain to know my newly conquered fear, I belted out "I'm not afraaaaaaaid. I'm dreeeeeeaming and I'm not afraaaaaaid anymore." As if realizing that I had somehow conquered a fear and passed a test (yes, my ego did get sparked in that moment), I was overcome with the automatic response of excitement and became unconscious. Flat out. Gone. My eyes reopened in the dark, quiet room of purring cats and breathing lungs. It was night and I was back in my bed.

Whether you recognize it or not, you've likely encountered many experiences throughout your life where your emotions have pulled you out of presence. You were calm, grounded, and experiencing life, then an emotion swept over and suddenly you were too high or too low to think clearly or act consciously.

The key to remaining empowered, in control, and present while also allowing ourselves to feel our emotions, is through ensuring that we're consciously working with our feelings rather than allowing our emotions to unconsciously work through us. Remember, our goal is to be empowered, not confused, lost, and out of control. By remaining present, witnessing the truth of what's going on and staying aware of your emotions, you gain control and step into your power.

THE HIDDEN LANGUAGE OF INTUITION

WHEN WE ARE OPEN AND RECEPTIVE TO FEELING the subtleties of our senses, it awakens deeper levels of awareness, intelligence, and sensitivity within us. This includes our sense of intuition.

While some may relate intuition to the mind's ability to match patterns and systematically process information through the subconscious, I see a different, more heart*felt* side to intuition. I see it as the heart's natural ability to listen, sense, and feel. As if woven together in the realms of telepathy and clairvoyance, intuition is our ability to access a hidden language mapped out in the field of consciousness; the network of connection that ties all living things together. Through intuition, we have access to this connective field. We can acquire information, guidance, understanding, and awareness. While some of us can make sense of it, much remains an undiscovered mystery.

Chances are that anyone who doesn't feel connected to their intuition has just misplaced it. For a lot of people, it is discarded or muted in childhood. We might be told "Stop worrying so much," and "How would you know that?" and "Don't make up silly stories." We are encouraged to only believe what we see and only trust what others can affirm. This happens around the same time that we start giving up our curiosity and imagination, which are both important doorways to deeper realms of understanding.

Looking back through your life, how many times did you sense something before it happened? How often did you *feel* the *truth* of something in your heart without being able to explain why?

When I was 12 years old, I was on a quiet drive with my mom to run errands. Out of nowhere, she asked in a loud and frantic voice, "Becca!! Where's Becca?" With a bit of confusion, I replied, "She's at the farm," which was very normal since my sister Becca had a horse and went there everyday. There was seemingly no reason for my mom to be so immediately and frantically concerned about Becca.

However, she was. Immediately, she pulled the car off the side of the road and grabbed some quarters for the nearest payphone. With confusion and intrigue, I followed. As if she couldn't dial the numbers fast enough, she called the number for the farm and as soon as someone picked up, she asked, "Where's Becca!?" The voice on the other side said, "She's right here, but she's not doing well. We think her arm is broken; she just fell off the horse."

Becca had been riding horses for years and never once fallen. However, on that day, her horse was stung by a bee and bucked her off, flinging her body through a fence. As a result, her elbow was broken, her knee was dislocated, and both her wrist and ankle were sprained.

And my mom knew it when it happened. Like a strange sensation inside her gut, she felt that something wasn't right. Even though Becca wasn't late coming home and there were no clues to comprehend anything was wrong, my mom had a deep and intuitive awareness that allowed her to access information beyond herself. As well, because she loved and cared for her children so much, her sense of intuition was especially strong with them since her heart was so open and activated within that connection.

Intuition is a powerful ability and it's something each of us has access to. Since we know that going into a state of protection blocks our ability to feel, we can then imagine how much our intuition comes to life when we activate our hearts and become sensitive. Because there is the field of consciousness that is so much bigger than the world we can physically see and understand around us, this sensitivity allows us to enter into that field of consciousness, awareness, and expansive understanding.

Your heart's ability to feel is similar to your eyes' ability to see.

If your eyes are open, you can see the truth

If your heart is open, you can feel the truth.

INTELLIGENCE OF THE HEART

THIS ACTIVATION AND RE-AWAKENING OF OUR senses has a major influence on our thoughts and how we see the world. With the opening of the cage around our hearts, our minds open as well. Through that process, we awaken higher levels of awareness and intelligence. While intelligence is often related solely to the mind and thinking, this expansion of both the heart and mind can be referred to as: *intelligence of the heart.*

However, most of us aren't in touch with or aware of the immense power of the heart and the intelligence that comes from it. As a result, when inquiring about one another's wellbeing or opinion, we humans often ask "What do you think?" rather than "How do you feel?" That's because we're often in our heads rather than our hearts.

Is that a bad thing?

Well, no and yes.

Thinking is an amazing and valuable gift. It's because we're able to think and use our brains that we're even here having this experience right now. It took a *lot* of thinking for me to organize my "thoughts" and compile all of the information in this book. And your ability to read these words and translate them into your own understanding requires the mighty presence of your thinking mind.

However, when we're living in a state of pain and fear, our thoughts go off on an unconscious journey without us (think back to *The Wave of Compulsion* in Chapter 7). Rather than being present, we're consumed by worrying and lost in a steady stream of compulsive thinking. We're stuck in our heads, which isn't a good thing.

When you ask certain people (especially self-help authors) about this duality of thinking and feeling, they'll often say that thinking is bad and feeling is good. However, the key to healing doesn't come from encouraging more duality; it comes from balance. It comes from being more conscious in the act of thinking *and* consciously nurturing our ability to feel. Essentially, *re*awakening the ability that many of us put to sleep early in life as it was an uncomfortable and undesirable experience.

While both are very important and very valuable, feeling and thinking are uniquely different. Our thinking brains tend to incorporate time, distance, patterns, and calculations to gain a sense of understanding, while our feeling is the emotional and physical response to the human life experience. Yes, your brain might allow you to draw shapes and color them perfectly or read music and play the exact notes on the page, however, unless you also allow yourself to be *moved* by the *feeling* of the experience, the end result may lack a certain depth and "heart."

When we allow ourselves to fully re-engage with our ability to feel and sense, we go from having an internal thinking and feeling network that is desensitized and disconnected to operating more holistically; more intelligently. With that, our overall intelligence is enhanced. Many people associate intelligence with being intellectual and retaining knowledge and information, when really, we can have a very high IQ and still not be reaching the full potential of our intelligence. True intelligence comes from a *full being* awareness: an activation of both the brain *and* the heart.

We've heard that humans don't use the entirety of their brain's capacity and that leaves us wondering—what would it be like if we consciously used our brains and our hearts to make decisions and formulate perspectives? How much more wise, perceptive, intuitive, and expansive would our overall understanding of life be?

By allowing ourselves to reach out beyond where only thinking can take us, we bravely let go of our attachment to what we think we know and open ourselves to trusting and leaning into the unknown. In doing so, we begin stretching out of the small cage we've been stuck inside for so long and reconnect with the network of consciousness that surrounds us. The unseen world of connection, information, and awareness that cannot be seen, but *felt*.

LEANING INTO THE FEELING
Self-exploration exercise

Now that you have a better understanding about the importance of feeling, let's do an exercise to bring you closer to actually *feeling*. As suggested in the previous chapter, do your best to come from a neutral and unbiased place. If you find yourself judging yourself or thinking "This is silly and a waste of time," observe that.

Also, keep in mind, if you've been neglecting yourself from feeling your deeper, more honest and intimate feelings for a long time, you may experience resistance to feeling anything undesirable or uncomfortable. That's ok. Take your time and take a step back if need be. However, please don't step back completely or underestimate the importance of *feeling* as this is an absolutely essential step in the process of healing. If you don't know how much you're really hurting, you won't know how much you need support. If you don't know you need support, you won't take action to receive it.

Our goal will be to begin in the outer layers of protection and defense, then move our way inward to find the pain and fear within.

1. To begin, bring your awareness to an experience where you were angry, irritated, or defensive in response to what someone did or said to you. This experience may be from your distant past or something recent.

    Was it a breakup or divorce?
    Did you have an uncomfortable conversation with your mother-in-law?
    Did your spouse do something that crawled under your skin?

    Allow yourself to really bring this memory and vision into your thoughts by asking yourself:

    What happened?

2. As you allow yourself to hone in on this experience, pay attention to your body and any physical sensations you feel in response. Do you feel tension or stress? If so, where? Your forehead? Your shoulders? Your chest? Your jaw. Take note of any physical feelings that may be in response to this experience.

    Do any additional emotions begin to arise as you bring this troubling experience into your scope? Anxiety? Confusion? Disappointment? Really ask yourself:

    How am I feeling?

3. Now, since you know that defense is a reaction to the tender feelings of pain and fear beneath the surface, give yourself permission to lean in closer, past the veil of defensiveness, and ask yourself:

    Where am I hurting?

    Are your feelings hurt by something they did or said?
    Do you feel taken for granted or underappreciated?
    Do you feel abandoned or disrespected?
    Really lean in and give yourself permission to be honest about where you're hurting. Remember, it's only you here. No one is judging you or thinking poorly of you right now, not even yourself. Take your shield down and tell the truth.

4. When you're ready, patiently and without expectation or judgement, ask yourself:

   Where am I afraid?

   Are you afraid that what they said was true?
   Are you scared they're going to talk bad about you to someone else?
   Are you concerned they don't love you anymore?

   Be as courageously vulnerable as you can and answer honestly.

5. When transitioning from a defensive state to a sensitive state, did you feel any changes? Whether dramatic or subtle, did you notice a shift in your senses?

   Did you feel a sense of relief?
   Did you feel inflated, then deflated?
   Did you suddenly feel more calm or present?

   Each time you give yourself permission to accept and *feel* the deeper feelings, you go from being internally disconnected, to reuniting with your true self.

6. Now, as best you can, imagine what pain and fear the *other* person may have been in as they were acting out and displaying qualities of protection and defense.

   Is it possible they were hurt by something *you* said or did?
   Is it possible they felt abandoned or disrespected?
   Is it possible they were feeling defensive and trying to protect their wounded heart inside?

7. Take a deep breath in, then release it.
   You're doing big work by courageously confronting your ego and allowing yourself to holistically feel. You're also strengthening your relationship with yourself each and every moment you're able to be more sensitive, aware and compassionate, rather than resentful.

   As we move forward into the coming chapters, we'll learn ways to *connect, release, comfort,* and *love* ourselves when we feel the discomfort of pain and fear.

EXAMPLE CONVERSATION

For this conversation, let's imagine that your partner recently said they "miss you" because you're always busy and distracted. Your reaction was, "That's absurd. Why would you miss me? We live together and we're always around one another."

"Yes," they replied, "But you're constantly on your phone or doing something. It's like you're not even here."

The conversation escalated into an argument, and you defended yourself and pointed out all the ways your spouse isn't present. However, something felt unsettling and important about what they said. Because the relationship means so much to you and you don't want to create disharmony, you're willing to take a look and see whether there's any truth to you being distracted and distant.

What's happening? What happened?

Investigator: Can you describe what's happening and what happened?
Witness: Yes. My partner said I'm not emotionally available because I'm distracted and on my phone a lot.
I: Are you?
W: No, I'm just living my life and they can stop being so controlling and needy.

Judgement awareness. Let's try that again.

I: Are you on your phone a lot?
W: Yes. I am on my phone a lot.
I: Exactly when are you on your phone?
W: Well, I'm actually not ever without it. I keep it beside me when I sleep. I take it on walks with me. I sometimes use it while I'm waiting in line or in traffic.
I: Why are you on your phone so much?
W: Because I'm bored and have nothing better to do.

That would be an exaggeration and false information. Let's stick to the facts.

I: Why are you on your phone so much?

W: I find that I'm anxious without it. I feel nervous if I don't have it with me.
I: So, the phone is calming for you?
W: Yes, I guess so. I feel calmer with it.

Interesting. That feels like something of importance. No need to judge myself or think I'm weak for finding my phone soothing. I just need to take note of it. Knowing that anxiousness is a sign of need, I wonder where it's coming from.

How am I feeling? Where am I hurting? Where am I afraid?

I: How often do you feel anxious?
W: A lot. I feel constantly upset and antsy.

Interesting. I wonder what's really going on?

I: When did you first start feeling this anxiety?
W: It's been intense for the past year.
I: Can you recall anything that happened last year that was traumatic or wounding?
W: Well, yeah. My dad passed away.

Interesting. I just felt a big sweep of solemn sadness wash over me. I think this might be a wound.

I: Have you processed your dad's death?
W: Not really. I thought I had, but now I'm wondering if maybe I didn't.
I: When you experienced the death, how did you feel?
W: Crushed. He was my everything. He raised me as a single dad and I never imagined life without him.

Ok. This feels big. This is definitely a wound. I don't feel frustrated anymore. I feel like I'm gonna cry.

I: Is it possible you've been distracting yourself because you're scared of feeling this grief?
W: Yeah, definitely. Crying is very uncomfortable for me. I don't know how to deal with sadness.

Knowing that my dad's death is a wound and somewhere inside I'm grieving, it must mean I need something to heal the pain.

I: In what ways are you soothing the pain?

W: Umm.. I don't know. Up until 30 seconds ago, I didn't even know I was in pain so I definitely am not doing anything to soothe it.

Knowing that we often protect ourselves with distraction, is there a connection?

I: Is it possible that you've been nervously distracting yourself because you don't know how to deal with the grief?

W: Yeah, definitely. My dad and I used to text everyday so I think I'm keeping the phone close even though I know he's not here anymore.

Wow, this is all feeling pretty sad.

I: What are you feeling right now?

W: I feel tender and sad.

I: What do you need?

W: I don't know. Maybe a hug? Even though crying's usually impossible for me, I think I need to cry for a while.

I: It seems your partner is genuinely reaching out for connection, could you talk to them?

W: Yes, maybe I need to tell them what's really going on and talk about all of this.

•

As we continue in the next chapter, we'll talk more about connection, friendship, and getting our needs met through seeking counsel to process the painful emotional hurdles of life.

FEELING TOOLS

Regardless of how insensitive and careless others can be,
I have permission to feel and be sensitive.

◆

When I acknowledge the presence of automatic and
reactive emotions, I can gain control by infusing them with
conscious awareness and transforming them to feelings.

◆

By paying attention to the subtle shifts in the energy
around my emotional responses, I can better understand
where the wounds are and what I'm really feeling beneath
my protection and defense.

◆

Each time I allow myself to feel the true essence of pain and
fear beneath the protection and defense, I gain confidence
and trust in myself.

◆

To awaken and strengthen my intuition, I can honor what
my heart feels and trust the authenticity and importance of
the messages it hears.

◆

By allowing myself to consciously utilize the strength of
both my feeling heart and thinking mind, I enter into higher
levels of awareness and intelligence.

❦

I have a feeling there is more to life than this.

Beyond this display of changing skies and moving parts,
A meaning that cannot be heard or tasted,
only felt.

Like a passageway leading to a sacred room
disguised within the vast mystery of clouds.

Though I cannot see it and I cannot prove it,
I know that it exists.

I can feel it.

One can point to the sky and wait
for the sun to burn the mist and still,
it cannot be seen with eyes.

For it is not a destination
or a place;

it is a feeling.

It is
here.

Inside my heart.

❦

GETTING YOUR NEEDS MET

Once we have clarity around what's really going on in our lives and can consciously recognize how uncomfortable (afraid and in pain) we feel inside, it becomes clear that we have unmet needs.

Ideally, you're at this point right now. You're recognizing, "I've been through some really uncomfortable stuff in life and I feel uncomfortable inside. Maybe instead of ignoring myself and avoiding where it hurts, I need to make some changes and show up for myself differently. Just because others haven't always shown up for me, it doesn't mean I can't show up for myself. Just because my needs haven't been met in the past, it doesn't mean I can't get them met now."

It's really at this point in the journey that you begin asking yourself:

<u>What do I need?</u>

While you may not know the answer to that question right now, change is on the way. You're about to build an entirely new relationship with yourself and become skilled in going beneath the surface to soothe the pain inside. Instead of soothing yourself with substances, you'll learn about hugging. Rather than being aggressive, you'll learn to be expressive.

Instead of seeking security and confidence through social media, you'll access it through building a sincere friendship with yourself.

This will happen through exploring four major needs:

- **Connect** (connection, friendship, community, counsel)
- **Release** (crying, speaking, movement, artistic expression)
- **Comfort** (warmth, hugging, nurturance, nature)
- **Love** (self-respect, discernment, compassion, forgiveness)

Through a plethora of tips, tools, exercises, meditations, and resources, you'll have everything you need to soothe and heal yourself. That's because you are powerful and you are your own true healer. You are the one in charge of your life, and when, not *if*, you get through this, you'll go from having a broken heart, to having an *empowered heart*.

◆

Now, let's continue on our journey together and get your needs met!

11.
CONNECT

*To deepen the connection with the self and others;
to experience healing, support, and wholeness.*

Not long after the hospital episode, we packed up our lives in Los Angeles and relocated to Austin, Texas. With Kurt being a Texan and both of us being musicians, it felt like a nice change of pace to leave California and embrace a lifestyle where we could slow down and have some space for our hearts to breathe.

As resistant to being domestic as we both were, it was no time before our little rented house had two cats in the yard and the world's best dog running around it. Suddenly, we weren't alone anymore. We had a family. We had plants. We had neighbors. We had friends. We had an 80-gallon fish tank with schools of fish. We had a route through the streets we would walk each night as the sun was setting, and above all else, we had a safe place to call *home*.

One of the two bedrooms in that sweet, humble home was our bedroom and the other was my office, *aka processing, writing, climbing, falling, crying, digging, exploring, questioning, realizing, observing, feeling, connecting* room. It was a safe place with a closed door where I could ask myself questions and patiently wait for the answers. It was a place where I could pace around in circles to avoid being led to the bathroom where I might be tempted to fall into the pit of despair.

Many times, I would routinely open the fridge and stand in front of it. I would gaze deeply into the shelves with a curious look on my face, then close it. Having become increasingly aware of how my anxiousness was influenced by unresolved childhood pain and what the addiction was doing to me as a result, I was feeling less inspired to eat and more inspired to call a friend or go out on a walk with my angelic guardian dog. Where once I was very protective and private, I had become more open and welcoming to friendships and connection with others.

In fact, each month, I would invite a dozen or so women over to honor our bodies, the moon, and our connection to it all. We called them "Merry Moon Gatherings" and together, we would sit in talking circles and create a space where everyone's heart could open. Dedicated to no judgment, we would give ourselves permission to listen, speak, and be heard.

As simple and uninteresting as that house may have appeared from the outside, it changed my life. It was the sacred temple that housed my prayers and dreams come true. Days turned into weeks, and weeks into months of sobriety from compulsive eating and bulimia. Like that lone wolf desperately seeking for so long, I finally felt reunited and connected. I needed to know that I wasn't alone and I needed to feel that I belonged. And I found it.

That's what happens when we allow ourselves to connect. Rather than being and feeling alienated in our protective shadows, we reach out and unite. We find our cable of connection inside and learn how to spark it to the world and people around us. In doing so, we experience the healing power of unity.

<u>Examples of ways to CONNECT:</u>
- Friendship
- Communication
- Intimacy
- Listening
- Sharing
- Relating
- Opening
- Reaching out
- Asking for help

I used to hear the word "connect" and think of a plug going into an electrical outlet or imagine a computer successfully hooking up to Wi-Fi. In many ways, energetic connection is similar. But it's more than just a physical or electrical connection of two things; it's the act of more than one thing *energetically* uniting.

Remember what happens when we've been deeply hurt and learned to close up? Our hearts break, the connection is severed, and we lose service. When we make the choice to heal and empower our hearts, we *reconnect* that energetic exchange within ourselves and one another. We take a giant, daring leap away from fear and towards trust.

With that, our understanding expands into:

"I'm not alone. I can engage with people and the world around me."

Piecing these steps together, we first take an honest look at where we are wounded, then we check in with how we're feeling as a result. From there, we make the choice to open up, rather than close down.

> Observe: *What's happening right now? What happened in the past?*
> Feel: *How am I feeling? Where am I hurting? Where am I afraid?*
> Connect: *I'm not alone. I can engage with people and the world around me.*

When we're feeling hurt, afraid, and uncomfortable in ourselves, what we often need is connection. We need to feel united and not alone. Rather than burying everything inside and feeling like we have to suffer alone in this world, we need to re-engage with others and feel the exchange of connection, which ties us to the life around us.

In the radiance of connection, our broken heart is fused back together. Our empty, longing hands are finally held, and that is something we all deserve. We deserve to know we are not alone.

SEEKING CONNECTION

AS WE'VE SEEN, EVEN THOUGH HEALTHY CONNECTION is often what we need, when we feel lost and separated, we often find ourselves seeking *anything* to help us feel better, whether it's helpful or not.

I call this *Seeking Connection*. We're seeking support to soothe the pain and a sense of wholeness. We're the lone wolf seeking a return to the warmth and inclusion of the pack. Unfortunately, we may find ourselves seeking connection through destructive ways or relationships that aren't healthy or constructive.

Examples of **destructive connection:**
- Social media (unconscious engagement)
- Compulsive eating
- Drinking alcohol to feel confident enough to socialize
- Destructive and judgmental camaraderie with peers
- Drug use
- Pornography
- Promiscuity
- Abusive relationships

While each of these things can offer a temporary sense of connection, they're not necessarily constructive or sustainable. We think we're experiencing a sense of connection and belonging, but in reality, we're acting from an unconscious state and being led further *away* from ourselves and the root of our pain and healing.

The solution?

Consciously observing and feeling that you're in pain, then making the decision to actively seek *constructive* forms of connection.

In many ways, when we seek connection, we're asking for help. This is very uncomfortable for many of us, especially if we've gotten cozy and comfortable behind our walls of false strength and protection. Asking for help may feel like shattering everything that seemingly keeps us safe.

In realizing that we don't need to struggle through it alone and allowing ourselves to seek support, we actively move towards getting our needs met. We take a step closer to creating and accessing a healthy, constructive support network, as opposed to an unhealthy one.

To do so, we need to continue being the investigator and study ourselves. Then, we'll notice when we open the fridge, reach for a bottle of beer, or worry whether anyone has liked our latest social media post, and we'll gain power and confidence in our own strength. Each time we notice, we disassemble the illusion and direct ourselves back to consciousness.

A FAMILIAL NETWORK

IDEALLY, THE CONSTRUCTIVE SUPPORT WE NEED would be provided from family. We would have a plethora of comforting arms, words, and ears ready to embrace our hurting hearts. However, it was likely within our families that we experienced the most significant and destructive wounding. Because of that, many of us don't feel safe, comfortable, or "at home" with our families. In fact, our family members may be the last people we would go to for support and a feeling of connection.

But let's take a step back... what is *family*? If you consider family to be your birth tribe, then it makes sense to feel that way. However, it's important to note that the essence of family is far greater and more expansive than the small group of humans you share the same blood with. Connecting with "family" can simply mean people who you trust enough to open up and be yourself with. "Family" can be a group where you *know* that you belong.

We often assume that it's solely within the presence of our fellow humans that healing takes place. As it was likely within the presence of a human that the wound occurred, this is easy to assume, but it isn't always the case. Yes, our connection to other humans is vital, but there are many ways to experience the healing force of family and connection.

Beyond the realms of human-to-human interaction, there are millions of incredible beings and ways to experience friendship and constructive connection. Yes, the tree in your yard may be a different species and have a different ancestry than you, but it doesn't mean you can't develop a deep and profound friendship. Sure, you talk rather than bark, but that doesn't mean that you and a four-legged friend can't unite your hearts and share an incredible familial connection with one another.

Even though our pain, fear, and sadness can make the world feel very small, it's not. It's a big, glorious planet filled with incredible heartfelt beings and opportunities for the exchange of life energy. We are nestled within a mycelial network of pulsating energy and opportunity, and we are completely surrounded by conscious, living, breathing beings who are capable and ready for connection. That includes yourself. You may not be the first person you think of when you hear the word "family" or "friend," but as you'll see, you are actually the most important friend you'll ever connect with.

Being included within this solar system of connection and belonging is not just something we want, it's something we *need*. We need to know that we're not alone and that we belong. We need to feel at home in our lives and in our bodies. We need to know that we're cared for and that we have family. When we allow ourselves to finally, truly connect with others, we leave our cold, solemn realm of suffering and reawaken in a realm of belonging.

Rather than excluding ourselves due to insecurity and fear of judgment, we must allow ourselves to step forward and engage, to reconnect with the life around us, and to birth a deeper understanding of family. This is something I call "constructive connection" or "a familial network of connection." It's a way of shifting our perspective from seeing that we are alone to understanding that we are surrounded by life.

Examples of **constructive forms of connection:**

Self
- Journaling to share and hear personal thoughts and feelings
- Sitting in a meditative space
- Going for a walk by yourself
  (We'll talk more about nurturing your relationship with yourself in the coming chapters)

Human interaction
- Speaking with a friend, counselor, therapist, or elder
- Taking a class with other people
  (dance, writing, art, cooking, music, yoga, meditation)
- Joining an online or in-person meeting group with shared interests and wounds

Animal kingdom
- Equine therapy
- Spending quality time with pets and animals
  (volunteering at an animal shelter if you don't have any animal friends)
- Bird watching

Plant kingdom
- Being around trees
- Growing a garden
- Raising house plants

Earth and sky
- Looking and studying what's on the earth's surface
  (rocks, soil, seashells, sand)
- Watching the sky
  (the stars at night or looking at the clouds)
- Spending time in, near, or around natural water sources
  (lakes, streams, rivers, oceans)

I realize that some of these things may seem childish and unnecessary. Perhaps you're thinking, "Sorry, but I don't have time in my busy life to go looking at rocks or staring at the sky. I have more important things to do." Yes, I understand why you may feel that way—a lot of us feel that way and we act upon it. We associate moments of rest, playfulness, and stillness as time wasted. Rather than allowing ourselves to naturally engage and connect with people and the world around us, we spend every waking moment working, making money, and surviving.

This all makes sense… until we find ourselves sad, alone, lost, and suffering, trying to fill a void in our hearts that no money, drink, or job promotion can fill.

Guess what? Shutting yourself inside a cage and spending every moment distracted and working your life away is not living—it's suffering—and you don't deserve that. You're done suffering.

If you really want to heal those aching wounds inside, give yourself permission to receive the connection and support you deserve. Take a step back and look at your life from a new perspective. Look around you at the miraculous family of life that you are part of and rather than holding yourself hostage away from it all, engage with it. Go for a walk, stretch your body, write in your journal, or call a friend.

You deserve to know that regardless of how dysfunctional and unavailable your birth family is, you are *surrounded* by a family of friendship and support. That network exists in humans, animals, plants, and every living, breathing, divine form of connection.

FRIENDSHIP

WHAT DOES "FRIEND" MEAN? IT CAN MEAN something different to each of us, but what does it mean to you? Does it symbolize someone who shows up for you when you're feeling down? Is it someone who is unconditionally loving without judgment or shaming? Does *friend* mean someone who is willing to say it like it is and be honest when others won't?

For a lot of us, a friendship is connecting with someone who is trustworthy and who listens; someone who honors us with the respect of being important and loved enough to be heard. Being a good listener requires presence, so it's safe to say that a good friend is someone who's present.

Often, we don't understand who our true friends are until we're going through a challenge and really *need* someone. And we're more apt to reach out to someone who we trust and feel safe with in those moments of hardship. However, not everyone can be present enough to be a good friend.

Imagine you have three friends and you're seeking support after a traumatic experience. Your heart is hurting, you feel tender and insecure, and you need help working through it. You explain to each friend, "I'm really going through it right now. My heart is aching and I feel like I'm falling apart."

> <u>Friend 1</u> replies: "Is there ever a time when you're not falling apart? What is it this time?"
>
> <u>Friend 2</u> replies: "Sorry, I've got too much stuff going on right now. Just try to perk up and focus on something positive. You'll get through it."
>
> <u>Friend 3</u> replies: "You are? Ok. Let me finish what I'm doing, it'll take me five minutes. I want to give you my undivided attention. Let's talk and you can tell me everything that's going on. I love you and you're not alone through this."

Which friend do you feel safe to open up with?
Which friend do you feel the warm exchange of connection with?

Which friend do you trust?

Chances are, you feel safe with friend number three, who is dependable, supportive, and present. The friend who is willing to show up with unconditional love and support to listen to what you're going through.

What if you don't have good friends like that? What if you don't know anyone who is unconditionally loving, listening, and supportive?

If you don't know anyone like that, maybe it's time to start making new friends with people who are honest, kind, and genuinely caring. But to connect with kind and trustworthy people, you have to be able to recognize when you come in contact with them. To do that, you have to step outside your cage and be more sensitive and discerning about how you *feel* in the presence of other people. You will likely feel a subtle *shift in your senses* when you come in contact with different people.

Imagine there's a really pretty, popular woman who you work with. She's everything you wish you could be. She wears trendy clothes, is outspoken, and has a plentiful following on social media. Just being her friend makes you feel important. However, you feel a bit insecure and down on yourself when you hang out with her. You're always the one who reaches out to her. While she's mostly nice, she says judgmental and destructive things about other people, and you find yourself not speaking up very much because you're nervous that her criticism will potentially come your way.

Now, imagine there's another woman at work who is very kind and at times, you almost feel embarrassed by how much attention she gives you and how little you give her in return. She's compassionate and engaging, and since you gave her your number last week, she's already texted you twice asking whether you'd be up for hanging out. You were "busy" both times because you weren't sure you wanted to spend time with someone who's not really your 'vibe.'

Well, consider this: how many kind, good people have you potentially disregarded because you were too protective and too judgmental to recognize them? How many fun-filled, incredible, heart-warming opportunities have you missed out on because your fear and insecurity held you back?

Some of us aren't popular and don't have a lot of friends but that doesn't mean we aren't capable of *being* good friends.

A good friend is someone you can trust, open up with, and explore the magical mysteries and adventures of life with. Give yourself permission to look around at all of the amazing people who are just as hurt, wounded, and wonderful as you are. Forget about popularity and what you have in common—make friends with someone you don't have anything in common with and learn something new! Find those kind, caring, and trustworthy people who could use a friend as much as you could and re-explore what true friendship feels like.

Also, it's important to note: some people are in a lot of pain and have not received the healing they need. They may be seeking connection from you and their needs may be asking for more than what you're able to provide. Maybe they're reaching out daily and it's beginning to feel unhealthy and overwhelming for you. If so, you may need to practice discernment in how you interact with them. While you may not be the one to help them, it doesn't mean there's any reason to judge them or be hurtful towards them. You can still be an honest and supportive friend by helping them find the right support they need, which might be in the direction of a trained therapist, coach or counselor.

How would you describe a true friend?

PLANTS AND ANIMALS

IN 1966, AN INTERROGATION SPECIALIST NAMED Cleve Backster was a polygraph expert for the CIA, and he had an idea. He hooked up his polygraph machine to one of the plants in his Manhattan office. Full of curiosity, he was intrigued to see whether the detector would show any response from the plant's electrodes.

As happens in the field of interrogation, he needed to create a threat to the plant to read its electrode response. He tried putting one of its leaves in a cup of coffee. Nothing. The plant didn't seem to care.

Then he set a leaf on fire. Immediately, the dial went so ballistic and the pen flew off the chart. In awe, he found some matches, lit one, and took a few swipes at the leaf. The polygraph continued to show the plant's extreme reaction to being burned. When he returned the matches and the threat had subsided, the plant relaxed and felt safe again.

This was a profound, life-altering discovery: plants are far more conscious, sensitive, and advanced than most humans had realized. The realization inspired Cleve to devote his life to the study of consciousness beyond humans. As his true purpose had finally revealed itself, he continued his research for nearly 40 years and brought to light the importance of "primary perception," a term used to describe the awareness that exists in plants.

Far beyond the work of Cleve Backster, many scientists and researchers have explored and confirmed additional evidence to prove the awareness in plants. In fact, research shows that plants also have the ability to count, see color, and even respond to music. While they don't have physical brains (that we know of) they clearly show signs of being aware of their surroundings and actively respond to them.

If plants are capable of this level of awareness, what about animals? Given that some parrots have the ability to speak human languages and chimpanzees have shown the ability to use keyboards to answer questions, how consciously aware are animals? Since they have eyes, ears, brains, hearts, emotions, and almost everything that we humans have, is it possible they have the ability to feel and genuinely care as much as we do? I believe so.

I can honestly say that our dog and two cats were a major part of my healing and recovery from addiction and suffering. It was as if they knew and could feel exactly when I was struggling. In the moments where I felt alone and filled with anxiety, the cats would lay directly on my head, or on my heart, and purr until I had relaxed and fallen asleep. When I would eat a meal and feel persuaded to fall into my bulimic tendencies, my dog would lay her paw on my leg and look deep into my eyes, filling me with a very direct sense of love and connection. In many ways, the animals were (and still are) my best friends. They surrounded me in a furry family of support, and because of that, I knew I wasn't alone. That's something I needed in order to heal. I needed to know that I wasn't alone.

Maybe the trees, grass, and beautiful potted Ficus in your office can't talk or give you verbal advice, but who's to say they aren't listening? Who's to say they don't love and care about you? Who's to say there isn't the potential of an incredible friendship waiting to be?

Look around at what appears to be a pile of leaves, a sleeping cat, or a bird perched on your window and give yourself permission to lean in a little closer. Feel the essence of life within and feel the invitation to be united in a world of connection that reaches far beyond what your eyes can see.

Have you ever had a very close friend who wasn't human? What are some experiences you've shared together?

FRIENDSHIP WITH THE SELF

NOW FOR A VERY IMPORTANT QUESTION:
What kind of friend are you to yourself?

How often have you needed support or someone to remind you that you're not alone, yet you yourself don't have time to be there for yourself? When you feel sad, disconnected, confused, and in need, what then? You may speak about how friends, lovers, and family members have abandoned you and not been there when you needed them, but what about you? At what point did you sign a waiver to always be too busy, too good, or too damaged to show up for yourself? Who is abandoning who?

To better understand what kind of friend you are to yourself, ask yourself:

How do I talk to myself when no one else is around?

I mean inside your head, when no one else can hear you: what do you say to yourself? Do you say hurtful things? Are you judgmental? Do you force yourself to put on the backpack of shame and trudge around with your head to the ground?

If you've been a neglectful friend to yourself, it's not your fault. Most of us weren't trained to be good friends to ourselves or to one another. Instead, we were taught to be disconnected and desensitized. We learned to drown out the truth with the constant buzz of avoidance and distraction. Rather than feeling safe enough to be present and allow ourselves to be open, sensitive, and receptive, we learned to be closed off and divided away from our true selves.

A good question to ask yourself is:

Is my tendency to be harsh, judgmental, and uncaring toward myself really serving me?

If not, then a better question might be:

What kind of friend do I want to be to myself?

Do you want to be someone who says, "Is there ever a time when you're not falling apart? What is it this time?" What about when you feel alone and desperately in need of someone to surround you in support and unconditional love—do you want to be there for yourself?

If you really want to rise up and live out the potential of what you're capable of, then treat yourself as a nurturing, warm, and caring friend would. What makes a good friend? Remember, someone who cares and someone who listens.

What does it mean to listen? It means allowing your ears, eyes, and heart to be in the present moment and join the person who is speaking, even (especially) if that person is you. Rather than focusing on what you have to do or what's happening next, stop what you're doing and *listen*.

Rather than abandoning yourself in a time of crisis, show up and be there for yourself. Really lean in, listen to yourself, and respond like the true friend you're capable of being. *Are you ok? What happened? How are you feeling? Let me finish what I'm doing, it'll take me five minutes. I want to give you my undivided attention. Let's talk and you can tell me everything that's going on. I love you and you're not alone through this.*

While you're not fully entitled, in charge, or capable of choosing how relationships unfold with others, you are completely empowered to determine what kind of relationship you want with yourself. It's something you decide to nurture and care for... or not. When you look back at all you've been through in your life, doesn't it make sense to treat yourself with kindness, honor, and respect? Wouldn't it benefit you (and everyone in your life) to commit to stop being abusive and instead listen to yourself and be a good friend?

Each time you make this choice to be a true friend to yourself, you begin seeing things differently. You begin showing up differently and being a better friend to everyone else as well.

What kind of friend are you to yourself?
What kind of friend would you like to be to yourself?

JOURNALING: A SACRED DOORWAY

WHAT IF WHAT YOU REALLY NEED IS TO BE ALONE? For a lot of us who spend a majority of our time tending to other's needs, sometimes it can be confusing when we feel both overwhelmed and lonely at the same time. As if we're missing something, yet couldn't possibly fit one more thing into our busy lives.

Well, in honor of nurturing a healthy and strong friendship with yourself, sometimes what you need more than anything, is nothing. Just some alone time with nothing to do and no one else but yourself. Time to relax, reflect, listen, and be heard. A very powerful way to achieve this very necessary and medicinal alone time is through writing in a journal.

Journaling is a powerful tool to nurture our friendship with ourselves and to feel heard and held in our own presence. It's also an incredibly useful way to confront our avoidance and honor the truth within us. Whether we're feeling contemplative and uncertain about which path to take or disconnected from ourselves and longing to reunite, we can embrace journaling to be honest with ourselves and gain advice, insights, and support.

I journal almost every day, and for many years, I've utilized writing as a way to check in with myself and hear how I'm feeling. In fact, this very book came from hours, months, and years of studying, reflecting, understanding, and journaling my experience of suffering and healing.

I also keep notebooks around me (in my purse, in my car, beside my bed) ready to scribble insights at any time. Each time I sit down to provide counsel to someone, I have a notebook and pen to actively listen to two voices: the voice of the person I'm helping and the one offering insight from within me.

I often see a vision when I'm writing:

Completely surrounding me is a world that I cannot see. A fantastic, mystical, magical world of infinite wisdom and possibility. It's as if I'm floating in a different dimension. This land of mystery and intrigue is the realm of collective awareness and it's only accessible when I'm in a calm, relaxed, and open state. If I try to look at it, it disappears—it's invisible. If I want to enter this realm, I have to completely relax and open a channel in my heart to this sacred space. The more I relax, the more open the channel is. When I'm completely relaxed, I fully enter this unique land of mysticism with access to everything. Every thought, dream, memory, and doorway yet to be discovered.

Because the universe is so vast and expansive, there is a *lot* we don't understand and a lot to the mystery of existence that we can't see. When you allow yourself to be a curious student, taking notes from teachers and guides who live within your heart, you will find worlds of possibilities and realizations waiting to be realized. By allowing yourself to write creatively and freely, you open yourself to what exists beyond your physical vision and welcome higher levels of seeing and understanding.

If you've tried writing down your thoughts and feelings but nothing comes, stick with it and keep trying. Like building trust in any friendship, it may take time to feel safe enough in the presence of yourself to be open and honest. Try not to judge yourself and trust that whatever makes its way onto the page is of importance.

If you find yourself veering off your original topic, reflecting on memories you'd forgotten, just go with it. See where it takes you and be open to what is trying to be revealed. You may discover that it's not just pain and negativity that needs to be relieved from your being but also incredible insights, profound wisdom, and dream visions that you're ready to awaken.

ANONYMOUS SHARING

THROUGH THE YEARS SPENT ON MY OWN JOURNEY of healing, I'd discovered the profound benefit of overcoming shame and pain through not just looking at it, but opening up and talking about it. While it was something I began doing frequently with myself through journaling, I also found that conversing with others was extremely helpful and healing. In an effort to share this awareness, I began creating safe, warm, and intentional spaces where people could gather in the gentle presence of others and feel secure enough to look at their own pain, talk about it, and also see how their situation was similar to others. In support of that, I started organizing and facilitating talks, workshops, and retreats around the country.

The biggest hurdle was: *how are a group of people going to push through their fear and shame enough to share their uncomfortable truths with a room full of strangers in a daylong workshop?* Even when people are together for a week (or years), they hold back their heavy secrets due to not feeling safe enough, which is completely understandable since most of us have dealt with the deep discomfort of having been judged or chastised at some point. But if they don't feel safe and secure enough to speak up, their truth won't be told, and that would defeat the purpose of us gathering to release our heavy burdens.

The other issue was the potential shame aftermath. Even if someone felt comfortable enough to share their truth with others in the safe environment of a workshop, they might realize that they're now surrounded by a group of strangers who know their story. And, they might worry that if they randomly ran into one another at the grocery store, the other person may potentially try to talk about intimate content from the workshop. *Not good.* In fact, that's a recipe for more wounds and more shame.

So, I came up with a solution called *anonymous sharing.*

It goes like this: Each person is given a sheet of paper and has 20–30 minutes to write. The instructions are: "Write something you are ashamed of and ready to let go of. Please do your best to make your writing legible and do not sign your name." Everyone finds a remote, secluded area to write in, and as they write, there is meditation music playing.

With the sacred beauty of the music, I found that pens were quickly meeting paper and tears were falling. There was a heartbreaking chorus of people giving themselves permission to write their truth. Each person entered an anonymous space of sharing, where they were able to release the intimate pain. Then, they each folded their papers and returned them to me. With puffy eyes and tender hearts, we reunited in a circle.

Each person was handed back a random sheet of paper. To not build stressful anticipation, I offered each person the chance to "Share the story on your paper when you feel moved. Because we won't know whose story is whose, when a story has been read, look around at the circle and say, 'I hear you. I see you. Thank you.'"

As the fear of being judged, criticized, or gossiped about contributes to so many of us remaining silent and internalizing our pain, this approach opens a space. A space where people can share without anyone knowing who is sharing. Each person may experience multiple benefits of anonymous sharing, including:

- Confronting the avoidance that has contributed to the silence
- Feeling heard
- Observing the similarities within each of the stories
- Experiencing connection
- Building trust
- Releasing the burden of carrying a secret

I can tell you right now, regardless of financial status, background, ethnicity, or physical appearance, *everyone* had a story. Everyone has been through it and *everyone* understands suffering. There were stories of deceased siblings, childhood abuse, rape, divorce, attempted suicide, racism, abortions, alcoholism, drug use, bulimia, porn, illness, and so much more, many of which had never been shared before.

Though the characters were different and the scenarios were unique, each painful story echoed the one before, as if everyone was hearing their story being told and retold but with slightly different variations each time. As the stories exited the bodies and entered the circle, it seemed that each participant stepped back from identifying with their own painful lineage and began dissociating from it. They stopped feeling the need to carry it.

When initially entering the space, I would often ask, "How's everyone feeling? Anyone nervous? Uncomfortable?" Many hands would timidly rise. After anonymous sharing, the previously nervous group of strangers felt a deep, sincere connection to one another. By the end, it resulted in teary-eyed hugs and compassion for themselves and each other. Rather than feeling uncomfortable and alone in their struggles, they felt heard and understood. What's more, they felt a sense of belonging in the presence of one another.

If you had the opportunity to anonymously tell the story of something you are ashamed of and ready to let go of, what might it be?

PRESENT LISTENING

HAVE YOU EVER CONTEMPLATED WHY SOME OF YOUR close loved ones don't seem capable of engaging in this deeper and more intimate level of conversation with you? Especially if they don't seem to really listen? It's possible they're like a lot of people in this world and so rather than being able to *go there* with you, they incessantly talk, interrupt, or ignore what you're saying. As a result, they fail to listen, feel, or sense what you're sharing.

If so, there's a reason for it: they're hurting and they're scared. They're afraid to be confronted by the shadows they've been avoiding within themselves, which they might see reflected in you. They're afraid to share the seemingly scarce energy and attention that they are desperately holding onto. And they're afraid to build intimacy as it may lead to potential wounding.

The act of listening is a sacred exchange of energy and connection. By shaking a constant, noisy rattle, they keep the energy moving outward rather than inward. In doing so, they feel a little safer and stop engaging in the exchange of energy.

This challenge was faced by a woman I worked with named Shannon. She was originally seeking support with habits she wanted to shift and patterns she was ashamed of. Though she was beautiful, radiant, and outwardly confident, she struggled with insecurity and lack of self-worth.

Shannon was continually aggravated by her dad, who was not a present listener. "He cannot listen. He interrupts. He speaks over me. I'll say something and he'll respond as if he didn't even hear what I just said. Sometimes I wonder if he's trying to make me insane. Honestly, I don't blame my mom for having left him."

While our focus was predominantly on building a stronger and healthier relationship with herself, the topic of her dad's inability to listen often made its way into our sessions. Feeling that it was important to put energy there, I inquired more about him.

I asked if she knew anything about his childhood or what his upbringing was like. "He had it pretty rough. I guess my grandma was an alcoholic and he pretty much raised himself. He had other siblings and was like the parental figure in the family." Sensing that her father had probably been neglected and had residual wounds from not receiving the attention or care he needed, he was stuck in a state of need and seeking attention. He needed to know that he wasn't alone and he was attempting to access that through his daughter, Shannon.

With the intention to guide her towards compassion and healing, I asked if she'd ever asked him questions about his childhood. She exhaustedly replied, "No. I'm usually trying to get him to stop talking; the last thing I want to do is encourage him to talk even more."

Knowing how nutrient-rich and valuable present listening is, I offered a suggestion, "Would you be open to having a more heartfelt and honest conversation with your dad? I get it that he doesn't listen and it's really challenging to deal with him, but what would it feel like to create an intentional space where you invite him to talk about his deeper wounds? Maybe it sounds counterintuitive, but I imagine there's a sincere opportunity for connection that you're both seeking from one another and I have a feeling that you're the one to initiate it."

Inspired by the idea, Shannon opened up to her dad about the work we had been doing together and explained the benefit of bringing attention to the wound. She inquired about his childhood and he was very moved by Shannon expressing deeper interest and care for his wellbeing. Tenderly, and in a much more patient voice than she was used to, he shared some heartbreaking experiences that she was unaware of. Naturally, this opened the cage around her heart, and she felt compassion for him. As a result, it strengthened her sense of connection to him. Having finally been heard, her dad transformed into a much calmer and more present listener for Shannon, which is what *she* needed.

Shannon was frustrated with her dad for not being a good listener, but in reality, she wasn't being a fully present and caring listener for her dad. As their connection grew and deepened, she was able to more comfortably voice where her needs weren't being met in their relationship. To her surprise, he wasn't even aware that he'd been interrupting her and was very apologetic for his actions, which were clearly unconscious and unintentional.

As their connection was the missing link, their relationship strengthened and so did Shannon. Gradually, she became a more confident, compassionate communicator and encouraged her dad to find a therapist to get the long-term constructive counsel he needed.

So often, with our busy lives and our complex needs for survival, we discount what others are going through and give negative attention or no attention at all. We call ourselves "family" or "friends" but we often don't offer the time or space to actively show up, listen, and connect in the way that our loved ones need.

As two hearts each supply one half of the whole in a relationship, it's important to ask ourselves whether we are really opening ourselves up and providing our half? Perhaps we're so carried away by focusing on what the other person isn't providing that we overlook what we're not providing, and we miss the sense of connection we seek.

SOCIAL MEDIA WITH INTENTION

SOCIAL MEDIA IS SEEN AS A PLACE OF CONNECTION, friendship, and information sharing. It's an online community where many of us feel seen and heard. It's also a place we might go to for information about what's happening with our loved ones, our communities, and the rest of the world. While it's not a news source, it's often seen as one—and because of that, we might consider what we read on social media to be the *truth*.

Without wanting to go too far down the rabbit hole, social media platforms are privately owned corporations (i.e. businesses) that are making *a lot* of money from our attendance and involvement. This means they're biased environments that are often not authentic, pure, or honest reflections of what's really going on in the world. Yes, there are real friends, real stories, and real events involved. However, beyond that, it can be a war zone of distraction and ego; an environment that supports unconscious and addictive behavior.

Because online networking has become such a prominent way for our species to communicate and gain a sense of connection, it makes sense to continue our relationship with it. However, there are keys to ensure that it's a constructive relationship: *conscious intention* and *discernment*. This way, you don't get pulled and persuaded by the unconscious haze.

Discernment: perception in the absence of judgment with a view of obtaining spiritual direction and understanding.

Here are some tools to implement discernment and make sure your time on social media is constructive, not destructive:

1. Before entering, clearly ask yourself:
What am I seeking right now?

Most social media platforms are designed to be persuasive, alluring, and highly addictive, so be mindful that you're entering into someone else's well thought-out maze. As if you are a recovering alcoholic walking into a liquor store to track down a bottle of water, it's essential that you ground yourself before you open the door and get clear on what your intentions are.

Are you seeking correspondence with a specific person? Do you want to inform your friends about an event? Are you curious whether anyone has remembered your birthday? Don't be afraid to get very consciously clear about your intentions and actions.

2. Determine how much of your valuable time and energy you want to offer:
How long do I want to spend on there?

Your life is very important and so are each of the moments you have to be alive. There are a lot of things you could be doing with your time. Go ahead and offer yourself a social media window but be discerning about how long it lasts. *Five minutes? Fifteen minutes? Thirty minutes?* Again, try not to be afraid of clearly stating your intentions and your needs.

If you answered the first question with "I'm bored. I just wanna hang out and see what people are up to," then consider signing off social media. That's the response of someone who is unknowingly about to enter an unconscious state and an experience they are not in control of. If you're bored, go outside. Find a park near your house. Call a friend. Teach yourself to play guitar. Get a book on astronomy. Track down a magnifying glass and lay in your backyard. Do something *real* in this wonderful real world.

When you finally realize your worth (I hope I get to be here when it happens!), you'll realize that social media needs you more than you need it. You are *that* valuable.

COUNSEL

SOMETIMES, YOU NEED MUCH MORE THAN ALONE TIME, a quick chat, or even a long heartfelt conversation. Sometimes, you need a trained, skilled listener who can constructively help you process the pain and struggles. You may not have anyone in your life who seems able to handle going *there* with you, but gratefully, there are people who can. Whether it's a psychotherapist, counselor, or life coach, there are people who have invested years of research, study, and practice into assisting others through the process of healing. As a result, they are knowledgeable, experienced, and capable of helping you through those challenging times.

The issue is, not everyone feels inspired or enthusiastic about considering the support of psychotherapy or counsel. Because much of our culture identifies seeing a therapist as meaning you have "something wrong" with you, there may be resistance and judgment towards psychotherapy and other forms of mental health support. We may even deny ourselves the support we need for fear of being perceived as "messed up," "crazy," or "psycho." Especially when we've been indoctrinated with the age-old belief that vulnerability means weakness, it makes sense that we are resistant to being vulnerable enough to seek help.

The reality is, regardless of what you're emotionally and mentally going through, when you are consciously aware of the need for counsel and actively seeking it, you're taking a step towards healing. You're moving in the right direction, which is a sign of your healthy mental state. Someone may judge you or shame you, but that's a glimpse into *their* mental state, not yours. For the most part, someone who can't understand the benefit of mental and emotional support may be in denial and is probably in need of constructive counsel themselves.

It's also possible that you've seen a therapist in the past and feel like you've graduated from ever needing to go back: "nope, no problems here." Well, just because you and your ex-wife saw a therapist 12 years ago doesn't mean you're forever healed and beyond the need for counsel. As you're always growing, always changing, and always experiencing new pain, there will always be new reasons you may need support throughout your life.

What if what holds you back is the intimidation of walking into a stranger's office? Especially when you have to attempt to feel safe enough to dig into the wounds, pain, and suffering that even you are not comfortable looking at. That's understandable—you've been through a lot and have every reason to be apprehensive.

However, if you don't feel safe, you probably won't open up and if you don't open up, there's no point. To resolve this, try to find someone who you feel really comfortable with, who you feel a natural desire to open up with. Do some research on therapists, counselors, and coaches in your area or find someone you can speak with over the phone or video chat. Then, move forward with the intention to align with someone you feel you can trust.

Also, be patient with yourself and with the person you are seeking counsel with. Trust takes time to acquire, so it may take a few sessions before you are ready to unfurl your truth. If you've tried and it's just not aligning, there is someone out there who you will resonate with—it may just take time to find them.

Perhaps it's the price that feels intimidating or out of reach? Consider this: *how much would you spend to fix your car if the engine was broken and you couldn't get anywhere until it was fixed?* Probably a lot. If your heart is broken, does it not deserve the same care as your vehicle? Even though we can't actually see into our minds or into our hearts, the world within us requires the same care, attention, and maintenance as the world outside us. If the therapy is just out of your financial means, consider exploring practitioners who are willing to work with your budget or look into online sites and apps that offer more affordable counsel.

By allowing yourself to open up and connect with someone who can assist in your healing, you not only welcome your own healing but also encourage the healing of your family, your marriage, your friendships, your business, and your future—and that's worth more than anything you can put a price on.

PLANT MEDICINE

I'm very mindful that sacred plant medicine is a controversial topic and it definitely doesn't resonate with everyone, nor is it the right path for everyone. In sharing about it, I don't encourage the use of it. However, because this form of therapy was instrumental in my healing (and saving my life), I feel it would be insincere to not talk about it. Please feel free to skip this section if it's not for you.

IF YOU ASKED ME WHO MY GREATEST TEACHERS in life were, I would probably say, "addiction, dreams, dementia, Dove (my dog), and psychedelic plants." You might tilt your head in a look of confusion. However, psychedelic plants have played a major role in healing for me and millions of people across the globe for thousands of years.

While they often have a negative reputation, they are far more medicinal, healing, and awareness-evoking than the mind-numbing drugs they're often perceived to be. In fact, through years of in-depth study and research, scientists have made leaps and bounds in discovering the healing effects of psychedelics on mental and emotional health. Gradually, they have realized that psychedelic plants are indeed *medicine*. With that, these sacred plants are slowly recovering their honor and being legalized in certain places in the US.

What makes them so powerful you might wonder? Well, these unique plants have psychoactive, mind-altering qualities that shift your perception of reality. Since so much of our understanding of reality is woven with and reliant on stories from the past, they quickly break down the cage walls and bring us to a state of presence.

In many ways, this shift from unconsciousness to consciousness can be a startling and uncomfortable experience for anyone unprepared to witness the truth so intensely. Especially those who have not invested time into observing their wounds, or who are living in a thick-walled cage of unconsciousness.

Engaging in this form of healing isn't about having a fun thrill, losing yourself, forgetting everything, and having a good time. Instead, it's about conscious listening, contemplation, and *remembrance* of the suffering, pain, and wounds within. Things that may not be described as *fun* but could definitely be described as *necessary*.

In general, we should be extremely mindful and cautious with anything that alters the mind. However, I refer to psychedelic plants as a form of healing therapy because that's what they were for me and that's what I needed—something to crack open the thick shell of unawareness and shine a light into the dark corners where I was hiding. Unlike you, I wasn't open, willing, or courageous enough to consider talking to someone or studying a pathway of support. I was deeply stuck inside myself and killing myself because of it.

Through the expansive awareness shown to me in the deep space of shamanic plant ceremonies, I saw a glimpse of what was possible. I was able to look directly at what I was avoiding and in doing so, go into the heart of my pain. Once I knew how to confront the avoidance, look at my wounds, feel my emotions, and let go of everything I was bottling up inside, I no longer needed the medicine. Like seeing a therapist, I only needed to be with them for long enough to alter my perspective, let go of the past, and become more present. Long enough to encourage me to go within myself and find the clues and answers to heal myself from the suffering.

THE ELDERS

HAVING SPENT YEARS AS AN ELDER CAREGIVER, I've had the opportunity to witness the sincere power of healing that can happen in the presence of an elder. They are the valuable wisdom-keepers who carry important knowledge and guidance for us to learn from. In many ways, elders are like trees: calm and still, patiently watching us as we run and stumble in circles of haste. Maybe we don't see them, but they see us, and even though we don't think we need them, we do.

Regardless of outside appearance, there is an entire universe of knowledge and wisdom within the mind and heart of *anyone* who has lived the human life experience. Whether they're 4 or 84 years old, each human carries within themselves a unique book of sacred insight and life experience and we have much to learn from one another. You may be surprised at the hidden jewels of wisdom within, especially those who have lived for many decades and witnessed the effects of war, political change, and cultural transformation.

Are you concerned about death? Ask someone who has courageously said goodbye to almost everyone they've ever loved. Are you curious about love? Talk to someone who was married to their spouse for 50 years and they can tell you about patience and resilience. Are you trying to get over how unhappy you are with your body? Speak to someone who can no longer walk without a cane and would give anything to move their hips and dance like you.

I realize that some people are "old and cranky." They're very challenging to be around and the last thing you want to do is refer to them as a wise "elder" and intentionally hang out with them. If that's the case, my suggestion is be patient and believe in the power and contagious ways of consciousness. The reality is, they may never have received the healing they needed and as a result, have not evolved out of a dense and contricting ego. However, just because they're not conscious and present, it doesn't mean you can't be.

While it may not be comfortable at first, experiment with being a compassionate and present listener. Feel the hurting child in them and believe in the consciousness and wisdom seeded deep in their hearts. Through doing this, you not only create a supportive environment for them to rise into their more present and wise self, you also nurture your own consciousness. Essentially, you strengthen the wise elder inside of *you*. And that's something this world needs. We need wise, grounded, compassionate beings to lead, guide, and pass on awareness to others.

So, contradict the race of life and slow down enough to compassionately walk alongside someone who could use your company. Let yourself be humbled and learn all that you can. In doing so, you make this world a better place.

Can you think of an elder in your life who might appreciate spending time with you?

OPENING TO LIFE
Meditative vision exercise

Now that we have a better understanding of the importance of seeking and accessing connection, it's time for a meditative vision exercise. This meditation is offered to help you experience a sense of expansion and openness to strengthen a channel within you for connection.

If possible, please find a quiet, comfortable place to sit outdoors in the fresh essence of nature. Whether seated in a chair on a patio, on a bench in the park or directly on the grass, it's our intention to expand outward into the awareness of the life surrounding you, and being in nature is a wonderful way to do this. If being outdoors isn't possible or desired, please find a comfortable and quiet space to rest your body.

◆

1. In whatever position is most comfortable for you, try your best to fully relax your body. If you don't feel comfortable in your body, do your best and know that this practice may help.

    When you're ready, take in a full breath of oxygen.... then... exhale.

    Repeat this intake and release of breath three times.

2. Now, bring your awareness to your chest, where your heart is beating within.

    As you breathe, feel the air entering your nasal passage and moving down, filling your lungs. As your lungs fill and release with each breath, feel your chest expand outward, then inward, bringing revitalizing oxygen into your being and releasing it.

Repeat this inhale and exhale of breath three more times, keeping your awareness on your breath moving in and out of your lungs.

3. Next, bring your awareness downward, to the area of your solar plexus, just below your heart, near your stomach.

Imagine that within this area is a small spark of light, about the size of your eye. As you breathe in those full, revitalizing breaths of oxygen, imagine that this small spark of light expands in size and brightness with each breath.

Hold this vision as you welcome a full breath in... then out. Repeat this three times.

4. This spark of light is symbolic of the light within you. It is the spirit of your being that grows in brightness, warmth, and intensity with each moment of your conscious attention and recognition.

Feel the light's center point in your solar plexus, and as you continue to feed it with your awareness and nurture it with your breath, feel it grow brighter and stronger. As if the light has rays like the sun, feel the streams of light reaching up and out into the rest of your being.

Repeat this inhale and exhale of breath three times, visualizing the rays of light reaching up and down, filling your entire being with light.

5. Now, visualize the rays of light being so bright and so powerful that they reach out beyond your physical being and fill the space around you with light. As if the center of your being is the sun itself, your solar plexus is where the rays connect and unite in an orb of bright, white light. Feel the warmth of this light in your being and as you breathe out, visualize the rays reaching out in every direction, completely surrounding you in light.

Continue this for three breaths.

6. Bring your awareness to the space around your physical body and the other life that is near you right now.

   Are there trees?
   What about a cat or a dog?
   Perhaps some potted plants?
   Maybe some birds?
   Are there some ants crawling around?
   Are there people?

   Even if you're unable to see them from where you're sitting, sense them around you and take a moment to scan the area around you for living beings.

7. As if you and each of the beings surrounding you are freed from being seen and identified by physical forms, visualize each life form as a similar spark of light with rays coming out from it. Instead of seeing trees, birds, humans, and a dog, visualize each one as the same bright, warm, and bodiless light that you are inside.

8. Now, visualize the rays of light from your being reaching so far that they begin touching and connecting the other rays of light emitted by the beings around you.

9. Visualize the light rays becoming so interwoven and united that the beams become one solid beam, connecting each of you in a weaved rope of light.

   As you visualize this, allow yourself to bring in three full and nourishing breaths of air... in, then slowly out.

10. Allow yourself to feel the innocence of each being you are now connected to. See where the tree was once a seed and where the dog was once a puppy. See where the bird was once a fledgling and where the humans were once small, innocent children.

11. Feel the innocence within yourself, and through a tender and sacred glance, visualize yourself when you too were a small, precious, and trusting child.

Feel the same heartfelt spirit within you that has always been inside you since the moment you were born.

Feel how much that sacred being deserves to be loved, acknowledged, and surrounded with support and appreciation.

Feel how deserving and equally important all the beings surrounding you are right now.

As you inhale, then slowly exhale, allow yourself to know that you are not alone.

Know that you are surrounded with love, light, and the many beings who see you, feel you, and appreciate that you are here.

EXAMPLE CONVERSATION

Let's imagine you're going through a rough patch in life and starting to feel really down. You've dealt with depression before and you're starting to recognize the signs. In an attempt to better understand what's really going on and figure out a way to not go tumbling face-first into a pit of depression, you decide you're ready to look beneath the suffering to see what's there.

What's happening? What happened?

I: Can you describe what's happening?
W: Yeah, I'm struggling a bit.
I: In what way are you struggling?
W: Well, I sometimes drink quite a bit of alcohol.
I: When and how much are you drinking?
W: Typically, I don't drink that much but on the weekends, I tend to let loose.

That answer is pretty vague. I need more clear details.

I: When and how much are you drinking?
W: I drink one or two glasses on weekdays and drink a lot more on weekends.

Interesting. I'm definitely showing signs of avoidance, I must be hiding something. I need more clear answers.

I: Exactly how much are you drinking on weekends?

W: I don't know exactly. I don't know because I'm drunk a lot of the time.

Ok. I just felt a shift in energy, like a bit of discomfort and shame came up. Before I felt fine, then when I heard myself say "drunk," I felt something else. I should ask more about that.

I: How often are you getting drunk?

W: Every weekend.

Yeah, I'm definitely feeling something stirring inside. Something I don't want to look at, which I shouldn't have to. Is this exercise even necessary? Does this stuff even work? This all seems pretty stupid and useless. I'm not going to—wait! Judgment awareness. Wow. I just caught myself. OK. This is tender for me. I need to stick with this.

I: Why are you drinking?

W: I don't even know. I stopped for a long time, then started up again a few months back.

I: Did anything in your life shift a few months ago?

W: Not really. Nothing that I can think of.

I: Ok. Can you think of any other reasons why you started drinking again?

W: Honestly, it's pretty pathetic. My friends invited me out and I guess I thought I was alright to just have one drink. Then, before I knew it, I started drinking again. Every day since then, I've been drinking. I'm a total idiot.

Judgment awareness. I don't need to be hard on myself; I just need to observe and study what's going on. If I'm calling myself an "idiot," I'm showing aggression and that's a sign of defense, which means I'm protecting myself, which means I have some unmet needs, which means there's some pain inside me. I need to dig in further to find it.

How am I feeling? Where am I hurting? Where am I afraid?

I: Are you hurting somewhere inside? Do you feel disappointed, sad, or ashamed?
W: Yeah. I do. I feel bummed out and ashamed of myself. I was doing so good for so long. I was on such a good track. I'd been losing weight and feeling really stoked on life. Now I'm depressed and feeling like I used to. Now I'm like my dad.

Interesting. That feels like a tender spot. As soon as I said "dad," I just felt a shift in senses, like a wall dropped inside. I went from being normal to being really calm. Well, kind of calm, kind of sad. I should find out why.

I: Can you describe your dad?
W: My dad is a loser.

Judgment awareness.

I: Can you describe your dad?
W: My dad is a sad guy. He lives alone and I don't even really know him anymore. My brother and I take turns visiting him but it's depressing so we don't see him much.

This feels like a lot. This feels like a wound.

I: Is there more pain around your dad that you avoid looking at?
W: Yep. I'd say there is. He's calmed down a lot but he used to be really hard on me and my brother. There's a lot of old stuff I try not to think about.

I feel another emotional shift inside, like a rush of anxiety. Knowing that anxiety is a response to pain, it feels like there's more to my dad and my childhood that's still hurting me. Definitely a wound.

I: Are you hurting inside?
W: Yeah. I think so.
I: Does any of your sadness around your dad have anything to do with your drinking?
W: Yeah, it probably does.

I'm not alone. I can engage with the people and world around me.

I: Have you tried talking to anyone about all of this?
W: No. My friends won't understand. I opened up to a girlfriend once and she just cried. I think it made her feel awkward and we never talked about it again.
I: Are you open to talking to someone or joining a support group?
W: Maybe. That feels embarrassing.

Oh man, I remember my dad's shame and embarrassment around all of his issues. I really don't want to turn into him.

I: Would you be willing to research some local support groups and commit yourself to reaching out to try connecting with them?
W: Yeah. I don't think it can get much worse than this. I'm game to try.

CONNECTION TOOLS

Even though I may not have felt safe and confident enough in the past, I can be honest about what I'm going through now and know that I'm strong enough to reach out and seek the counsel I need.

◆

A true friend is someone who shows up, listens, and offers unconditional acceptance. It's time for me to be a true friend to myself.

◆

There are more than just humans in this world. I can explore a sense of connection and friendship with plants, animals, and nature.

◆

If and when I engage with social media, I can set constructive intentions and parameters for how long I plan to partake so that I remain conscious, present, and empowered.

◆

If my needs for counsel aren't being met, I can consider reaching out to a therapist or counselor who can help me work through the painful struggles and challenges in life.

◆

Elders are a very important and often underappreciated part of our cultural family. Perhaps it's time for me to create friendships with people who are in the later stages of life.

*Trust was a tree growing directly from your heart,
with arms reaching out,
to the world around you.*

*Then,
life happened.*

*painful words,
sharp stones,
and
aching goodbyes
happened.*

*Slicing into the bark of your being.
Cutting away at the sacred branches of your trust.*

*Sometimes,
you imagine yourself opening and reaching out,
and you stop.*

*You get glimpses of twinkling warmth,
and you freeze.*

*The cage door slams
and you contract back into yourself.
Back into
the reasons*

*not to believe
not to open
not to try.*

*Rather than lush leaves speaking to the sun,
you carry the sad stump of fear within you.*

And there you sit,
alone
trapped
within the cold emptiness of caged walls.

Persuaded by the winds of distrust.
You have forgotten

to feel,
to know

that the beloved tree of trust may have been cut down;

However,
in its place is a seed

waiting for you
to show up.

To be present.

Waiting for you
to open,

to expand.

Waiting for you
to remember

to believe
again...

12.
RELEASE

The action or process of releasing or being released; to set free.

As the days of feeling recovered and clean from addiction turned from weeks into months and eventually years, my life stopped being so much about my own survival. No longer was I hanging on by a thread, trying to make it through each day. The cup of my spirit was previously running out but was now being filled and refilled each day. I was beginning to feel stronger in my body and in my mind, and more able to offer others time, energy, motivation, and support in *their* healing.

After we left Texas, we spent some time in Colorado and then a stint in Ojai, California. There, my heart began pulling my focus and concern towards my mother. Each time I spoke to her on the phone, it was clear that her forgetfulness about what she had for breakfast and the overlap of memories was more than just old age.

Motivated by her wellbeing, Kurt and I moved back home to the small town in Washington State where she lived. We rented a house outside town and I got a job at a friend's shop, two blocks from her house. Each day, I would check in, making sure she had her needs met and meals taken care of. For the first year, that was enough. She was always happy to see me and we filled our days working in her garden, entertaining her dog, and preparing meals together.

However, over the months and eventually years, her dementia progressed, and it became clear that the leaves of her memory were slowly drying and falling away. I imagine it was harder for her to see and consciously recognize, but I noticed. I could see the little changes and missing pieces, which started as small cracks and eventually grew into caverns.

In those early years—before we came together as a family to care for her—my grief wavered between fully inspired motivation to the hollow sadness of feeling her slowly fade into the distance. I tried everything to help: changing her diet, finding the right supplements, and making sure she was getting enough exercise. It didn't work.

As the house we rented was 25 minutes from town, my daily trips to visit her gave me hours alone in the car where I would shuffle through my playlists to find the songs that helped me accept and process my grief. I would hold the wheel while staring at the road and wail a deep ache of sorrow from my lungs. Each time, being with the truth of my feelings and what was happening made my pain feel heard, seen, accepted, and released.

One afternoon, as we were cleaning her cupboards in the kitchen, I felt a question rising to the surface, longing to be freed from my timid grip. It was a question whose answer I feared wholeheartedly.

"What if you forget who I am?"

With sincerity, as direct and determined as a mother attempting to save her child from harm, she said, "I won't. I will never, ever forget you."

"But what if you do?"

My eyes started streaming at the shocking thought of being near her, only without her having any connection or recognition of who I am.

She paused and stared at me, without words or expression, as if suddenly realizing that there may actually be a time when she would forget; where the fierce strength of the mother-child connection would not be strong enough to keep her arms wrapped around her children, tethered by knowing.

She looked directly through my eyes, into my heart and with sincerity and regret, she said:

"If I forget you, I won't mean to. If I do... I'm so, so sorry."

We held out our arms to one another and let ourselves cry. We sobbed like children mourning the death of a mother; both of us holding tightly to the connection braided between us; the gift of awareness and recognition that suddenly became more valuable than gold.

So easily, we could have turned away from the overwhelming sadness of her memory loss and the slow unfurling of her identity. We could have pretended it wasn't happening or allowed ourselves to be lured by irritability, which is so often the way grief is temporarily numbed, especially when saying goodbye to someone we're not ready to leave.

We didn't.

Instead, we felt the depth of fear and pain and opened ourselves to it. We looked into the grief and spoke directly to it, calling its name like a songbird summoning the morning light, reaching into ourselves and out to one another.

Our hug and tears lasted a while, and in many ways, they are still wrapped around me now. I often call upon that memory of looking into her eyes and hearing her words. Like an angelic whisper, I feel her apologetic sorrow and her spirit hovering over me as I do the small and trivial tasks of bathing her body, withstanding her orneriness and explaining, and re-explaining, who I am.

Telling this story to you right now has me in tears. It's a tender and heartbreaking tale, yet it's not meant to be tucked away and hidden inside me. I don't need to stuff down my sorrow. In fact, none of the pain, sadness, or grief that any of us feel is meant to be locked up and stored inside us.

Release is the art of *letting it go*.

Examples of experiencing RELEASE:
- Crying
- Talking
- Apologizing
- Writing
- Singing
- Drawing
- Stretching
- Walking
- Laughing

While connection is the channel that unites us with one another, release is letting the energy move and flow out of that channel. As if finally freed from the clutches of the cage, when we release, we set free what has been blocked and protected within us.

One way to think of this is: "I don't need to hold onto this any longer. I can let it go."

For some time, I placed release before connect on the path to empowerment. To me, directly after the act of feeling came the need to release. I saw that I was hurting, I felt sadness, *I cried.* I saw that I was angry, I felt frustrated, *I talked about it.*

However, something felt out of place when I described the transition from feeling directly into release. Yes, I was grieving, then finding the ability to talk about it, but *who was I talking to?* Usually, caring friends and supportive listeners. Perhaps I was hurting and finally able to cry, but *where was I crying?* Often, when I was on a walk or writing in my journal.

It was *because* I felt safe and trusting enough in a space of connection that I gave myself permission to finally open up and *release.* Then, I witnessed the same thing with so many people I worked with—the initial sessions of building trust, then the eventual opening and release. It became clear that connection is integral to the sensation of safety required to release. Its solid, secure foundation allows the release to take place. That's why we move from connection *into* release.

In order, we first identify the reality of where we're wounded, then lean in to feel and understand the pain. Once we've accomplished that, we have a better idea about what we need and can begin getting our needs met by reaching out for connective support, then constructively releasing the energy.

<u>Observe</u>: *What's happening right now? What happened in the past?*
<u>Feel</u>: *How am I feeling? Where am I hurting? Where am I afraid?*
<u>Connect</u>: *I'm not alone. I can engage with the world around me.*
<u>Release</u>: *I don't need to hold onto this any longer. I can let it go.*

Just like the need to connect, release is a very important need. For most of us, it's something we need to do frequently. Daily even.

Each day, you eat various foods that provide nutrients and energy. Your body digests and absorbs the valuable ingredients needed for survival, then performs a very natural function of extricating and letting go of the rest. This process is essential on your journey of being alive and having an active, living body. It's not a choice of whether you *want* to let go. It's a matter of what *must* occur for you to continue being healthy and alive, because there's only so much room inside your body to hold onto the extra matter that doesn't belong there.

This is similar to what happens when that channel of connection opens and we allow ourselves to release the emotional energy built up inside. Whether it's anger, sadness, joy, grief, or love, each feeling encompasses energy that needs to move and be relieved from our beings.

What happens if we don't release it?

We become emotionally and energetically *constipated*. Our hearts and minds get overstuffed and packed with the burden of everything we are holding onto inside. We become weighed down by the toxic sludge of our pain and fear.

Sound like fun?

Not really.

The solution?

Letting it go.

Each time we open up and talk or cry, we untangle ourselves from the pain and release that heavy pressure from within. We become free. This is something you, me, and all of us deserve: to be free from suffering. So, let's learn how to do it!

COMING CLEAN

HAVE YOU EVER HELD A SECRET INSIDE you for a long period of time? Maybe in order to protect it (and yourself), you lied when speaking with someone else about it?

What was it? Did you cheat on your partner? Did you get a DUI and hide it from your parents? Did you get an abortion and never tell the father?

Have you ever freed that secret?

Let's imagine you haven't.

What does that *feel* like?

Chances are, whether you're consciously aware of it or not, it probably feels grimy and heavy inside. It feels like thick mold is coating the inside of your heart. You may feel weighed down by the shame and self-judgment of perceiving yourself as weak or a liar.

Think back to that house inside where unconsciousness grows like mold and all the windows and doors are boarded up with fear and pain, those windows and doors are the outlets and access points for expression and energy exchange.

By allowing ourselves to consciously observe, feel, connect, and release the emotions and stories within us, we take down the boards that have been protecting us for so long. We swing open the door to let the fresh, cleansing light of truth wash our beings clean. Like bringing in the cleansing light of awareness to transform the areas of unconsciousness in our lives, that same frequency of cleansing ignites when we release the emotions, memories, fears, truths, and words stored inside us.

This experience of release happens by opening up and talking about it. By communicating, writing, sharing, crying, and expressing ourselves.

I remember how absolutely terrifying it was to talk to anyone about my secret habits and food addictions. Inside, I knew I wanted to open up and talk about it all, but I was so ashamed and scared of what others would think and how they would react. *Would they judge me? Would they think less of me? Would they stop wanting to hang out with me?*

I would fantasize opening up and telling the truth for weeks and even months. But by the time I was able to say something, I was so overcome with emotion and anxiety that the words just spewed out into a pool of broken sentences and exhausted tears.

Yet, however difficult and uncomfortable it was to finally open up and share my undesirable truths, I always felt a sense of relief afterwards. Like some part of my mind, body, or heart had been lifted, cleaned, and rinsed off. I also felt strangely empowered each time—as if the fear that had been holding me hostage was losing its power over me.

Through honoring the truth and choosing freedom rather than suffering, my friendship within myself became stronger and stronger each time I opened up. With that, I began building self-trust like a bridge between my mind, my body, and my heart.

Just like brushing our teeth and washing our clothes for personal hygiene, it's equally important to keep our minds and emotional selves clean and healthy. By continually giving ourselves permission to open up and clear out our thoughts, emotions, and fears, we live in a cleansed and healthier state.

I imagine you've heard the phrase *"coming clean,"* and that's exactly what the act of releasing allows us to do.

Come clean.

VOICING YOUR TRUTH

WHAT IF THIS ALL SOUNDS INCREDIBLE but you're too shy, insecure, and terrified to step out of your cage of safety and open up with others? As we've talked about in previous chapters, a lot of us aren't comfortable being honest about what we're going through and have been through. We feel far too much shame and insecurity to tell people what's really going on.

However, knowing the importance of connection and release, it's worth us confronting this fear and overcoming it. One way to start is simply to ask yourself:

Am I apprehensive to open up and be completely honest with others about what I'm going through and what I've been through? If so, why?

Here are some potential reasons to consider...

I don't want to be judged or abandoned.

How many times have you tried talking to someone and they didn't seem interested or like they had the time to listen? What about times where you shared an intimate truth and someone seemed repulsed or scared? Maybe at some point someone called you "a downer" or "dramatic"? Did you decide to withhold what you were going to say and opt not to talk to anyone? If you have been discouraged, judged, or rejected by others in the past, you may be fearful of sharing your tender wounds from fear of being rewounded.

I don't want to weigh anyone down or make them uncomfortable.

If your emotional pain feels like a heavy burden to carry around, there's a chance you don't want anyone else to carry that burden either. For this reason, you may choose not to talk about anything uncomfortable for fear of making others uncomfortable. Instead, you bury it down and withhold it, and do your best to let others believe everything is "fine" when it's not.

I don't know who to connect with.

Many people just don't know who to talk to about what weighs on their heart. Perhaps you've tried talking to friends or family and it didn't go well? Maybe you worked with a counselor or a therapist and it felt like a waste of time and money? After enough unsuccessful attempts, it's not uncommon to think "no one understands me," which can lead to feeling alone, alienated, and misunderstood.

Essentially, we opt *not* to open up with other people because we're afraid. We're ashamed of what we're going through. Because we know what it feels like to be judged, neglected, and let down, we do everything in our power to avoid that. So, we avoid putting ourselves in a vulnerable and intimate space of honesty.

Unfortunately, shame thrives on secrecy, and if you allow your fear to control you, then you make the choice to remain silent and locked inside the cage.

You don't deserve that. Remember, you're done suffering.

In order to free yourself from that cage of entrapment, you have to know that you're safe and strong enough to do so. This means you have to courageously reopen your heart to trust. You have to push past your fears and apprehensions and explore what it's like to connect with the world around you.

How do you do that?

Using your voice.

Your voice is a powerful gift that you were given for a reason. Just like a cat that meows, a dog that barks, or a bird that chirps, you have a voice that allows you to communicate and share messages with others.

To actively connect with the support you need, you have to utilize this sacred tool by speaking up and voicing your truth.

This means giving yourself permission to say:

"I'm hurting right now."
"My heart aches."
"I'm scared."
"Do you have any time and availability to talk?"
"I need help."

By allowing ourselves to not just acknowledge the pain but also voice it, we do something to change it. We begin to transform the fear and avoidance into honesty and communication. In doing so, we build strength, confidence, and trust in ourselves.

In giving ourselves permission to explore trust, it doesn't mean we've suddenly figured out how to never get hurt again; it means we're making the conscious decision to live life *regardless* of what might occur.

Because pain is a natural and inevitable circumstance of life—like birth, like death—we can't prevent it from happening or keep ourselves locked away from it forever. At some point, we have to come out of our cage and give it another try. We have to trust that even though we've experienced hurtful people and wounds in the past, there are also plenty of kind people in this world and the future is filled with fresh, unknown, wonderful experiences just waiting to happen.

Do you ever find yourself holding back your voice?
What would it feel like to fearlessly use it?

THE INTENTIONAL SPACE OF SHARING

ONE THING TO KEEP IN MIND: not everyone is ready to look at the truth, let alone talk about it. While you may have discovered a newfound desire and passion for talking about your feelings and needs, not everyone will be interested in joining you. For this reason, it's important to use discernment in who you choose to open, process, and release with. That way, you work towards healing and not the regeneration of more wounds, pain, and shame.

A great way to find this out is to simply communicate your desire to communicate. This may sound redundant, but it can be very helpful in prefacing what you intend to accomplish through communicating, and it can be a good indicator of whether the person is ideal to speak with.

Say you've had a lot on your mind and are ready to finally talk to your loved ones about some deeper truths, feelings, and needs that you've been withholding. Yes, you can opt to randomly open the conversation at the dinner table during a family gathering or you can find a moment to invite them into an intentional space of presence and sharing.

The invitation could sound something like this: "I've been taking a deeper look at myself lately and realizing that I can be distracted, closed off, and not present. I don't always open up as much as I'd like to or listen to you as much as I'd like to. If you're up for it, I'd love to find some time to take a break from our busy lives to sit together and connect. What about sometime this weekend?"

Along with this inviting and intentional space, you might also consider creating some gentle guidelines that you both agree upon to ensure the space is safe and constructive to both share, such as:

1. Each person has the opportunity to be both the "speaker" and the "listener."

Perhaps one person speaks for 10 minutes, then allows the other to speak. Then, you take turns and continue until each person has had the opportunity to share how they're feeling while receiving the beneficial reward of being heard.

2. When the speaker is speaking, the listener holds a committed intention to not interrupt them.

Because interrupting is so common, especially when we're feeling scared or uncomfortable (feelings that may arise in a space of sharing), you can hold yourselves accountable by listening when it's your time to listen, not interrupting and injecting your viewpoints or opinions.

3. The meeting can have a designated start time and completion time.

Some can easily talk for hours without effort while others would prefer to keep conversations short, so it's important to meet in the middle where everyone is comfortable. Does that mean a one-hour talk? Two hours? Together, you can decide what feels right.

Maybe they'll be up for this, and maybe they won't, but by offering the invitation, you give them the option to partake or not. You also give them the opportunity to be better prepared being brought into a conversation that could be uncomfortable or traumatic for them.

Importantly, if they agree to join you in conversation and it turns out that what they share is unkind or not aligned with what is true for you, it should not determine how you feel about yourself.

Why? Because each of us was gifted the human life experience and a lifetime of lessons, challenges, and opportunities to grow. No two individuals are the same and no one is here with the exact same to-do list. Each of us is unique and that includes our spiritual path.

When you follow what you know is right in your heart and speak your truth, how others react and respond should not determine how you feel about yourself. If your truth is not appreciated, respected, or aligned with what someone else feels or believes, that's ok. It's not your responsibility to get everyone to think or act the same. It won't happen. Each of us is allowed to be different and it's those differences that make the world such a dynamic and versatile place.

This is a vital understanding for those who want to share with their loved ones that they're homosexual or transgender. While some of us come from open-minded families who are welcoming of sexual, racial, and religious differences, many of us don't. Many come from parents and families who follow strict, devoted belief systems that don't accommodate or encourage freedom of the heart and body.

I know numerous tender-hearted and caring people who grew up extremely close with their parents and siblings but were literally abandoned on the streets when they found the courage to speak openly about their sexual truth. Essentially, they were wounded for speaking honestly to their loved ones. For some, that trauma and pain of being separated and exiled from their families was painful enough to consider or even attempt suicide.

I'll say it again, *when you follow what you know is right in your heart and honestly speak your truth, how others react and respond should not determine how you feel about yourself.* That goes for opening up about being gay or letting your mother know that you're in love with someone of a different race. It also applies when you let your friends know that you're not into bad-mouthing people anymore and when you finally feel ready enough to tell your brother that you are addicted to heroin.

Your intention isn't to hurt anyone. It's to bring the conscious light of awareness to areas that are shadowed with shame, fear, and unawareness. When you come from a place of presence, honesty, and love, you are bringing that into the world. Maybe it won't feel like it in the moment and maybe it won't be reciprocated by those you share your truth with, but eventually, it will make sense.

By devotedly following the path lit within your heart, you'll be guided to a true family of friends and loved ones who are strong enough to welcome your truth and appreciate each of your unique, divine qualities.

A GOOD CRY

Even though crying may not be something we allow ourselves to do very often (or ever, in some cases), it's something we naturally know how to do. We cry when we're sad. We cry when we're filled with joy. We cry when we're overwhelmed with laughter. Deep down, we all *know* how to cry—we were born doing it. Literally, most of us were born crying.

In fact, **crying** is actually really good for your body as it:

- Improves your mood
- Improves your vision
- Protects your eyes
- Clears your sinuses
- Strengthens your ability to communicate
- Kills bacteria
- Releases toxins

Yet, at some point, crying got a really, really bad reputation. As if there was a campaign to keep the humans shut down, unhealthy, and desensitized, some slandering lies and accusations began circulating like...

"Crying is for babies."

"If you cry, you're weak."

"Don't cry, get over it and be tough."

My friend, these statements are not true and they don't have your true health or wellbeing in mind. They are part of a belief system that originated from a place of pain, fear, and suffering. Whoever told you these things was hurting; they were stuck inside their own cage. They didn't have the strength or understanding to stand up to the false narrative and honor the truth that crying is *healthy, natural,* and *necessary*.

For many people, to cry in front of someone is often an experience accompanied by shame, embarrassment, and a verbal apology. We feel bad for crying. We apologize for bringing others out of their cozy cage and doing anything that encourages them to feel. So, we avoid it. We swallow our tears and pretend they're not there. We bury away our feelings and convince ourselves that we're stronger than feeling; that we can *handle* it all.

When someone *else* cries, we instantly feel care, compassion, and tenderness—and that in itself is terrifying for a lot of us. Raised in a culture that avoids anything remotely resembling vulnerability, we're not comfortable or prepared for the connection and intimacy that other people's tears evoke in us.

In an effort to do whatever we can to make it stop, we often say, "hush, no, no, don't cry." While these words may come from an innocent intention to soothe someone's pain, it doesn't necessarily do that. It just encourages the person to swallow their tears back down, rather than openly expressing and releasing the energy held inside them.

In other words, when we hush someone from crying, we're saying: "When you cry, it awakens feelings of care and compassion and I'm not sure what to do with those feelings because I'm uncomfortably comfortable being separated from my feelings. I associate your crying with pain and because I'm not comfortable looking at the pain; I would prefer that you stop expressing it. So please, sshhhhh. Stop crying."

While it may feel unnatural in the moment to simply hold space for someone who is crying, it's the most supportive thing we can offer others while they have the experience of release. In being strong enough to push through the avoidance of intimacy and feelings, we surround them with safety and permission to continue healing through the sacred act of crying. We allow them to feel safe and accepted, which helps them to release judgment towards themselves.

Whether it's you crying or someone else, being in the presence of tears is a direct route to your heart. Like a golden key that instantly unlocks the cage, it opens us to expansive realms of compassion, sensitivity, and feeling.

Because we've been so misinformed for so long, the act of accepting tears is courageous, rebellious, and revolutionary. It's a reflection of true strength, confidence, and intelligence within our minds, bodies, and hearts. Essentially, when we give ourselves and others permission to cry, we're saying: "I am not afraid to acknowledge, feel, and express this moving experience of being alive."

Have you ever apologized or felt bad for crying?

What would it feel like to allow yourself to cry anywhere, anytime?

Even if it was uncomfortable in the moment, would you do it for the betterment of your health and wellbeing?

WASH THE PAIN AWAY

YEARS AGO, I VOLUNTEERED FOR AN ORGANIZATION in Texas that offered a youth leadership program. Each year, the organization would gather children from around the world in the hill country of Austin, where we sang songs, went hiking, and played games. We also engaged in sharing circles, where the entire camp would gather in an intentional space and offer a welcoming atmosphere to open up about painful life experiences.

From an outside perspective, you might not sense any major wounds behind the radiant glow of those children with such huge smiles, bright eyes, and beautiful laughter. However, as we entered the safe space of sharing, their painful stories began unfurling. In sharing these stories, it brought forward an immense amount of connection and compassion for each other.

One encounter that was deeply moving and forever broke my heart open was being in the presence of a group of young girls who had survived the war in Congo. They had been relocated to the safety of the US but had seen horrendous traumatic events and experienced painful wounds that were hard to imagine, and even harder to forget.

Sitting beside me, I saw where their memories were woven with the painful tears, and those tears needed to be detoxed and released from their bodies.

After making sure they were comfortable and knew there was no pressure to share, I explained how important it was to *get it out*. With courage summoned from deep within, they were ready to tear down the wall of silence. With trembling hands and in the presence of 60 or so people, they let it go.

They spoke of civil war, gun violence, refugee camps, and genocide. They shared the terror of what they experienced in 2004 when armed groups attacked their camp, forcing them to run for survival. The violent attack took 166 lives and left many others physically and psychologically wounded. Though their bodies were not scarred, their hearts were torn open and carried the scars of what they had seen and felt that day.

All of us became humbly silent as we wept alongside them. Their voices and tears stretched our hearts wide open.

While a sense of stillness, exhaustion, and raw tenderness followed, there also appeared to be vulnerability, lightness, and liberation from finally speaking the truth about what they had been through. It was as if the dam that withheld the pain was finally cracked and there was an outlet for some of the memories and feelings to release. Somehow, they felt it was safe enough—that *they* were safe enough—to look at the pain, talk about it, and release some of the withheld pressure.

Afterwards, we returned to our cabins. With heartfelt motivation to soothe what was so tender inside us, I grabbed my guitar and a group of eight girls sat together in a song circle. To let the energy of emotion and pain continue releasing, we sang "Wash the Pain Away." When the sound of the pouring Texas rain started overpowering our voices, we stood up and one by one leaped out into the rain.

The rain was like an alarm reminding everyone to *get it out and wash the pain away*, and we were running through the camp, laughing, screaming, and encouraging everyone to do the same. Eventually, there was a hive of around 50 children, and we found ourselves in a giant pool of mud, which quickly turned into a loving chaos of dirt flying everywhere. It was deeply freeing, fulfilling, and cleansing for our aching hearts.

Each step—the opening up, the speaking, the crying, the singing, the running, the screaming, the laughter, the mud-throwing—was remarkably healing on our mission to release the pain and wash it away.

No one deserves to be weighed down by the burden of their pain. While it may not be comfortable to open up and let it go, it's necessary if we want to transform our lives from a state of fear and suffering to a state of confidence, peace, and self-acceptance.

While each individual's experience is uniquely their own, what I personally learned that day—in the presence of courageous children who allowed themselves to observe, feel, connect, and release their pain—has stayed with me all of these years. Like a guiding light, it filled me with profound awareness of the transformation that is possible when we feel safe and supported enough to observe our wounds, feel the pain and allow ourselves to release it.

And by going through the experience together, profound trust and a lifelong friendship was birthed between the girls and I. We joined our hearts like family and to this day, we are still united in an indescribable sisterhood that has lasted many years and been a cherished friendship in my life.

THE POWER OF A MAN'S TEARS

FOR MUCH OF MY LIFE I SAW FEMALES AS SUPERIOR to males. I felt that women were handed the short end of the stick, and if they were given the entire stick, they would turn it into a wand and heal the world. I imagine I was strongly influenced by my single mother, who was an activist and a survivor of abuse, and because I grew up witnessing such profound injustice from males.

In reality, the injustice is palpable. Men are the ones creating the majority of violence, rape, and abuse. They rule almost every country and dominate the governments, banking industries, militaries, police forces, medical industries, entertainment industries, oil industries, auto industries, stock markets, and human trafficking. It's easy to feel overwhelmed and repulsed by the fact that women are continually enduring so many wounds and cycles of trauma, and men often have a strong hand in it.

What's more, having been a young woman who grew up with cultural pressure to be thin, attractive, and popular to be accepted and feel worthy, I resented the small, suffocating boxes and bodies that women were continually forced to fit inside. Most girls and women deal with some form of shame and insecurity as a result of the societal narrative and that was something I grew to detest.

Being female felt so challenging, while males seemed to have a free ride.

However, as I continued on my journey of healing and became increasingly honest through fearlessly looking at my wounds and releasing my story, my views began to alter as I began to notice a startling pattern. At many of the talks, workshops, and counsel sessions I facilitated, I realized that males have in many ways been just as abused and mistreated as females, but their wounds are disguised and overlooked.

They would quietly and shamefully share that they hadn't cried since they were young. Or they had been sexually abused but didn't feel confident enough to tell anyone. Or that their mother caused many of their psychological wounds. Many had dealt with suicidal depression and didn't know how to be vulnerable enough to seek support.

This makes sense when you realize that the majority of men have been conditioned from a very young age to not cry, feel, process, connect, or release their feelings, tenderness, or pain. Even though boys express a wider range of emotions than girls do as infants, boys are typically discouraged from showing their emotions as they get older due to traditional ideas about masculinity and gender roles. From a young age, they're often told "boys don't cry" and for most of their lives, they learn to bottle up everything inside and lock it away. By adolescence, the majority of young men feel embarrassed about crying. This is also the age when young men begin experiencing depression and feelings of sincere loss and displacement.

How many tender, caring, vulnerable, open-hearted young males and adults are forced to build cages around their hearts and swallow their feelings and tears? How many young men (and women) go off to war because they're already desensitized and afraid, and they just want to feel connected, worthy, and part of something?

When we don't speak up, cry, open, share, connect, and release the bottled-up pain from within us, we become silent. We board up all the doors and windows to the room of our hearts and cut ourselves off from feeling, sensing, caring, and being alive in this world. Unfortunately, silence equals violence. When we silence our hearts, we become depressed, shut down, and *violent* and *that* is where many men end up.

If we don't take the giant and courageous leap to welcome males of every age into this important work of vulnerable empowerment and emotional freedom, we will continue to experience the imbalance of a culture and live in a world where the desensitized and broken-hearted are irrationally and unfairly leading the way.

Every time a man allows himself to cry, the collective pain is gradually transformed and we are one step closer to healing our entire species from this painful web of collective suffering.

Do you know any males who would benefit by feeling safe enough to cry?
Can you think of any ways that you can personally provide a welcoming space of safety to allow them that much-needed experience of release and healing?

THE CHILD BEHIND THE MASK

I WAS ONCE ON A FLIGHT FROM DENVER TO SEATTLE, seated beside a beautiful elder couple. While it was hard to tell their ages, she appeared slightly younger than him and he looked around 80. My heart felt tender sitting beside them and without pulling my usual "are you headed out on an adventure or headed home?" I opted to be silent and leave our trio of seats as a quiet place of rest during the flight.

The flight was relatively uneventful, and when I heard the preparation for landing announcement, I felt inspired to ask whether there was anything interesting happening in the paper he was reading. In response, he grumbled a low growl of distaste for the "*** of *****" that was president.

Entertained and admiring his gusto and passion for politics, I chuckled and exchanged a warm look of compassion with his wife, who responded with an exaggerated eye roll, which said, "you have no idea what I put up with." Then, his skin turned red with fury and the floodgates of anger opened wide. As if his life depended on it, he began ranting a slew of hatred and angst that honestly had me contemplating which attendant to wave down should he have a heart attack.

Clearly, it wasn't good for him. Whatever he was experiencing at that moment wasn't healthy or sustainable. With concern for him, I waited until he stopped for air and then said, "Wow. Yeah, that guy has a lot of problems." He retorted, "Yeah, he is a problem."

I offered, "I wonder sometimes though. I wonder what it must be like to be him. To be surrounded by so much pressure and have so many people needing something from you all the time. I try to imagine what got him into politics. I wonder what pressure his dad put on him. I bet he did it for his dad. He's been trying so hard to be what everybody else expects him to be that he doesn't even know himself. Honestly, he seems like a sad puppet to me. It's possible he's been that way his whole life, a sad puppet who is just trying to please his dad."

Not entirely sure if I was getting through to him or adding fuel to his fire, I glanced at his wife who had leaned in and was listening intently to each word I said, then looked over at him, then back at me. With sincere concern for his wellbeing, I said, "You don't have to be angry at him. Your anger isn't going to solve the situation or get him out of office. It's only going to make you suffer and honestly, life's too short to be suffering."

Like an eagle releasing its talons from its prey, his face began to relax and he leaned back into his chair. He gently folded his paper and with a calm and somewhat deflated voice, he quietly said, "You might be right. I guess I'd never thought about it that way." There, like icicles melting in the warm sun, I saw his eyes moisten with tears. I leaned over and warmed his shoulder with my hand, then offered a smile to his loving wife, who stared at me with eyes as wide as the moon.

Still uncertain if I had said too much and made them both uncomfortable, I handed her a CD that had my contact information on it. I explained that if they ever wanted to connect, my email was there. I got off the plane and felt my heart ache for this beloved man and his sincere care, which displayed itself so painfully through his anger.

A week later, I received an email. It was from his loving wife. She wrote, "I want to thank you for what you did. I've been married to my husband for 35 years and never once had I ever seen him cry. That was the first time ever and he has been a different man since. Thank you for that."

THE FLOW OF THE RIVER

AS YOU'VE SEEN, ANGER IS A NATURAL WAY that we defend and safeguard what we love and care for, so we don't need to be judgmental or hard on ourselves when we feel angry. We also don't want to bottle up unexpressed feelings of anger as that can be detrimental to our health and wellbeing, causing us to feel anxious, weighed down, and stuck (suffering). Because anger consists of built-up fear, pain, and unconscious emotions that need to be freed, it's essential that we consciously acknowledge and feel it, then constructively *release* it all from our beings.

Unfortunately, a lot of us *don't* do that. Instead of constructively working through the uncomfortable feelings and releasing the energy, we end up being aggressive (or passive aggressive) and destructive, such as:

- Saying something hurtful or judgmental

- Raising our voices and yelling at someone
- Throwing something
- Breaking something
- Physically hurting someone

Hurt someone? Do you really want to *hurt* someone? Do you really want to create wounds and trauma that will potentially generate shame, sadness, and suffering in someone else?

No, you don't. In our hearts, no one does. However, we might be. We might very well be choosing to destructively release our anger and there are numerous reasons why.

1. We don't know how to constructively release it.

We've become so familiar with releasing our pent-up pain and fear through aggression that it's all we know. Our anger often happens when we're in an unconscious state, meaning many of us don't know how to control our anger. It just kind of happens. We just get angry.

2. It feels good.

In the moment, with all of the adrenaline and hormones pumping, it may feel somewhat exciting and enjoyable to release our pent-up energy through losing it. Like holding our breaths until we're blue and then finally exhaling, releasing our rage can feel like releasing a burden.

3. We don't see our anger as problematic.

There is a common narrative that approves, justifies, and encourages anger that is distructive and aggressive. As it's associated with strength and power, it's often perceived as a way for seemingly "confident" people to display their *tough*ness. (We'll revisit this when we get to the final chapter and talk about true strength and power.)

The issue with utilizing anger as a means of release is that it often creates more wounds, trauma, regret, and shame, which ultimately adds to the weight of what we're carrying.

Unless you're literally trying to save someone's life and need that fierce dose of adrenalin for the super human strength required, becoming aggressive isn't the solution. Relieving yourself by raising your voice, yelling, and intimidating others isn't the long-term resolution needed to heal and make the world a better place. Perhaps it might feel relieving to swing your fists through the air, but the moment they come into contact with someone or something, your actions become destructive.

It's always important to remember that anger is a response. It's the *effect* from the *cause* of pain and fear. It may look like a treacherous mountain with lava spewing out, but really, it's an innocent, tender stream of tears trickling out. Just like my seatmate on the plane, unless you carefully remove the mask of defense and give that stream somewhere to go, the pressure builds and you get sucked into the cycles of suffering.

You're stronger than that. You know that defense leads to suffering and you have the power to choose differently and more wisely. Rather than getting pulled into the enticing game of fireball ping pong with someone, you can choose to honor the truth of what's really going on and take off the mask. By allowing yourself to observe, feel, and release what's really going on inside, you have the power to remain present and decide whether you really *want* to get angrily aggressive or not. If you don't, you can make the choice to consciously take action to work through the situation, rather than unconsciously react to it.

Let's imagine you're feeling anger towards your coworker, Tom. You have been working on a project together and every time you share an idea or contribution, he interrupts, dismisses it, or puts you down, as if what you have to say is unimportant and unwelcome. You begin to feel fed up and angry.

In that moment, you have a choice. You can either say (yell) "What is your problem, Tom? Stop cutting me off. This isn't your solo project, you ****, and you're not the ****ing boss. Stop acting like a *****."

You could definitely react that way, but chances are, the boss will mysteriously walk by right then and see how irrational and unprofessional *you* are, which doesn't help you or the situation.

Rather than reacting with anger and being pulled into the cycle of suffering, try to remain present and constructively work through the situation. By utilizing what you learned in the previous chapters, observe what's going on and check in with how you're feeling. What are the layers? What does it feel like inside you? Where is the pressure building? Maybe even consider calling up your old friends, the investigator and the witness to see what they have to say.

Observe:

What's going on right now? What happened?

I'm pissed off. I'm trying to do my job and literally can't because this person keeps preventing me from speaking or doing anything. I feel SO frustrated.

Feel:

Where am I hurting? Where am I afraid?

It's hard for me to tell where I'm hurting because I'm so angry, but I guess I feel hurt. I feel picked on. This feels really unjust and unfair. I feel helpless and picked on like when I was a kid. Afraid? I guess I'm concerned that he's going to take all of the credit and I'm going to look useless. It makes me concerned about losing my job. I'm scared of losing my job. I'm pretty concerned about finances right now and losing my job really freaks me out.

Connect:

I'm not alone. I can engage with the people and world around me.

I need to ground down. I actually really love this job and I need to stop allowing other people to get in the way of my joy. I think I'm gonna go for a walk on my lunch break and get some fresh air and gather my thoughts. I might call up my friend this evening and see if they have any advice.

Release:

I don't need to hold this in any longer. I can let it go.

Honestly, I feel really pent up inside and need to get it out. I'm sick of being silent. I need to tell him that his communication style is not working for me. If that doesn't work, I'm gonna request a group meeting with our supervisor so we can figure this out, but first, I need to cool off. I think I might wait until tomorrow before I say anything. I can tell I'm triggered right now and I don't want to react out of pain. I want to act towards a solution.

Once the hidden emotion is revealed, the blocked energy has a place to be released, like the flow of a river. Sometimes it feels like a weight is lifted. Sometimes it feels like you need to sob and wail. Regardless of what it feels like in the moment, each time you master the art of removing the mask, you feel more empowered, grounded, and confident in yourself. You take the wheel away from fear and you empower the force of consciousness inside you.

From a more grounded and balanced space, the next time your coworker interrupts you and cuts you off, you can reply with, "Hey Tom, that doesn't really work for me. While I appreciate hearing your ideas, we're producing this project together as a team and it's essential that we both have the ability to bring our voices and ideas forward in order for this to all thrive to its full potential. If collaboration isn't feeling aligned for you, let's schedule a meeting with the boss and discuss some changes that can be made."

Maybe he'll respond well, and maybe he won't. That's up to him. You just continue working on yourself and honoring what you know is right, with the intention to be as present and honest as possible. By allowing yourself permission to speak openly and honestly, rather than spewing aggression, you rise up into your true, present self.

THE APOLOGY

LEARNING TO GROUND OURSELVES AND CHOOSE a conscious release rather than being swept away in an unconscious wave of emotions isn't always easy. It takes patience and practice. One way you can stretch beyond your comfort zone and let go of what's stored within you is offering an apology.

This can be easier said than done, especially when we've gotten very comfortable living behind the seemingly secure walls of the cage. Apologizing means confronting the part of us that is attached to constantly protecting and defending ourselves. It means courageously admitting that we were wrong, which means bringing attention and awareness to our vulnerability. This may not be comfortable, especially if we've spent much of our lives striving *not* to feel exposed or vulnerable.

Acknowledging that we were wrong also means admitting that we were the ones who created a wound, and as we talked about, no one wants to be the bad guy. Chances are, you're hurting inside and your wounds need care and attention, so the moment you acknowledge the wounds you've created, it might feel like you're drawing that much-needed, valuable love away from yourself.

Well, here's another perspective: in apologizing, you're empowering yourself by releasing some of your pain and shame. You're courageously confronting the part of you that is living in scarcity and you're holding yourself accountable in a very honest and necessary way. You're saying, "I've done something that I don't feel good about. Because I care about you and your wellbeing, I want the wound I've created to be seen and soothed through the light of awareness. I'm holding myself accountable through this verbal acknowledgement and it is my intention to do better."

This became clear to me when I was 16 years old and serving as the art director of a summer camp for girls. Traditionally, they would never have hired a 16 year old for a position designed for a professional, and an adult. But due to their lack of staff and the four-page mission statement I submitted with my application, they felt somewhat obliged to assign me to the role.

It was a very enriching experience to be away from home and surrounded by fellow staff from around the world. Together, we shared a passion for supporting the youth and a desire to spend an entire summer camping in the woods.

The director of the camp was a force of nature. She had the spirit of a mother bear and the fierceness of a lion. We were encouraged to adopt nicknames for the summer, and she was formally referred to as "Hawkeye."

Hawkeye appeared to never veer away from the path of integrity and honesty. She was the refreshing breath of contrast and culture that I needed, having grown up in a small town of predominantly white people in Michigan, and feeling restricted and stuck. She was open-minded and biracial, with a strong, confident voice. She saw everyone as equal and everyone as special and if you veered from that perception of yourself, she would make sure to get you back on track.

With months of continuous camp songs, mosquito bites, scraped elbows, stomach aches, missing luggage, outhouse drama, and patching up of leaking tents, the staff would at times get tired, exhausted, and irritable. In one of those moments, Hawkeye released her frustration in a commanding and unthoughtful way. She directed her energy towards me, and dealing with heightened insecurity (and pretty severe eating disorders), I took her careless words to heart.

Offended and deflated, I walked away and took refuge in my crafts room where I kept myself busy cleaning, organizing, and preparing the God's Eye materials for the 20 campers arriving to class that afternoon. Not long after, Hawkeye came to find me. With slumped shoulders and a look of shame and sorrow, she solemnly walked up to me and said, "Hey Punkin," (yes, that was my camp name) "I'm really, really sorry. I've got a lot going on right now and I really didn't mean to vent it on you." Understanding that we were all exhausted and stretched thin, and with a touch of wanting to move past the discomfort of receiving an apology, I quickly replied "It's ok. It's no big deal."

With a look of determination, she said, "No, it's not ok. It's not ok how I acted and it's not ok for you to be treated like that. You deserve to be treated better than that. I need to be held accountable and I need to look at myself right now." Then, she said something that stuck with me for all of these years. With tear-filled eyes, she looked deeply at me and said, "Sometimes an apology isn't about the other person. Sometimes it's what you need. I need to apologize right now."

So easily, we don't apologize. We don't feel the repercussions of our actions. We say or do something careless or hurtful and we convince ourselves that they're fine and we're fine—and that's not fine. If we're trapped inside our desensitizing egos, we don't find this jewel of awareness that Hawkeye found that day: the permission to be humble and benefit from the empowerment of releasing unnecessary shame. Whether I forgave her or not didn't matter—she needed to do it for herself. She needed to step outside her lonely, cold cage and know that she was doing what she could to heal the wounds she may have created.

When you apologize, you don't just offer healing to the other person. You bring yourself out of the shadows of suffering and welcome both of you into the light of consciousness and love. Though it may feel like you're giving yourself when you apologize, you're actually receiving. You're receiving strength, wisdom, freedom, and the permission to release what feels so heavy and burdened inside of you.

*Can you think of anyone in your life who you owe an apology to?
What would it feel like to let go of the fear holding you back
and finally apologize to them?*

WRITE A LETTER

WHAT IF INSTEAD OF GIVING AN APOLOGY, you feel you're owed an apology? Maybe someone wasn't there when you needed them or maybe they physically or emotionally hurt you in ways that were painful and unjust? Maybe they broke things off in your relationship and left you feeling abandoned, and you're still hurting because of it?

Ideally, you would be able to find an intentional space of sharing and speak directly with them. You would communicate the desire to connect, then you both would have the opportunity and willingness to share what you are feeling, say what needs to be said, and heal the old wounds.

Unfortunately, not everyone is interested, supportive, ready, or still alive to reciprocate this level of communication. Maybe it's been many years and that person is not in your life or in this world anymore? Maybe you've tried and they're not open to talking about it? Maybe you don't know how to get a hold of them?

Maybe they're in your life and you *could* speak with them but you don't feel emotionally or physically safe doing so. If they're living in a state of prolonged suffering, it's possible that they won't have the skills, courage, or ability to properly hold the space you need. It's also possible that over the past twenty years, they have calmed down, become wiser, and transformed their once raging temper into being loving, kind, and patient.

Let's imagine there is still a part of you that needs to tell them how their constant yelling, hitting, and neglect was extremely damaging to you when you were growing up. You need to tell them what it felt like for them to side with the stepparent instead of you. You've considered bringing it up with them, though you feel pretty certain if you do, it will send them into a deep hole of shame. Sadly, there are instances when healing our pain directly involves someone else and it seems impossible because we're not able or comfortable speaking directly to them.

Regardless of whether they're involved in the conversation or not, you need a clarifying release to happen inside you. That way, you *can* transition out of protection into feeling at ease. If the damaging wounds happened in your youth, it's likely that there may still be an inner child who is hurting and needs to be acknowledged. In these cases, I strongly encourage you to give yourself permission to use your voice and speak up.

If it's not comfortable or doable, you can still accomplish this release through writing a letter. Ideally, with an actual pen and paper. In doing so, you give yourself permission to say anything and everything that needs to be shared. Explain how the experience made you feel. Share how it impacted your life and what it has been like holding it inside you. Explain the pain, fear, sadness, anger, and regret. Maybe tell them how sorry *you* are and how you never meant to hurt *them*. Whatever needs to be said, release the pent-up fire, tears, shame, and pain, and let the letter be as long as you need.

Then, I strongly suggest that you consider *not* sending the letter.

You are writing this letter to them, but you are doing it for yourself. As much as you may have immense pain, anger, regret, shame, or rage that needs to be released and shared, it's not about them anymore. This is about you finding your voice, being heard, and releasing the feelings taking up space inside. If you send the letter, it may generate fresh wounds and a new knot of pain to work through. You don't need that right now. Instead, let this be something in honor of your own release—a healing experience that you are granting yourself, for yourself.

Remember, you deserve to be freed from the suffering. Allow yourself the incredible gift of release because you deserve it. If and when they are ready to be freed from their suffering, they will need to confront themselves. However, their actions are not your focus—*yours* are.

With this all said, if it feels intuitively aligned to send the letter, offer yourself at least one good night's rest before sending it. Take a deep breath and sleep on it in case you need to edit some of the steam out.

THE LANGUAGE OF MUSIC

MUSIC HAS THE ABILITY TO AWAKEN US ON A CELLULAR, emotional and spiritual level through vibration and sound, and I believe it is one of the most healing, soothing forms of release that we humans will ever come into contact with.

For me, music provided counsel, support, connection, and release through the years of suffering. When I was sad and felt tears building up, I would put on music and listen to someone openly expressing *their* heartache and it allowed me to do the same. When I made my own music, it allowed me to open up and express so many withheld feelings—in a healthy and constructive way. The pain was released from my heart through sound. It enabled me to nurture a deeper connection with myself and be comforted by the message I needed to hear.

Music has such a sincere ability to offer us healing benefits, including:

1. Listening

Listening to music can help you tap into emotions you may be avoiding or unable to access. Maybe crying is hard for you? Well, there are hundreds and thousands of musicians who have mastered the art of expressing their feelings through sound—and by sitting in the presence of their heartfelt and intimate expression, you can follow their lead to your own heart.

If you are limited in your taste in music, try exploring new styles and genres. You are constantly changing and evolving, and so is your taste. Just as you are learning to practice judgment awareness in yourself, consider practicing judgment awareness when listening to music. Allow yourself to be free from the restriction of always having a strong opinion or judgment. In doing so, you may find that there are entirely new worlds of sound that will move you.

2. Creating

Creating music is something that everyone has the ability to do but perhaps not the inner permission to allow. One reason why many of us feel apprehensive about making music, especially singing, is because at some point we were discouraged and shamed for trying. Maybe we were told "Ow, you're hurting my ears," or "don't quit your day job."

The truth is, for thousands of years, every culture around the world has engaged with feeling, expressing, releasing, and celebrating the life experience through singing and playing instruments. Only in recent years has music been categorized as an elite profession or a gladiator spectacle with competitions of who can out-sing the other.

As the sacred and divine art of music has become entwined with fans, likes, views, comments, and followers, it has become part of the collective ego. It has shifted from a healthy expression of self into something up for constant judgment and opinions. For this reason, a lot of people are afraid to even try to sing in front of anyone else out of fear of judgment.

I'm here to tell you: when you sing and make music, not only are you not hurting anyone, you're actually healing yourself and making the world a more beautiful place. You don't have to be apprehensive about it and you don't have to be a professional. The reality is, like blinking or breathing, creating sound is a natural ability that you were born with as a means of sharing and releasing your feelings. Birds do it, dogs do it, cats do it, and humans do it. You deserve to access this ability you were born with. You deserve to fully embody it without feeling ashamed.

By opening up through singing and making music, you are reclaiming your birth right to express yourself. It will not only free you from the weight of emotional blockages—it will help you develop strength and confidence in yourself.

Don't sing for other people; sing for you!

ARTISTIC FREEDOM

I REALIZE IT MAY FEEL LIKE I'M GUIDING you back to preschool with these suggestions—write letters, sing songs, draw pictures—but honestly, they are profoundly healing tools for release.

Creating art is similar to creating music as it's a direct channel to connecting with yourself and expressing emotions and feelings that need an outlet. It's also similar to music in that it was captured by the world of profession and industry as something reserved for those who are "good enough."

You may hear people say "I'm not an artist," or "I can't even draw a stick figure." This happens if we lose our childhood permission to simply engage with the act of creating, instead focusing on the end result. It's about the journey, not the destination. You have all the permission in the world to immerse yourself in the fantastic realms of color, shape, and texture and express your feelings through painting, sculpting, sketching, building, crafting, and creating.

This isn't about what you end up with, what others think, or whether it will sell or not. It's about giving yourself freedom and permission to open, express, and release the feelings and energy inside you.

Do it for *you*, not them.

EXPRESSION THROUGH MOVEMENT

SOMETIMES, WHEN OUR EMOTIONS GET stockpiled and stored inside of us, we need more than a good cry or a conversation. We need to *move* it out of us. Because our bodies physically store so much of what our hearts are carrying, a lot of healing can take place through the release of physical energy.

Perhaps you're not an athletic person and don't fancy the idea of moving your body? Perhaps you have mobility issues and going for a walk isn't an option? All of us are shaped differently and live very different lives, so what works for one person won't necessarily work for another, and that's ok. Whatever you are capable of engaging in is good enough.

Some examples might include:
- Walking
- Stretching
- Yoga

- Dancing
- Running
- Martial arts
- Hiking
- Swimming

Whether it means going for a long walk or standing in your backyard throwing mud and punching the air, let that swell of energy move *through* and *out* of you. By letting your body move and release pent-up emotions and feelings, you strengthen the connection of mind, body, and heart. You also safely and constructively release energy from your being. The goal is to get into your body and release the energy and emotions stored inside.

Keep in mind, it's important to do this with the intention of feeling freedom, not to lose weight or meet some unmet need for attention and acceptance. This isn't about anyone but you. Let it be an uplifting and cleansing experience that brings you closer to yourself and the emotional freedom you deserve.

Are there any ways that you long to physically express yourself and haven't due to fear or shame?

Who is benefiting from you holding back and saying "no" to yourself?

What would it feel like to prioritize your own wellbeing by fearlessly and freely expressing yourself?

GENTLE THROUGH THE DETOX

DETOXING EMOTIONS AND STORED ENERGY is similar to cleansing the body of physical toxins and it's not necessarily clean, pretty, or comfortable. In fact, you may experience physical discomfort in response to what you're emotionally processing.

What comes up and out of you emotionally and energetically has likely been inside you for some time. So you're not introducing new discomfort, you're just becoming aware of it and releasing what's already there. With that said, it can feel jarring or unsettling to look at the undesirable feelings and memories that were previously out-of-sight and out-of-mind.

One thing to continually remind yourself of through the process is that it takes time. All the layers of fear and pain didn't happen overnight; they accumulated over time. Therefore, they won't necessarily all peel off in a day.

For this reason, it's important to be patient and gentle with yourself through the process of releasing and cleansing. Self-care, compassion, and finding the right support network is beneficial and at times essential. As we move ahead, we'll talk about strengthening our ability to comfort and love ourselves, which helps us be kinder and more gentle with ourselves through whatever discomfort we may experience in life.

LETTING OTHERS FIND THEIR OWN WAY
Meditative vision

In preparation for the exercise, try to find a comfortable and quiet space to sit or lay down. Ideally, a space without distractions or interruptions.

◆

1. Imagine yourself on a small island. Whether the land is surrounded by sand and turquoise waters or cliffs and the deepest blue sea is your choice.

2. Imagine that lined up next to you are all the people who you need personal, energetic, psychic space from. Maybe your little brother? Your spouse? Your client? Your neighbor? Who do you need space from? Go ahead and bring them into focus and add them to the queue.

3. One by one, let them walk forward and meet you by the water's edge. (No, we're not about to throw them into the water). Now, visualize a beautiful little boat coming along the beach, and for each person present, there is a boat with their name on it. Literally visualize each individual's name painted on their boat.

4. Work with one person at a time and just focus on that person. Think of what they would love and place those items in the boat for them. Do they like playing music? Place an instrument in the boat. Do they like birds? Maybe they'd like some binoculars. Get creative. I always like including some fresh drinking water and a warm blanket and a pillow in case it's cold or they need to rest.

5. Next, pack them some food. What do they love eating? Find some nice snacks for them and hand them a packed lunch as you help them into the boat.

6. Watch them light up with enthusiasm, "Oh my goodness! A ukulele?? Wow, is that a birdwatching guide? Thank you!" Look how joyful and content they are. Watch them become so focused on the beauty of their surroundings and the wonderful assortment of projects that they've completely forgotten you're there. Now, they have a safe, comfortable, fulfilling journey to set out on with themselves.

7. Watch as the boat gently turns away from you and with your hand, give the boat a gentle push (not a shove, just a push). As you do this, say something along the lines of, "May you find joy

and contentment in this beautiful place. Safe travels. Goodbye now."

8. Then, watch them go so far away that their little boat becomes a speck on the horizon and you can't see them or hear them anymore. They're gone!

9. If there's someone else standing in line, welcome them forward and repeat the process until you've let go of everyone and anyone who you need space from.

10. Then, imagine yourself on your own private island. What do you want to do? What do you need? If it's much-needed rest, allow yourself to curl up and go to sleep. (This meditation is really useful at night time.)

EXAMPLE CONVERSATION

FOR THIS CONVERSATION, WE'LL SHIFT out of the separate investigative and witnessing personas, and we'll explore what it's like to speak in first person, directly to and with ourselves. We'll continue this style of self-inquiry for the remaining conversations in the book.

◆

Imagine you're feeling exhausted and down lately. Maybe you've been working long hours and feeling increasingly stressed and uninspired with your life. Because you've experienced depression before, you feel it happening. To turn things around, you're ready to ask yourself some questions and get to the heart of what's going on to get your needs met.

What's happening? What happened?

I: Can I describe what's going on?
W: I feel tired of life. I wake up wishing I didn't have to get out of bed.

I: How long have I been feeling this way?
W: For a while. Maybe three or four months.
I: Did anything significantly wounding happen three or four months ago?
W: I can't think of anything. It's all been pretty boring for a while.

I need to be more specific.

I: Can I better describe how my life is boring?
W: There's just not a lot going on. I spend most of my time working and going through the motions each day. I feel like a machine. I'm tired of it. I'm beginning to wonder what the point of being alive is.

Hmmm, this sounds like depression. I must really be hurting somewhere inside. I also hear myself exhausted with work. I need to go deeper and find out what's going on.

I: Does my job fulfill me?
W: No. It used to when I started but ever since I got promoted and started working more hours, it's been really stressful. I feel like I don't have time for anything else.

This feels important. I definitely feel troubled by my job. I wonder where that's coming from.

I: Can I explain more about feeling stressed?
W: Yeah. Even though I'm just sitting all day looking at the screen, I feel really anxious. It's like I'm bored and anxious at the same time.
I: Are there key moments when I feel this anxiousness?
W: Usually at night, after I get done with work. I just feel anxious, like I need a glass of wine or something to calm me down and unwind.

Interesting, that sounds like need, meaning there's definitely deeper pain in there.

How am I feeling? Where am I hurting? Where am I afraid?

I: Do I feel any deeper feelings of sadness about anything in particular?
W: I don't know. Some people have serious problems. I don't deserve to complain about my life and whine about my problems.

Judgment awareness. It's important to not put wounds on a scale. If I want healing, I have to be neutral and just listen to myself.

I: Where am I hurting?
W: I guess I feel pretty lonely at times.

Ok, that's interesting. I just felt a shift in senses. I definitely feel like I'm getting deeper into what's going on.

I: Does this pain come with any fear?
W: I sometimes wonder if I'll be single forever and that makes me scared. I question if I've made the right choices. I'm making good money but I'm scared of spending the rest of my life alone.

Ok. I feel like I'm going to cry. There's definitely some pain here.

I'm not alone. I can engage with the people and world around me.

I: How have I been connecting with the people and world around me?
W: I haven't. When I'm like this, I just want to curl up under a rock and fall asleep forever. I actually avoid people altogether and since my job shifted to being virtual, I rarely leave the house.

This doesn't sound healthy. I need to engage with others.

I: Would I be open to exploring some forms of connection?
W: What? Like, talk to people? No way, the last thing I want to do is be around people and look at their perfect lives with their perfect relationships.

Ooooh, I'm sensing myself being defensive around the topic of relationships. This is definitely a wound that I'm guarding and protecting.

I: If I'm not ready to hang out with people, am I willing to at least get myself out on a walk or spend time in nature?
W: I guess so. There's the new walking trail they recently put in near town. Maybe I'll get myself out on that tomorrow.
I: What about inviting a friend to go with me?
W: No. I don't want to be around people right now.

Hmmm. I'm catching myself saying that I'm lonely then actively avoiding being around anyone. That doesn't work. I've gotta start somewhere.

I: Am I open to going on a walk tomorrow and next week, inviting someone to walk with me?

W: I guess so. I don't really have many friends. Well, actually, my neighbor Sheryl is always asking how I'm doing. I don't think of her as a friend but she's really nice and caring. I like the way I feel around her and she has a super cool dog. I bet she'd go with me if I invited her.

I don't need to hold onto this any longer. I can let it go.

I: Am I willing to explore some form of creative expression to get the energy moving and release some of this pain in me?

W: Maybe. I have those paints I got at that garage sale last summer. I think they're in a closet somewhere. I guess I could stop in town after the walk and find some paper or canvas to paint on. I'm not great at painting but I'll give it a try.

I: Ok, so what's my game plan for tomorrow?

W: After work, I'll go for a walk, stop in town for some art supplies, then try to do some painting.

Wow, this actually sounds kind of fun. Maybe my life isn't as boring as I thought. I wonder if Sheryl likes to paint...?

RELEASING TOOLS

Each time I allow myself to acknowledge the truth, feel the truth, and speak the truth, I welcome the cleansing light of awareness into my being and come clean from within.

◆

Crying is a natural and necessary form of release.
Next time I feel myself needing to cry, I can do what's best for my mind, body, and heart and give myself permission to say yes.

◆

If and when I feel myself tempted to release anger through a form of aggression, I can go deeper within to explore what the underlying feelings are, then express those.

◆

Though I may feel resistant at first, I can offer myself permission to apologize to strengthen my integrity and self-confidence and experience healing through the release needed.

◆

I give myself permission to make music and listen to music as a means of expressive release, regardless of what anyone else thinks.

◆

There are many ways that I can release the energy of my pent-up emotions. I can give myself permission to be creative and find constructive outlets like art, writing, and movement to express myself.

*Each time someone allows themselves to release
the tears that weigh heavy on their heart,*

*a strand from the rope that ties us all to the suffering
is broken
and we become that much freer.*

13.
COMFORT

Freedom and relief from pain or constraint.

I'T'S NEARLY IMPOSSIBLE TO SUSTAINABLY CARE for someone else (especially someone with a mental illness) unless you also practice the sacred art of caring for yourself.

A lot of people tried relaying this message to me over the years. They would see me taking on the role of caregiver and say, "that's going to wear you out" or "you can only do that for so long." While I appreciated what appeared to be concern, I also felt apprehension receiving advice from anyone who had never actually been a caregiver for a loved one with dementia, especially a beloved mother.

How could they know what I'm going through or what I needed?

Then, as the years passed and I became deeply familiar with what "caregiver burnout" felt like, I began to reflect on all those times people tried to explain to me how important caring for the self is. Slowly, I came to understand that *I can't keep giving energy without receiving it.*

If you are anything like me, a caregiver by nature, and have an inclination to put others before yourself, the art and act of *receiving* care can be challenging.

Gratefully, a heartfelt encounter welcomed me to that awareness.

I was feeling low. I felt sad and I felt heavy, for no known reason. I didn't think too much of it and went about my day, doing chores and daily routines. I made mom some dinner, helped her bathe, and tucked her into bed, then went into the kitchen.

I thought, *What is going on with me? Am I premenstrual? Why am I so down?*

Nope. Not that time of the month.

Am I hungry?

Nope. I just ate dinner.

Do I need a sweet treat? A little pick me up?

Nope. It's too late at night, the sugar will keep me awake.

What is going on with me?? Why do I feel so heavy and sad?

Without any other ideas about what I might physically need, I took a shower and went to sit on my yoga mat (by the way, yoga mats are incredible even if you don't do yoga. I don't do yoga but I do like a welcoming place to sit and stretch on the ground.)

I asked myself, "What's going on? Are you ok? What do you need?"

I asked as though I was asking someone else. I genuinely addressed myself in a warm, direct, and inquisitive manner. As I did this, I felt my hands lay upon my arm and gently wrap around me like how I would comfort a child. I could feel that I was sad, but I didn't know why. I felt myself paying close attention and leaning into the part of me that was grieving instead of telling myself to bury it down as I had done for so many years.

My tender and quiet self responded, "I don't know. I don't know what's wrong. I don't know what I need. I just don't feel good. I'm just down."

I felt overwhelming compassion and warmth sweep over me, and I replied, "It's ok, you don't have to know. We can just sit here together. I'm not going anywhere." My hands continued to wrap around me and the genuine exchange of warmth and love surrounded me. I felt myself deeply caring for me, who was also deeply appreciative to be receiving that care.

I held this (her, myself) for about five minutes, gently rocking back and forth with my eyes closed.

Then, I slowly leaned in and gently asked, "Do you want to talk about it?"

She quietly answered, "No, I'm not ready. I don't know what's wrong."

I replied, "Ok, no problem at all. You don't need to tell me anything. No pressure. I'll just hold you. I'm not going anywhere."

After five more minutes of gentle, soothing warmth, I felt a twinkle of movement in my heart and my tender self said, "Ok. I'm ready to talk."

I exclaimed, "You got it! I'll go and heat up the hot water bottle and get the bed cozy."

Enthusiastic to help, I zipped into the kitchen, heated up some water, positioned the pillows, chose the coziest blanket, placed my journal beside me, and curled up in bed.

I said, "OK, please just share whatever you're feeling. I'm listening. I won't judge you or rush you. Just share and release whatever comes up."

Then, I picked up the pen and journal and let my timid, hurting self speak.

First, she spoke about how exhausted and deeply sad she was watching mom slowly die of dementia. I let her open up, and together we cried. Then, she (I) began opening up more and sharing painful memories from childhood; memories from the years of addiction and self-abuse—distant, faint, and nearly forgotten memories. Numerous times I thought to myself, *I've been clean from bulimia for years, why is this all coming up right now?* However, in honor of my commitment to create a safe space with no judgment, I didn't question for too long. I continued listening and watching the words fill the pages with memories and tears.

When I was finished, I had filled six pages and felt a strange yet familiar sensation. I was infused by a deep, maternal force of love and compassion, similar to how I feel after offering support and counsel to someone who is hurting.

However, this time, it was for myself. For the first time, I experienced what it's like to truly show up as a caregiver *for myself*. This was an exceptional and strange new experience for me.

How many times and for how many years had I told myself that what I was feeling was not allowed, not welcome, not important enough? How many times had I abandoned myself in a time of crisis and said, "Stop complaining. Just go eat something! Grab chocolate, grab a drink, go online, do whatever—I don't care—just go away!" For how long had I unknowingly been generating painful wounds from self-neglect?

The next morning, I opened my eyes and felt a joyous lightness in my body and in my heart. I felt mentally clear and refreshed, as though the divided pieces of me had been united. I felt heard. I felt seen. I felt *comforted*. I felt *whole*. That's what being comforted feels like. It's being soothed and healed with an incredible force of nourishment.

Examples of ways to experience COMFORT:
- Warmth
- Kindness
- Nurturance
- Breathing
- Being heard
- Hugging
- Sleeping
- Spending time in nature

The definition of **comfort** is: **to ease or alleviate feelings of grief or distress.**

However, because so many of our wounding experiences left us feeling so uncomfortable in ourselves, many of us *don't* ever feel relieved of our grief and distress. Instead, we end up anxious, stressed, and in a prolonged state of need and discomfort.

At some point, we have to stop what we're doing and tend to where it hurts. We *have* to care for ourselves. We need to ease the pain and return to feeling safe and comfortable in our hearts, our bodies, and our lives. As connection is the channel of flow that unites us with all of the life around us, receiving comfort is the ability to let that energy move inward and be absorbed and received in our beings.

In many ways, this internal message is:
"I'm ready to be comfortable and receive the care I need."

Especially when we've allowed ourselves to open that sacred channel of connection and release our pent-up emotions, it's vital to create a warm, nurturing flow of energy to soothe our tender, exposed insides. In releasing, we let go of what doesn't belong. Through comfort, we receive what does belong.

In progression, the steps would unfold like this:

<u>Observe</u>: *What's happening right now? What happened in the past?*
<u>Feel</u>: *How am I feeling? Where am I hurting? Where am I afraid?*
<u>Connect</u>: *I'm not alone. I can engage with the world around me.*
<u>Release</u>: *I don't need to hold onto this any longer. I can let it go.*
<u>Comfort</u>: *I'm ready to be comfortable and receive the care I need.*

Now, many of us shrivel up at the thought of allowing ourselves to receive. We're much more comfortable giving than receiving. Because of this, we starve ourselves of comfort and nourishment while propelling a false narrative that we don't deserve it or are strong enough without it.

It's not true and it's not sustainable. You're not indestructible and you're not saving the world by pretending that you're a superhero made of steel. You are a soft, gentle, vulnerable being who needs nourishment, care, and comfort, just as much as every baby, child, teenager, young adult, adult, and elder deserves it.

Even though you may not have received the comfort you needed in the past, let's change that. Let's learn about the many ways to soothe and comfort ourselves so that you can become even more skilled at getting your needs met!

TEMPORARY COMFORT

THERE ARE A LOT OF THINGS THAT FEEL COMFORTING. Food is comforting. Alcohol is comforting. Watching TV is comforting. Sadly, even though something might feel soothing and good in the moment, it won't necessarily meet your needs. Unless you're consciously understanding the pain behind the need, you can easily get caught in a cyclone of temporary comfort and end up even more uncomfortable in yourself.

So, what's the difference?

Well, temporary comfort is like pain medicine. A painkiller eases and alleviates the feelings of distress but only for a while. For those minutes or hours, you have a highly sought-after sense of relief. You feel calm, at ease, and free from pain.

Then, it's over. The pill wears off, the pain returns, and you're left once again with the throb of discomfort inside. By taking a pill (or eating a candy bar or having a cocktail), you may think you're actively comforting and tending to the pain but you're not. You're just *pacifying* the pain for a short while until it eventually bubbles up again (and again and again).

In that sense, temporary comfort is also like junk food. It's not sustainable. What you really *need* is a well-balanced, nourishing meal to give you strength and energy, but you settle for a quick high that temporarily appeases the sensation of hunger. Maybe you feel better for a moment, but very soon, the sensation of comfort wears off and you're hungry again (while also feeling taxed and drained from whatever junk you just put in your body.)

Examples of **temporary comforts:**
- Compulsive eating
- Television or movies
- Shopping
- Social media
- Video streaming
- App games
- Video games
- Caffeine
- Cigarettes
- Alcohol
- Sexual stimulation
- Pain relievers
- Drugs
- Sleeping pills

Maybe you're thinking, "What's wrong with a little comfort? That's better than no comfort at all, right?" Well, perhaps. However, if you're reaching for comfort because you're avoiding the pain, your efforts are coming from fear and living in fear is not comfortable. You're trying to alter your state of being because your state of being is *uncomfortable.*

The reality is, if you're hurting and uncomfortable, you don't need temporary relief; you need long-term healing. You need to acknowledge the reality of where the deeper discomfort and pain is coming from (the wound), then shine the light of conscious awareness onto it. Then, *care* for it. Soothe it with your attention. Recognize the healing support you've always needed, then let yourself receive it.

Can you think of any ways you may comfort yourself at times with unsustainable forms of temporary comfort?

BEING COMFORTABLE

BY CONSCIOUSLY MOVING *toward* being comfortable rather than unconsciously fleeing the discomfort, we reach a place of true, long-term comfort within in ourselves.

Here are some **constructive ways we can receive the healing support we need** (rather than temporary comfort) when we're feeling uncomfortable:

- Allowing our bodies to sleep and rest
- Giving and receiving hugs with ourselves and others
- Taking a warm bath or shower
- Engaging in a meditation practice or entering a meditative space
- Writing in our journals
- Eating healthy and balanced meals
- Drinking a glass of water
- Walking or sitting in nature
- Cuddling with animals
- Resting with a hot water bottle
  (a specially crafted rubber bag that can be held to your body)

Receiving our own comfort and care means giving ourselves permission to care for ourselves as much as we care for those we love. It means having the courage to show up, listen, and open both arms with infinite acceptance and support. It means allowing ourselves to uncomfortably weep, slouch, stutter, and be slow moving—without judging or scolding.

We don't always know why we're hurting or what we need to feel better and that's ok—we don't have to. Do you force everyone you love to have a written explanation of why they're hurting for you to grant them a hug? Do you tell them to sit up straight, stop crying, and look presentable when they're sad?

No, you don't. You love them and you show up for them. You wrap your arms around them and you hold them and comfort them. And, this is the same level of comfort that you deserve and need.

When you let yourself receive genuine, healthy and constructive forms of comfort, you realize you're not as reliant on the temporary comforts as you once were. Rather than being dependent, you begin feeling at ease and more comfortable in yourself. With that, you are less *in need* of something to make you feel better because you already feel better. You're not hurting anymore.

CREATING MEDITATIVE SPACE

MEDITATION IS AN ANCIENT PRACTICE OF STILLING the mind and bringing awareness inward. It brings clarity and calmness into the mind and body, and quite honestly, it would drastically change the world if everyone integrated it into their lives.

However, meditation requires a direct relationship with stillness and for many of us, that's not an easy thing. Especially when we've mastered the art of avoidance. Being still can feel incredibly overwhelming and intimidating. If we're dealing with anxiety, insecurity, anger, restlessness, and/or an addiction, the thought of sitting still for extended periods can trigger more anxiety, which is not the direction we want to head in. We want to work towards relieving anxiety and feeling secure and more comfortable, not *un*comfortable.

Since meditation is also something many of us have tried and not successfully accomplished or stuck with, there may be a shameful cloud of *"I can't"* that emerges when thinking about it, which is also not supportive or helpful on our journey of healing.

So, here's a different approach: rather than setting a goal of mastering meditation and potentially shaming yourself for not reaching it, allow yourself to enter an intentional *meditative space.*

What is that? It's giving yourself permission to consciously relax your body, rest your mind, and release the cage around your heart. It's finding a window of time (15 – 60 minutes ideally) to step away from your emails, phone calls, text messages, and obligations to prioritize and nurture your relationship with yourself.

You may have a busy life with lots of people to care for, so early in the morning or the 10 minutes during your lunch break are the only windows you have, *that's ok*. Whether you're on a bus, at your kitchen table, on your sofa, or a park bench, find somewhere you feel physically and emotionally safe enough to let your guard down and fully relax your mind and body.

The goal is to give yourself time with yourself. Rather than focusing on all that surrounds you, it's a special and sacred opportunity to relax and rest with yourself, without sleeping.

If silence is challenging to achieve due to city noise, a full house, or personal intimidation, there are many meditational albums available that will take you on a beautiful and sonic journey of relaxation. (Note: *a good pair of headphones can be worth their weight in gold.*)

If your mind tends to wander and fill up with to-do lists, needs, and compulsive worrying, you can say, "Dear busy mind, I know you're looking out for me and want to take good care of me, and I thank you for that. But right now, I need to spend some quality time with my heart. As soon as we wrap up, I'll check in with you and we can continue talking… but not right now."

By doing this, you begin a practice of experiencing healthy connection and comfort that doesn't pull you further from yourself and into the realms of unconsciousness. Instead, it brings you deeper into your true self within the space of conscious awareness and intention. By managing your thoughts, you also develop interior boundaries from compulsive thinking and practice healthy communication and discernment.

This is something I've found helpful when working with people. At the end of each session, we take 15 or so minutes to enter into a quiet, meditative space. I recap the memories and insights discovered through the session, and gently weave the visuals and feelings into a guided meditation where the receiver can relax and absorb the newly discovered awareness. Sure, we might spend 90 minutes sorting through the pages and pieces of the past by working through fears, patterns, and visions for the future, but relaxing in a meditative space together for 15 minutes is just as, if not more, healing than the session itself.

Through these guided meditations, I've discovered that people often benefit from the company of others to give themselves permission to stop and be still. Somehow, if we're in it together, it's more comfortable and safe, which is another gentle reflection of how much we humans benefit from connection and presence with one another. For this reason, you might consider pre-recorded verbally guided meditations to welcome you into a meditative space, or try guided classes or courses where you can be united with others in the shared space of stillness.

Or if you feel called to begin a traditionally structured meditation practice, I recommend exploring and finding an approach that feels aligned for you (ideally one that doesn't generate self-judgment or shame). Perhaps you can think of meditation like an instrument—it takes time, patience, and practice to learn your way around and get to the point where you are making beautiful music and not just noise.

If you were to integrate a practice of bringing meditative spaciousness in your life, how would you do it?

THE SOOTHING RELIEF OF SLEEP

ONE OF THE MOST IMPORTANT WAYS THAT we humans can give ourselves the soothing comfort and relief we need is through physical sleep and rest. However, because so many of us are constantly in a swirl of trying, striving, and surviving life, we don't always get enough rest.

Maybe you're caring for a young child (or an 80-year-old one) who wakes up through the night? Maybe you've taken on the nightshift to cover the bills and aligning your body to sleep with sunlight is proving difficult? Whatever the reason, if you're not getting enough sleep, you're probably well aware of it.

Even though each of us (on average) will spend a third of our lives sleeping, we often overlook it or view it as a chore or nuisance. We see it as something we have to do; something that limits us from being more productive. If we're tired, we quickly reach for caffeine or something else to stimulate us and keep us in motion.

The issue here is that sleep is absolutely vital for our wellbeing, and when we're deprived of it, it deeply affects our body, emotions, energy level, and perspective on life. Like going without water, you can only go so long without sleep before your body begins to shut down and you *suffer*.

In fact, studies have shown that **a lack of sleep** can:

- Impair your ability to think clearly
- Limit you alertness, comprehension, and concentration
- Increase your risk of heart disease, heart attack, high blood pressure, and stroke
- Contribute to symptoms of depression and anxiety
- Cause your skin and organs to age faster

What's the solution?

Explore the idea of seeing sleep for what it really is: a healthy, necessary, and enlightening experience. Engage with it and honor it the same way you would a loved one, a career, or an activity that you cherish. Place it on the front burner of your intentions and carve space for it in your life. Cancel plans and prioritize it. Let yourself be reunited with it and fall in love with it.

Why? Because it is one of the most important and invested relationships you will ever nurture in your life. You literally cannot live without it. While your body is resting in a deep state of soothing paralysis and your organs are regenerating, your spirit is traveling to far off dreamlike galaxies.

Whether you consider yourself a meditative person or not, sleep welcomes you into the holy corridors of sacred stillness and you are reuniting with the expansive network of universe-wide connection. That is something you not only deserve to experience—you *need* to experience it.

If ever you stumble into the trap of thinking that sleep is just a gap of nothingness in your daily routine, take a moment and think again. Sleep is a sacred, soothing, intimate, nourishing and vital part of your life. Regardless of how much other people fail to appreciate it, you can choose your own path. You have permission to make a date with yourself to rest in the comforting warmth of a good sleep.

HOME IS WHERE THE HEART IS

SPEAKING OF SLEEP, WHERE ARE WE MOST LIKELY to find that regenerative and supportive space to rest? Well, for most of us, it's when we're home. Yet, if you ask a lot of people when they're most happy and free, they'll often say when they're traveling and visiting a new place; when they're *away* from home.

Why is that? Even though travel can offer us stimulating new perspectives and awaken curiosity and presence, a lot of us feel happiest when we're not at home because home is an uncomfortable place for us. It's a place we might associate with being boring or uneventful. Maybe it represents duty, struggle, and confrontation with challenging people (especially ourselves).

It's also likely that for many of us, our most prominent wounds happened within the home. Maybe it was an unsafe place where mom would release her rage or the place where your parents would argue late at night? Maybe your home growing up was really messy and so you still feel uncomfortable and insecure having people over to your house? Or maybe home was where your brother lived out his final days before dying of cancer, so home still feels like a sad and depressing place? Regardless of how distanced we are from our childhoods or where we lived in those times, our perception of home may still be affected by those wounds from the past.

Home can also be a breeding ground for self-abuse. Whenever I had time alone at home, it was an opportunity to binge and get lost in my secret and destructive comforts. It was also where I was more apt to say hurtful things to myself and allow shame to become a toxic slew of self-judgment. Yes, my early years included a lot of abuse within the home, but it wasn't my dad or my sister who had continued that destructive behavior into my adult years: it was me.

For that reason, I never felt at home. I would try to make rented houses and apartments feel like home. I would desperately paint the walls warm tones, put fresh flowers in vases, collect cozy blankets, and light candles in every room, and still, I felt restless and uneasy. Sure, I might be able to take a bath and relax for a few minutes, but it was just a matter of time before the anxiety would bubble up again.

What does it mean to feel "at home"?

It means to feel safe, secure, and at ease. It means to feel a sense of belonging, where we can comfortably *be* ourselves without fear or protection. When we talk about allowing ourselves to feel comfortable, it means allowing ourselves to experience these feelings of safety, security, and ease. We feel at *home* with who we are, right here in this moment, without fear standing in the way.

How do we do this?

We expand ourselves outward to look at the bigger picture. We look at the reality that we are only having a very temporary life experience. Not long ago, we were born. Not far from now, we will die. While this body and life seem like all there is, our heartfelt spirits are part of a life force that is more expansive and infinite than anything we can perceive. Yes, the roof over your head may be your "home," but it's only your temporary home. Your *true* home is so much greater and more profound than any pile of stone, cement, and clay. It's the tapestry of majestic and expansive oneness from where you came and where one day, you'll *return* to.

How do you access this place?

By being comfortable enough with yourself to be present and go within. By giving yourself permission to lean in and touch the vastness of existence through the tether found in the incredible stillness of the moment. Yes, you've been afraid for a long time and shocked out of being at home in yourself, but you don't need to be afraid anymore. You can take down your walls and know you are safe now.

Regardless of what's happening in your life, what experiences you've been through, or what pain you're still feeling from it all, you have permission to remember the truth: that you're home and you belong here. That your spirit is infinitely woven into the space beyond time and regardless of what painful and heartbreaking lessons life presents, you don't have to be afraid. You have permission to feel safe, secure, and at home right here, right now.

When you realize this, the saying, "the home is where the heart is" has a lot more meaning.

What does the essence of "home" feel like for you?

DIVINE MOTHER NURTURANCE

COMFORT AND REST ARE OFTEN ASSOCIATED with the soft, nourishing, soothing safety of a mother's love. Unfortunately, not all of us have (or had) a healthy relationship or connection to our blood mother. Maybe she was so distracted with the stresses of life that she was neglectful and wasn't there when you needed her? Maybe she dealt with a lot of trauma and was deeply insecure? Maybe she played out her need for safety through controlling your every move? It's also possible that you never had the opportunity to meet her and have felt disconnected and abandoned since birth.

For those reasons, we may not necessarily feel warm and relaxed when we hear the word "mother." Instead, it may bring up feelings of contraction, separation, and anxiety.

However, if we allow ourselves to expand outward, beyond our actual birth mothers and connect with the frequency of what a mother is capable of, we begin to discover something profoundly beautiful and valuable in our process of healing.

What I'm referring to is the soothing warmth of *divine mother nurturance.*

This wise, powerful, radiating warmth is often emitted through a mother, but not exclusively. As if streaming directly from an ocean of love, it cannot be contained, encapsulated, or even fully described. It's unconditional and much bigger and more expansive than any one human being. Like blood, like oxygen—it's fueled with vitality that lives and flows through us. It connects us and unites us like an umbilical cord to infinite and divine consciousness. Through it, we have access to unlimited compassion, forgiveness, and care for the wellbeing of ourselves and one another.

Regardless of whether you consider yourself woman, man, transgender, non-binary, elder, or youth, we all have access to this powerful, soothing warmth of divine mother nurturance within us. This electric stream of unconditional love is what soothes babies to sleep and inspires animals to entrust humans with their lives.

This powerful understanding came piercing through the clouds when I became the mother to my mother. Like a sacred changing of the guards, where once she soothed my worried mind to sleep and rubbed a soft hand upon my back, we changed roles. No longer was she cast as the "mother" in our relationship. She didn't have the ability or capacity to hold such a weighty role. She had to step down from the noble throne of motherly comfort and care, and I had to take the seat.

At first, I resisted. The tender child in me couldn't unbind the grip I had to her love. I needed it. Her nurturing warmth was necessary for my survival. However, as the mourning child in me began soothing the confused child in her, the divine mother began beaming through me and surrounding her in unbreakable strength. She was no longer my mother.

I was now *her* mother.

How could this be? She wasn't birthed from my body. She's 42 years *older* than me. It doesn't matter. Deep love is timeless and formless. It's not exclusive to any one person, gender, or age group—everyone has access to it.

It's this same radiant glow of maternal warmth and care that I feel for each person I offer counsel to. For years, I've struggled calling them "clients" because they feel more like my children: the gentle hearts I foster until they're strong and empowered enough to love and care for themselves.

Gradually, it became very clear that this profound nurturance and love channeling its way through me was actively healing other beings, and I started wondering why I wasn't offering it to myself?

Why do my clients deserve the soothing warmth of my nurturing love, but not me?

Why does my mother deserve the soothing warmth of my nurturing love, but not me?

Why do my pets deserve the soothing warmth of my nurturing love, but not me?

Why does my husband deserve the soothing warmth of my nurturing love, but not me?

The truth is, I *do* deserve to receive it, and honestly, I have yet to discover anything as calming, wholesome, and fulfilling as when I offer love, care, and nurturance to myself.

You too have this ability and you deserve to access it. You have the power to contradict what you've been led to believe for so long—that you have to suffer through life and desperately seek comfort outside yourself. You're done suffering and you're ready to let it go.

Next time you feel yourself drifting into sadness, loneliness, or shame because you're hungry for nurturing love, remember that you have permission to feel what's already inside you. You deserve to feel as secure and safe as a child in the arms of a loving mother, in the arms of yourself.

WARMTH

WHILE WE'RE TALKING ABOUT MOTHERS, it's important to acknowledge the sincere power and warmth of the womb, the sacred pod of comfort that exists inside a woman.

Oops, did I lose you? Was that too *far out* there?

Yeah, I can understand that. There are a lot of reasons why we close up, judge, and feel intimidated by talking about the warmth of the female body. Given how persuaded we are by fear and protection, we veer away from anything that resembles nurturing and intimacy. In a culture (and for the most part, a world) dominated by the facade of being tough and acting strong, we're very reluctant to immerse ourselves in intimate thoughts of warm, cozy wombs.

Well, I'd like to offer another perspective: regardless of whether you're comfortable thinking about it or not, you came from a womb. Your entire body spent months and months curled up inside one and your physical heart was beating inside your mother's womb within only five weeks of her pregnancy with you.

Maybe your experience in the womb was enjoyable or maybe it was challenging? A lot of us experienced abuse while in the womb and don't necessarily feel comfortable thinking about our earliest months of development. Regardless, what matters most is that the womb is a nurturing place you are deeply familiar with and something you've needed. You literally wouldn't be here, alive, reading these words right now if it weren't for the warm, safe, nurturing walls of your mother's womb.

Why am I bringing this up? Am I contriving a plan for you to somehow squeeze back in? Nope, definitely not. However, there is a lot to be said for what you experienced and relate to through the sensation of the womb.

What are those sensations?
- Warmth
- Safety
- Protection
- Nurturance
- Connection
- Love
- Care

So often, when we're hurting and feeling sad or alone, we crave warmth —and to feel safe, protected, and nurtured. While there's absolutely no way or need for you to return to your mother's womb, the soothing warmth it provided is something you can welcome into your life to experience comfort. You can create warm, safe settings to feel held and nurtured.

When we endure the shocking lightning bolts of trauma and the echoes of pain that follow, our nervous system can feel rattled and buzz with discomfort. Warmth is a direct and constructive way of not just soothing our emotional bodies but also our nervous systems.

Some examples of experiencing **soothing warmth** might be:
- Curling up with a warm blanket
- Wearing soft, warm clothing
- Holding a hot water bottle
  (if you don't have one, I recommend getting one)
- Sipping warm and relaxing herbal tea
- Taking a warm bath or shower

Whether it feels like something your mind remembers or not, your body and your spirit remember the safe nurturance of womb-like warmth. Because the core of your being is heat, it's possible that you'll feel a nostalgic remembrance of your true nature and enveloped in a more open, loving space by simply connecting with warmth.

Can you remember any occurrences in your life when you felt anxious or uncomfortable, then felt a shift in senses when you were warmed?

KINDNESS

IF YOU'RE ANYTHING LIKE ME, YOU MAY SOMETIMES associate being *kind* with being *nice*. For a long time, I grouped the two together and would question, "Why can't people just be nice? I know we're all hurting, but come on, people, be nice." Or, influenced by what I'd been told throughout my youth, "If you can't say something nice, don't say anything at all." As a result, I regarded anything that was unpleasant as unwelcome.

As I began healing from my suffering, I realized what I really craved was kindness, not niceness. Being *nice* comes with the potential baggage of smiling when you're not happy and putting on a performance to make others comfortable when you're not comfortable. Nice isn't necessarily what's needed in the world.

Kindness is different.

Similar to intuition and compassion, kindness comes from deep within us. Even though some may associate kindness with naivety or weakness, it's far from weak. Kindness is a super power. It's an uncontrollable, unthinkable force that swells up from the ancient wisdom of our hearts and encourages us to participate in a cosmic, karmic, benevolent exchange almost too vast for us to understand. In a similar way to our negative thoughts and judgments reverberating out and impacting those around us, kindness can do the same, but instead of sending shards of fear and pain, we wrap them in the healing force of love.

Showing kindness means to regard and concern for another's wellbeing. It means feeling love from a place of wholeheartedness and engaging with the act of sharing that love. Being nice is giving back the toy you snatched away from someone in the sandbox. Kindness is seeing someone sitting alone in the playground and offering them a warm and comforting hug.

Years ago, I got off work and stopped at the grocery store on my way home. Exhausted and loaded with a full cart, I pulled up to the register and dazed off as the cashier ran the items and bagged them up. She told me the total, I pulled out my card, she scanned it, the card was... denied. A bolt of shock and humiliation rushed through my system as I looked blankly at the checker and the people in line behind me.

We've all been in that situation. *Maybe it's a complication with the bank?*

Maybe I forgot to activate the card? "No problem, I'll just use a different card..." I didn't have a different card. I didn't have enough money. The card was denied because I was living in Los Angeles, scrambling to pay rent, and there was no money in my bank account.

Immediately, I mean—without a beat—the beautiful woman in line behind me handed the checker her card and said, "Add her groceries to my bill." Stunned, honored, and completely ashamed, I just looked at her. Her warm and kind eyes responded, *I know what it's like. You're not alone.*

Thinking back, I imagine it felt fulfilling for her to share. When we give, we too receive so much love from the experience. However, at that time, being bulimic, I wasn't able to accept her generous gift. I felt guilty and horrible having anyone spend their money on something that was going to be soon wasted and drained away. So, with tears in my eyes, I thanked her profusely and left the store with my head down and my heart full.

The reality is, I didn't know how to receive the gift of kindness from others because I didn't know how to be kind to myself. If kindness means sharing and showing love from a place of wholeheartedness, I was far from offering that to myself. When we're unwilling to receive our own love and care, we become deprived and feel like we don't have enough. When we feel we don't have enough, we become focused on survival and are more apt to be unkind to others.

Unfortunately, unkindness is contagious. When we're rude and unkind, we encourage others to be unkind and the cycle mutates, grows, and continues. Fortunately, kindness is also contagious. Each time you make the conscious decision to be generous, caring, and kind (to yourself and others), as opposed to coming from a place of lack, you nurture the collective force of consciousness and love, and give it fertilizer to grow strong.

While you definitely don't always have to be nice, by choosing kindness, you engage with a holy act of transforming your life and the rest of the world in the process. You fill other people's hearts and remind us all to be more present, generous, and caring towards one another. When you realize this, it makes a lot of sense to be kind to yourself.

Are you ever unkind to yourself?
How does that feel?
What would it feel like to be kind to yourself?

THE ALMIGHTY HUG

FOR AS LONG AS WE'VE BEEN ALIVE ON this planet, we've been using our arms, chests, and hands to hold, protect, and comfort one another. Whether we're cold, alone, sad, or scared, it's through the embrace of a hug that we instinctively and lovingly care for one another.

Similar to the healing benefits of crying, **hugging benefits the body** in numerous ways:

- Reduces stress and anxiety
- Strengthens the heart
- Boosts the immune system
- Strengthens communication skills
- Increases overall levels of happiness

Ironically, hugging is as rare, valuable, and endangered as crying. Like that same level of apprehension and resistance we feel crying in front of one another, many of us are more comfortable handshaking, high-fiving, or bro-hugging than we are welcoming each other in a warm and lasting embrace.

Why? Because we're afraid. We've lost trust in one another and are disconnected from experiencing connection and intimacy together. We've each been so hurt and wounded that exchanging a thorough hug feels too vulnerable, too exposing, and too generous.

This is something I learned by observing myself in intimate relationships over the years. When I was sad, hurting, and alone, I would more comfortably fire off words of protection and defense than allow myself to be honest and vulnerable. Rather than just saying, "I'm hurting. I'm sad. I need a hug," I would push away any form of tenderness and my soft fur would turn into the sharp thorns of a cactus. I would exclaim how my needs weren't met, how little I was receiving, and how unsupported I felt.

Yet, I was calling out those statements from a loud speaker that was squeezed between the bars of my cage. I was saying how much I needed comfort but not taking the courageous steps to receive it.

Have you ever tried hugging a cactus? It's really *not* that easy, or enjoyable. It's also not safe. Because most of us have been injured and bruised by the emotional wounds of life, if you're in a relationship with someone dressed up like a cactus who is saying "Why aren't you comforting me?", it can be confusing and scary to know what to do. You want to support them but you're dealing with your own lack of trust, and in an attempt to not get injured, you instinctively become protective and pull away.

The solution?

We must daringly take off the thorny cactus suit, show our vulnerable squishy selves, and *ask for a hug*. It may sound trivial and minuscule, but when you're protective and defensive, then stop, observe the truth of what's going on, feel the deeper pain, open yourself up to seeking support, voice what you need, and allow yourself to *receive* it—it's next level. Instantly, the mask falls crashing to the ground and your true and tender self has a warm invitation to emerge. Just one hug can truly transform you, the moment, and the future of any relationship.

A BREATH OF LIFE

BREATHING IS SOMETHING EACH OF US DO, and have done, steadily since the moment we arrived in our bodies. Like an instant refuel of energy and life force, we're constantly recharging ourselves with the rejuvenating gift of oxygen. However, like many aspects of the human life experience, we can become so distracted, busy, and swept away with our day-to-day lives that we quickly forget and under-appreciate breathing.

The reality is, each breath you bring into your body enters to your windpipes, passing through your bronchi, and eventually making its way into tiny air sacs. You don't just have a few of these magical little sacs of life—you have about 300 *million* of them. Around each of those sacs is a community of blood vessels called capillaries.

Every time you casually take in a breath of oxygen, the air passes through this sacred corridor and enters into the blood vessels. From there, the oxygen travels through your entire body and infuses each and every one of your cells. Not just a couple, not just a few—all 30 *trillion* of your cells. As this oxygen infuses your bloodstream with vitality, the carbon dioxide is discarded. How do you expel this waste product of carbon dioxide from your body? By exhaling—another holy act of existence that is often overlooked and taken for granted.

Why are we talking about all of this right now? Because breathing is one of the most powerful ways we can revitalize the consciousness inside us and reconnect with the present moment. Just by observing yourself taking in a breath of air, feeling it in your lungs, connecting with all that the oxygen is providing your body, then allowing it to release from your being—you get your needs met in multiple ways. Also, because the oxygen is providing your body (and life!) an invaluable service, you feel profoundly soothed and comforted when you realize that you're constantly being nourished and taken care of.

THE NATURAL WORLD

NOW, IF YOU REALLY WANT TO TAKE BREATHING to the next level and experience a profoundly healing exchange of connection, release, comfort, and presence—go outside. Leave your computer, your cell phone, your distractions, and go breathe some fresh air.

Because just as our bodies are engaged with this miraculous wonderland of oxygen, blood, carbon and life, so are the trees. In their own mystical way, they're doing something very similar. While our bodies are taking in oxygen and releasing a sludge of carbon dioxide, trees are completing the cycle and absorbing the carbon dioxide, then offering us the oxygen we need. In fact, just one tree will absorb more than 48 pounds of carbon dioxide per year and provide 260 pounds of oxygen—the very stuff we cannot live without. In that sense, trees are like mothers, surrounding us, nourishing us, and helping care for our bodies and needs.

So often, we humans feel untethered and out of control, as if we're unable to get our feet on the ground. Well, there's a reason we use the same term "grounding" as the *ground* of the earth's surface. Because it literally grounds us. It brings us back to balance and aligns us with our body and our center. In fact, when someone shares that they feel lost, anxious, and overwhelmed, I usually suggest they go outside and have a seat. Not in a chair, on the ground. Take the shoes off and let the body land on Earth.

For many of us, going outside and directly connecting with nature feels strange and foreign. In fact, a lot of us are intimidated by the natural world. It feels like a scary, wild, dirty, spider-crawling place. We feel much safer and more comfortable indoors with many layers of concrete and carpeting between our feet and the earth.

Why is that? Because at some point, we turned away from the wild within ourselves. The humanized and unconscious world we live in taught us to control, own, groom, cut, clear, and build. It taught us to fear the edge of the infinite power of the unknown and its greatness, to fear all that we can't understand or control. With that, we reach for axes, saws, and drills—anything that can help us feel in control and *seemingly* empowered in the presence of something so much greater than us.

It's that same need to "change what is" that has enraptured our minds, spirits, and bodies, forcing us to see the continual need for change in ourselves. Constantly, we are washed over by the belief that we need to groom, cut, clear, and build ourselves to feel maintained and known.

It's not true—you don't need to change anything about yourself to love yourself.

Just go be in nature and let its wild radiance and wisdom completely surround you. Let it speak to you in its warm voice of divine mother nurturance, reminding you how powerful, important, and equally insignificant you are. Let yourself be quieted and humbled by the perfection of its beauty, then, feel *all* of that inside yourself. You are the offspring of something powerful and divine, so feel its blood in your blood and accept the invitation to be welcomed into its lineage.

When you understand the mysterious and perfect beauty of the natural world, you become more aware of that wild, untamed beauty in yourself. The perfection that exists in you—just the way you are—without needing to change a thing.

How much time do you spend in nature?

What are some ways you could enhance and deepen your relationship with nature?

RECEIVING COMFORT
Meditative passage

If you're able, find a comfortable place to sit or lay down for this meditative passage. Allow a few moments of stillness before reading the words.

◆

1. Though your mind may be filled with thoughts and your heart aching with grief, you are welcome here.

   Are you afraid? Are you uncomfortable?

   Everything is welcome here. Every feeling, every doubt and every ounce of your body, is welcome here. Here, a place where judgment has no place and cruelty has no purpose.

   Allow yourself to bring in a full breath of life-giving oxygen...

   Then...
   Let it go.

2. To yourself, you may offer these words aloud:
   I allow myself in this moment to be as I am.
   I allow myself to feel safe where I am.
   I allow myself to feel accepted in who I am.

3. Look down at your hands and see the lines and the unique crevices acquired through the years. Then, turn your hands over and reflect on the many hugs, handshakes, shoulders, tears, and faces they have touched. Reflect on what radiant warmth comes from these hands and what all they are capable of. Remember what healing and nurturing comfort they have provided to so many others in need.

4. Then, gently lay a hand on your chest, facing inward, towards your heart.

5. Allow yourself to breathe in a full and clearing breath of life gifted from the trees, then out, releasing it. Allow your chest to feel the hand laid upon it and feel the warmth radiating inward towards your heart.

   Are you afraid?
   Love is more powerful than fear and your love is stronger in this moment.

   Are you uncomfortable?
   Your nurturance is more powerful than your pain and you are nurtured in this moment.

6. Then, as if your hand is a channel to the divine, feel your heart being filled with the soothing warmth of divine nurturance. Feel the light of love filling the inside of your body and shining so brightly that the outside of your body ignites in a light that is brighter than the sun.

   Everywhere warmth, everywhere light.
   Where the light touches, the fear evaporates.

   Everywhere warmth, everywhere light.
   Where the warmth reaches, the pain is soothed.

   Everywhere warmth.
   Everywhere light...

   Allow yourself to be here.
   In the warmth and in the light.
   Exactly as you are.

Worthy.
Whole.
Soothed.

This moment is your home and you belong here.

EXAMPLE CONVERSATION

Imagine that you've been frustrated and getting into a lot of arguments with your spouse. While a divorce feels like the best option, you're open to taking a deeper look at yourself to make sure there's nothing you could be doing differently to save the marriage. Finally, you're ready to look at yourself.

What's happening? What happened?

I: Can I describe what's going on?
W: My life is a mess and I hate my pathetic marriage.

Judgment awareness—let's try again.

I: What's going on?
W: My wife and I are talking about a divorce.
I: How long has this been going on?
W: Pretty steadily for the past eight months.
I: What do I sense is the cause of the problem?
W: Her. She's extremely annoying.

Judgment awareness—try again. Just stick to the facts.

I: What do I sense is the cause of the problem?
W: We argue a lot and we're both pretty unwilling to listen to one another. It's like we're always angry at one another.

I heard some key words like "argue" and "angry" that obviously symbolize the presence of defense, so I know there's pain hidden somewhere. I'll try to find it.

I: What do we argue about?
W: Everything.

I'm exaggerating and need to be more specific. I'll try again.

I: What do we argue about?
W: Honestly, it's really just me defending myself from her judgment and rude remarks. She says something untrue and mean and I just let her know she's wrong.

Ah-ha! "defending," another clue.

I: What kinds of things does she say?
W: She says I'm closed off and emotionally blocked. She says I'm not responsive or supportive when she's going through it.

Ok, we're getting in deeper. We're talking about feelings.

How am I feeling? Where am I hurting? Where am I afraid?

I: Do I consider myself closed off and emotionally blocked?
W: Maybe. Sometimes. It's always been hard for me to express emotions.
I: Do I recall a time when I was able to express my emotions?
W: Not really. Maybe when I was a kid. It's been a long time. To be honest, my lack of emotion has been the downfall to most of my relationships. I start out loving and affectionate, then over time I just close up.
I: When did I emotionally close up with my wife?
W: It started happening a couple of years ago.
I: Can I recall any traumatic or jarring experiences that happened around that time?
W: Well, yeah, I guess so. It wasn't a big deal but she got pregnant and had a miscarriage. We'd been doing in-vitro treatments to try and get pregnant. That was our last chance so yeah, we don't have any kids now and that was all pretty tough.

Ok, interesting. I just felt an energy shift. My stomach is beginning to turn and my lungs are tightening. I think I found a wound. I wonder if I'm still in pain and if my needs were met. I'll try and find out more.

I: What was that experience like for me?
W: Hard. It was harder for her so I just tried to stay strong and be a

rock for her through it. She was a wreck and I was just trying to keep everything together.

I: How was she processing the heartache and loss of losing the baby?

W: She cried a lot. Like, every day, for months. It was tough and actually a really sad time for both of us.

I: How did I support her when she was crying?

W: I just made sure she could take that time off of work so I worked every day and made sure we had food on the table.

I: How was I able to process my own grief?

W: I just worked and tried to stay busy.

Uh oh. That sounds like avoidance. Let's rephrase that.

I: Have I processed my grief about the miscarriage and not being able to have kids?

W: I don't know. It's hard for me to tell. I have trouble feeling anything so I don't know what I'm feeling. Really, I just feel numb most of the time. When I'm not numb, I feel frustrated.

I: Do we talk about any of this?

W: No. We did for a little while then we stopped. It was too painful. We just focused on other stuff and life got pretty busy with work so yeah, we don't really talk — unless we're arguing, which we do all the time.

So, we're both defensive and both trying to protect ourselves from the pain through avoidance. This must mean that we're both hurting, afraid, and not getting our needs met. Hmmm. That doesn't work. Neither one of us seems to be figuring out how to get through this. Maybe we need some help.

I'm not alone. I can engage with the people and world around me.

I: Do I need to process all of this and talk about it with someone?
W: Yeah, I think I probably do.
I: Do I need to grieve?
W: Probably. I'm not sure how to do it but I'm open to learning.

I don't need to hold onto this any longer. I can let it go.

I: Am I comfortable allowing myself to cry?
W: No, not yet.
I: Ok. What about pulling my guitar out of storage and dusting it off? Maybe I could write a song in honor of the child who never had the chance to be born.
W: Yeah. That sounds very sad but I need to do something. I'm pretty roughed up inside and feel like I'm carrying a huge weight in my chest.

I'm ready to be comfortable and receive the care I need.

I: What about allowing myself to feel comfort? Am I willing to welcome comfort and nurturance into my life?
W: What? Like curl up in fuzzy blankets and write in my diary? No, not interested.

Judgment awareness. Try again.

I: Since I feel so uncomfortable, am I willing to take action to feel comfortable?
W: I guess so. I'm not sure what that would look like. I'd be open to calling someone to come out and fix the hot tub. That was always a way that my wife and I would relax. We haven't done that in years.
I: What about sharing all of this with my wife and telling her how I'm really feeling and hurting?
W: I don't know. I'm not great at talking about my feelings.
I: What if it would save our marriage?
W: Ok. I will. I'm not sure how she'll respond but she always likes it when I'm sensitive so she might be grateful I'm finally ready to talk.
I: If she's not able to talk about it, am I willing to seek other counsel and support?
W: I think so. I don't think of myself as messed up, but I've definitely got some stuff to work through. I can't keep it all buried inside forever. I'm willing to try.

COMFORTING TOOLS

When I'm in need of comfort, I can choose something that leads to long-term comfort in myself, rather than a temporary, fleeting sensation of comfort.

◆

I have the ability to be loving, nurturing, and comforting. There is no reason why I don't deserve to feel this for and from myself. I give myself permission to comfort myself when needed.

◆

Though it may feel foreign and unnatural to prioritize my own needs, I will try to create a quiet, meditative space in my life to feel centered, grounded, and relaxed.

◆

*Sleep isn't just something I have to do—
it's something I get to do and
I give myself permission to receive it.*

◆

Being warm brings me to a calm and nurturing space of safety. When I'm in need of comfort, I can allow myself to be comforted through the experience of physical warmth.

◆

I don't have to struggle. I can ask for a hug.

◆

Breathing is one of the most necessary and remarkable acts that we living beings are fortunate enough to engage in. When I need to breathe, I can go outside and be immersed in a sacred and rejuvenating exchange with trees.

*I vow to better care for myself,
so that I may better care for you.*

14.
LOVE

To experience deep joy, admiration, and respect.

I UNDERSTAND THAT MARRIAGE IS SOMETHING a lot of people consider romantic and highly sought-after, but not me. At least, I didn't feel that way for a long time. Having experienced my parents' divorce and gaining a strong aversion to feeling controlled or trapped, getting married seemed like a big, bad idea. Like an opportunity for inflated expectations to explode into a million messy pieces, and for a lot of money to get wasted in the process. I also considered myself fiercely independent and had no intentions of allowing anyone to weaken my stance.

Withdrawn due his own distaste for *marriage* as just another word for "divorce," Kurt spent much of his life with one foot in and one foot out when it came to relationships. Like me, he had "street skills," and both of us were seemingly content in not needing (or trusting) anyone else to rely on or fulfill us.

Perhaps that's why it was so surprising when after almost a decade of walking side by side, he magically found it in himself to propose to me and in response, I crumbled into an instantaneous, sobbing pool of "yes!" Somehow, we had crawled through enough deserts and scaled enough mountains of emotion to feel unquestionably solid and secure in one another's arms. Finally, I was safe to unfurl myself from commit-o-phobia and welcome a new understanding of love and commitment. Rather than constantly guarding and defending my ego, I felt a sense of wholeness, abundance, and trust.

Could I have gone to this mystical place of love and union before Kurt and I had reached our 10-year mark? Yes, it's possible. Though, what allowed me to finally feel confident in stepping forward into matrimony was the trust and respect I had gained in *myself*.

For so long, I wasn't enough and didn't have enough, and now I *knew* I was enough. I knew in my entire being that I was worthy and that I deserved respect and honor. I also knew it wasn't Kurt's responsibility to provide that for me; that it was something I needed to witness, feel, and activate in myself, and I did. Every day, I devotedly practiced the art of getting my needs met. Because of that, I felt safe and trusting within myself. No longer needing to protect my heart, I was finally ready to share it.

The result? A deep sense of trust and allowance in exchanging my love with someone else.

Since neither of us ever imagined getting married, we weren't set on a white dress or diamond rings. Getting married felt more like an acknowledgment of how far we'd come than an attachment to where we were going. It felt like a celebration of love, and with that, an opportunity to circle with our loved ones and toast to the bittersweet beauty and evanescence of life.

I don't imagine my mom understood the storyline of what was going on, but it was clear from her bewildered smile and blossomed energy that she felt the sacred beauty of the experience.

As she doesn't have the mental capacity to consciously lie, it's nearly impossible for her to do so. Dementia plagued her with the holy curse of presence and honesty. With that, her expressions and reactions are often very telling of whether something is authentic or not. I suppose like a child or a life form from another planet—unaware of customs or the perpetual sugar coating on every human word and phrase—she is a meter for the wild and authentic realness of life.

That's why it was so heartbreakingly beautiful when she looked admiringly at the kind and gentle man sitting beside her and lovingly said, "I don't know who he is but he's a good man."

My dad. Her second husband. The man with whom she co-wrote her most infamous tale of suffering. The man whose painful past was washed away in the river of time alongside her own and whose wisdom and sincere love shined through as he led us in a sacred Hindu prayer at our beloved wedding ceremony (this chapter's poetic inspiration).

How was my father so different from my mother? How are any of us so different from one another when each of us has experienced the gut-wrenching pain of being wounded and each of us knows the deep ache of suffering? If I'm unwilling or unable to see the divine in those who have wounded me, I become the wounder and I remain the wounded. I remain suffering, scrambling, and reaching for my shield of defense every time my cage opens and lets any light in to my trembling heart.

I don't deserve that. I've suffered *long enough*. I'm done trudging through the thick swamp of struggle and swallowing swords marked with the same blood of my great, great, great grandparents.

It stops here. I choose a different path.

When I feel the walls of insecurity enclose around me, I choose to remain present and lean into the light of trust, rather than be engulfed by clouds of fear.

When I feel lost and alone, untethered from the light within me, I choose to wrap myself in the warmth of my own embrace and whisper, "I'm here, you're not alone," rather than telling myself to "go away."

When I feel the fire inside me begin to rage, I choose to utilize those flames as fuel for connection, compassion, and forgiveness, rather than fiercely defending myself and being scarred by the burns.

I am done being afraid. I choose love and *that* is what love is. It's a decision to boldly look into the eyes of fear and be stronger than it. Rather than run away in despair, we stand strong and solid, and we open our hearts even more.

Examples of what LOVE feels like:
- Respect
- Honor
- Compassion
- Forgiveness
- Appreciation
- Care
- Joy

When we have reached the place of having looked at our wounds and felt our own pain, offered ourselves the benefit of reaching out and reaching in, let go of what doesn't serve and feel worthy enough to receive what does—love is there. Love is the powerful force of strength that comes of that. As if all the steps prior were to prepare us for our purpose. Love is what our hearts were designed to do.

Love is also the frequency of exchange. Connection encourages us to open ourselves to the channels uniting us with the world around us. Release gives us permission to move energy out of those channels. Comfort lets us receive energy inward. Then, love is the flow that breathes the nutrient-rich energy in and out of our beings.

Rather than constantly patching up holes and tending to our broken pieces—when we're ready to fearlessly accept and love ourselves—we're fulfilled enough to share that greatness of life with others. This is deeply gratifying because it's something we need. We need to love. We *need* to receive it and we *need* to give it.

From this sincere place of wholeness, strength, and trust, our internal chant becomes, "Love is stronger than fear. I choose love."

Like a powerful step upward, into the realms of consciousness and light, love is the natural progression along our journey.

> Observe: What's happening right now? What happened in the past?
> Feel: How am I feeling? Where am I hurting? Where am I afraid?
> Connect: I'm not alone. I can engage with the world around me.
> Release: I don't need to hold onto this any longer. I can let it go.
> Comfort: I'm ready to be comfortable and receive the care I need.
> Love: Love is stronger than fear. I choose love.

Does choosing love sound like a huge feat that requires years of training and persevering and struggling? It doesn't need to. Love is something our hearts were designed to do and because of that, choosing love is the most natural, effortless, and enjoyable thing we can experience.

There's no need to sculpt ourselves into something we're not in order to access love. We just have to be ourselves and let the true nature of our beings shine through. We are not the dark cloud that blocks the sun; we are the radiant light of love that burns regardless of it.

With that, let's journey into the heart of love!

A POWERFUL FORCE

WHEN WRITING THIS BOOK, I WANTED TO PUT "love" in the title. I wanted to say "The Path from Fear to Love" or "How to Stop Suffering and Remember to Love Yourself." Then, after speaking with my dear friend Kelly Notaras (my mentor and coach throughout the beginning stages of writing), I learned that "love" isn't entirely popular. "It's kind of a cliché term that not everyone resonates with," she said.

"What?" I asked, "Who doesn't *love* love?"

Well, as it turns out, a lot of us. Even though we all share a deep need for love, many of us have become so disconnected from it that we don't light up when we hear the word. Instead, we think of silly Valentine's Day cards and tie-dyed hippies waving peace signs. Somehow, love became the uncool kid that people make fun of.

I see it differently. Love is pretty much the greatest, most powerful force that any of us will ever come in contact with—*ever*. It's mysterious and infinite, something that can't be contained or understood. In a sense, love is the essence of consciousness that gives a name to the energy exchanged through the network of connection. It's the healing glow of warmth that channels through the beam of divine mother nurturance. Like the food and water that our bodies rely on to live, love is the nutrient that our spirits must have in order to survive.

Does that sound really far out? Too gushy and woo-woo?

It shouldn't. Feeling united and connected with yourself and those around you in deep, benevolent warmth and intimacy is something you *need*. You need love and it should never be something that you frown upon or distance yourself from.

However, we often do. We're apprehensive to hug, we're embarrassed to cry, we're nervous to say "I love you," and most of us feel uncomfortable if a stranger smiles at us, thinking "Why are they looking at me? What do they want from me?"

When did this happen? At what point did we stop letting ourselves be vulnerable, open, trusting, and generous with our hearts? When did we give up on love and one another?

The answer is: when we were wounded and we learned that it's not safe to love—that's when. When we built up cages around our hearts and felt safer behind the thick walls of our egos than being united and connected to one another.

Well, guess what? It's not working. For too long, we've been choosing fear instead of love, and it's a failed experiment. Fear is not sustainable and it's not serving us as a whole. It's not evolving our species or expanding us into higher levels of awareness. Fear is actually killing us and destroying the planet, and if we want to do something to change that—something to save our species from annihilation—we have to choose love. We have to all step out of this big, huge cage and free ourselves.

When we decide to contradict the narrative that portrays love, tenderness, and sensitivity as weak, we reclaim our power. We honor our birth right to be open and caring, and we step into the power of our presence. Just as unconsciousness can't exist in the presence of consciousness, fear cannot thrive when there is love to outshine it. Love is the anecdote to the poison of fear, and it's time we cure ourselves of this deadly sickness.

SELF-LOVE

HAVE YOU EVER BEEN REALLY THIRSTY and tried drinking water from rain? Maybe you figured if you opened your mouth really wide, faced the sky, and waited for a *really* long time, it might work? Yeah, me too. It doesn't really work. Accessing love for ourselves can feel similar. Even though love is seemingly everywhere around us, pouring from the sky, we can still feel deprived, like we can't get enough.

If you have trouble loving yourself and feel parched, it's ok. It's not your fault and there's nothing wrong with you. The reality is, you might not know how. Maybe you were raised by wounded and hurting parents who didn't know how to love themselves and offered few examples of what healthy self-love looks like? Maybe you've been put down and judged for so long that you don't find anything noteworthy or lovable about yourself? Maybe someone from your past led you to believe you weren't worthy of acknowledgment unless you looked and acted a certain way and now you feel undeserving and unlovable?

Whatever it is, you may have learned (again and again) that you're not worthy of receiving the honor, respect, and appreciation that comes with love, not even from yourself.

As sad and alienating as that may feel, you're not alone. In fact, studies have shown that on average, 40% of people feel they don't have time to love and care for themselves, and 67% of people feel that their need for personal care is not as important as other's needs. If you feel anything like I did for a long time, loving yourself might mean pushing through a wall of shame and guilt to feel worthy of receiving care.

If 40% of us feel similar and don't feel we have time or ability to care for ourselves, we're not prioritizing our own wellbeing, which means we're not taking action to honor and respect ourselves. We're not showing ourselves love. If we did, we would prioritize our needs and take better care of ourselves. This is a systemic problem affecting much of our species.

You can get a very telling glimpse into how unhealthy our collective understanding of self-love is by looking up "**self-love**" in the dictionary:

> : the instinct by which one's actions are directed to the promotion of one's own welfare or well-being, *especially an excessive regard for one's own advantage.*
>
> : conceit; vanity; narcissism

What does that mean? Does it mean that to acknowledge and appreciate myself, I'm taking advantage of others and potentially causing them harm? Does it mean I'm conceited and vain?

If so, I can tell you right now I will do *everything* in my power to not let that happen. Because I don't want to hurt anyone and I don't want to be a conceited narcissist, I will actively not show myself love.

In other words, the narrative would be: *I don't want you to judge me or feel hurt by seeing me giving and receiving love to myself. Because I love you and I want you to love me too, I will make the choice to eliminate love for myself to try and receive love from you. I feel like I have to choose so I'm choosing your love for me over my own love for me.*

Kind of twisted, huh? It is, and sadly, it's very common. We deprive ourselves of our own respect, admiration, and honor because it makes us feel *less* conceited and *less* threatening; more assured that we are safely accepted and included in the pack. Instead of basking in the healthy and rejuvenating light of our own love, we stay powerless and hidden in the shadows of shame and insecurity. With our heads down and our confidence deprived, we hold ourselves in a state of *need*ing attention, approval, and acceptance from others. Essentially, we try to get our needs met by *not* loving ourselves and get stuck in a cyclical pattern of relying on the love received from others, rather than accessing it ourselves.

Frankly, this doesn't work. Relying on others in order to experience the love you need only keeps you held down, insecure, and in a prolonged state of need and that's not what *you* need. What you need is to be freed from all that suffering and feel wholly loved and respected within yourself, *regardless* of what anyone else is or isn't providing for you.

By saying "I love and appreciate who I am," you're not conceited, vain, or narcissistic. You're conscious, caring, and honestly speaking words of truth *to* yourself *from* your true self. Each time you're able to do this, you contradict the societal misbelief that self-love is bad and teach us all how to do it in the process. You shine brighter and make the whole world shine just a little bit brighter and feel just a little bit more love.

THE WOMAN IN THE MIRROR

YEARS AGO, I WAS TRYING ON CLOTHES WITH a close friend. She had just put on a pair of pants and while I thought she looked wonderful, she immediately began laying into how bad she looked and how fat she was. She turned back and forth, spinning her body to let her glued eyes see every single angle possible in the mirror, and with each new angle, a negative remark emerged.

I tried to get a word in but my voice didn't cut through, like I was trying to break up a dog fight. Each of her statements were harsh but also extremely sarcastic, which made it challenging for me to not agree, since sarcasm has a way of luring the spectator into non-consensual camaraderie.

Inside, I felt the heat of fierceness. Rather than relating to the woman beside me cracking snide remarks, I felt extreme concern for my beloved friend in the mirror who was being obliterated by the swinging claws.

Suddenly, I said, "Stop. Stop making fun of her. Stop saying those things. I love her. I love that woman," pointing to the innocent woman in the mirror. "She's my friend. Stop doing that to her." As if plunging a broomstick in the center of the fight, I broke it up. She stopped, like she was woken from a trance and looked at me, then back at herself, as if she was realizing just then, "Oh wait, that's a real person in there."

Maybe no one had ever stood up for her when she was previously picked on and abused, or maybe she just needed to be reminded that she deserved better? Maybe she had temporarily forgotten all the challenges she had been through and all the wounds she had experienced through life? I hadn't forgotten. I knew she was a good person who had worked hard and moved mountains to get through life's suffering. I wasn't about to let anyone else hurt her—*not even her.*

To empower our hearts, we have to stop hurting ourselves and stop forcing ourselves to suffer. Rather than continually seeing ourselves as less important, less pure, less talented, less capable, and less deserving of love than others, we have to know the truth: that each of us are equal and deserving of love as anyone and everyone else in this world.

Maybe your parents weren't able to love themselves or you enough to be an example of love, but that doesn't stop you from being stronger, more courageous, and more self-loving than anything either of you have ever known.

When you awaken true self-love, *you* become a profoundly loving and accepting parent to yourself. You begin taking care of yourself the way a nurturing, responsible mother or father would care for its young: fiercely, devotedly, and *unconditionally*. With that sincere devotion, you stop abandoning yourself in times of crisis and lean in closer instead.

The deep trust and security that is birthed within that connection begins transforming any feelings of shame, insecurity, and self-doubt. You reconnect with yourself the way you've needed to do since the pain of division broke you apart so long ago. You internally unite as a whole, complete being.

Instead of seeing yourself as the problem, you begin to realize that you're the solution. You're the reason you're alive and you deserve to be held, accepted, appreciated, respected, honored, forgiven, and loved wholeheartedly.

What would it feel like to honor and care for yourself the way a genuine and true friend would?

STEPPING BACK WITH LOVE

IN THIS NEW-FOUND SPACE OF SELF-APPRECIATION and acceptance, you become less inclined to stay in situations where others don't value you to the same degree. With that, you may find that you don't resonate with certain friends and peers as much as you once did. Rather than enjoying time with them like you used to, your connection may feel like a monotonous job you're exhausted with, except you're *not* getting paid.

While before, you may have mirrored one another in the seemingly fun-filled acts of distraction, temporary comfort, negative venting, and making judgments about someone else—now, you're not resonating with it. You realize those hangout sessions are pulling you away from the true friend who really *understands* you; who listens, honors and genuinely respects you: *yourself* (well, and your cat or dog).

What's the solution?

"No."

Rather than always feeling the need to say "yes," "ok," or "sure" and stepping into activities that you're not genuinely enthusiastic about, you can use the power of your voice to do what's right for you and take a step back. You have the ability and permission to use *discernment* and make decisions that are the wisest, healthiest, and best ones for you.

Instead of acting out of fear and insecurity, agreeing to do something you'd rather not do, you reach into the deep sense of trust within you and make a decision from there. You make a decision that feels aligned with your intuition, morals, and deeper knowing. The key to doing this successfully is doing so without judgment.

Imagine you've been dating someone for the past year and while there are a lot of things you really appreciate about the relationship, you're beginning to notice that your health is declining. They tend to spend most nights out late, so to spend time together, you're staying out late too. You've mentioned numerous times that you'd love to spend time together without partying and they become defensive. On more than one occasion, you've been in situations where they were driving drunk, and while you really do love them, you're beginning to feel that unless they join you in taking better care of your health, it may be a relationship you need to step back from.

In this moment, there's no need to judge them or scrutinize them for their personal struggle. You know that everyone is hurting and a lot of us tend to that pain by numbing ourselves and avoiding it. However, through discernment, you can decide whether it's healthy and right for *you* to engage in or not. You're being a good, solid, caring, and responsible friend to yourself. You are discerning between what feels right and what feels wrong.

While before, you may have felt insecure and in need of inclusion, attention, and reassurance that you're loved—now you love yourself. You realize your needs are being met in other, more constructive ways, and you aren't reliant on spending time with someone who doesn't fulfill you.

This practice of discernment—stepping away from others and closer to ourselves—is something I refer to as *stepping back with love*. It means we're willing and able to understand our needs and love ourselves enough to be honored in situations that aren't healthy, safe, or constructive for our wellbeing.

Here are some ways to **step back with Love**:
- Say "no" to an invitation
- Turn off your phone
- Be honest about how you feel
- Stand up for yourself (to others and to yourself)
- Speak from your heart
- Be silent and listen instead
- Do nothing
- Walk away

It may feel awkward and uncomfortable at first, and *that's ok*. Remember, trust is a tree that takes time to grow and it may take a while before you reach best friend status with yourself. However, each time you honor your truth, speak it, and show up for yourself, your inner best friend gains trust and belief in you. The connection within you grows stronger and you feel more solid in your voice and more confident in your relationship with yourself.

If the act of honoring and speaking up for yourself threatens your relationships, friendships, and aspects of your life, that's something you may want to look at. Ideally, you are surrounded by people who see your strength, appreciate it, respect it, and honor it. If they don't, you may need to step back with love.

It's important to remember: we can step forward in love or step back with love but never close ourselves to love. With compassion in our hearts, we can trust that by honoring and respecting our own needs in an authentic way, we encourage others to do the same, and that's something we want. We want everyone to experience a deeper sense of love and connection within themselves.

What are some areas in your life you may need to step back from to step closer to yourself?

THE GIFT OF COMPASSION

IF INTUITION IS THE ABILITY TO ACCESS AND understand a sacred, unseen world, compassion is the reason we've been gifted that ability.

Also known as *sympathetic consciousness*, compassion is our ability to feel and sympathize for the experiences and hardships of others. It's the awareness that: *You are hurting and I see you. I feel you. I too have been hurt and I know what pain feels like. It's very uncomfortable and I don't want you to suffer. I have a deep desire for your pain and suffering to end. You deserve to experience love.*

Unfortunately, because so many of us are living paycheck to paycheck, caught in an emotional state of survival, we don't feel we have enough for ourselves, let alone enough to share with others. So, we often avoid looking at or feeling the needs and suffering of others. As if to say to ourselves, "I've got too much to take care of in my own life and not enough time, energy, or emotional capacity to offer my valuable care to anyone else." Drawn in by the warm relief in the cage, we get caught in a pattern of avoidance and solely look at our own needs, our own dilemmas, and our own need for fulfillment.

If only we knew the truth that compassion doesn't take anything from us. It's a powerful and sacred river that flows around both the receiver *and* the giver. When we're willing to deeply care for something or someone who's hurting, we allow the healing light of consciousness to move through our beings and we too are healed.

Just think of the many people in this world who so courageously and devotedly offer themselves as support for others who are alone, struggling, and in need. On a daily basis, millions of compassionate and caregiving mothers, fathers, grandparents, step-dads, friends, daughters, neighbors, nurses, paramedics, and strangers are generously giving themselves to lessen the suffering of the world.

There are children who are nursing their mothers through cancer and grandparents who are signing papers to adopt grandchildren. There are teenagers parenting younger siblings and neighbors crawling into tiny spaces to rescue stranded kittens. There are teachers strategizing plans to save students from abusive homes and kids lifting up classmates who are bullied on the playground. There are people opening their homes to foster children and others who are fostering homeless animals.

There are such *good* people in this world doing so many good things and for the most part, they do it without any recognition at all. They offer themselves in service to make this world a better place because they care. Because they know what it feels like to be in pain and guided by compassion, they want to do something to help.

In ways, compassion is magical stardust that brings us out of protection and into the light of love. If we imagine this journey of empowerment like a board game, compassion lets us *move ahead 10 spaces*. It's a shortcut to experiencing genuine and sincere love, forgiveness, and connection, which is the pure, healing light of consciousness.

EMPATHY AND FEELING BAD

WHAT IF YOU FEEL RESISTANT TO AND intimidated about feeling compassion? What if when you've allowed yourself to really witness and feel the pain of others in the past, you end up feeling bad for people?

Well, there is a difference between *feeling compassion* for someone and *feeling bad* for someone. If we feel bad for someone, we are literally feeling bad for them. Somewhere inside, we think that to support them in their suffering, we need to feel bad *with* them and *for* them. In an attempt to show this, we often say, "I'm sorry," or "I feel sorry for you" when someone's going through hardship.

What does **sorry** mean? It means: **sorrow, sadness, distress, and regret.**

Basically, feeling *bad*.

I did this for a very long time. I felt bad *for* women who had been raped. I felt bad *for* the trees being cut down. I felt bad *for* soldiers coming back traumatized from war. I felt bad *for* animals being unfairly killed. I felt bad *for* children without enough food.

I felt bad because to me, that was showing care. That was showing love. When so many people are ignoring and turning away from the suffering, I didn't want to be another person abandoning those who needed help. So,

I joined them in the suffering. I thought that feeling bad *with* them was supporting them. With that came depression and feelings of judgment, frustration, and fire. I was angry at those causing harm and inflicting wounds. I was ready to fight against anyone I perceived as villainous. In many ways, that anger led me to generate and create more wounds, which wasn't helping anyone.

We don't help others by crawling down into the trenches of suffering and hurting alongside them. We don't need to join in other people's pain and hatred to prove our support and devotion to them. We don't need to wear similar bruises to feel camaraderie and connection. How are we going to truly help others if we're limping along ourselves? Two sufferers don't make a solution.

If you really want to actively help someone, overcome your own fears and be courageously present. As uncomfortable and distressing as it is to be present with someone grieving or hurting, it's the best thing we can do *for* them. You may feel the ache of pain, anger, and sadness in your heart for what they're going through, but because suffering isn't their true home (or yours either), you don't need to feed into the story of this being who they are. You can help them without offering unnecessary apologies and taking on their suffering as though you were the one who caused it (unless you actually *were* the one who caused it, in which case, offer a necessary apology).

Then, get out of your cage and offer them a hand. Instead of saying, "I'm so sorry that happened; that guy's a jerk. I hate him too," you might say "My heart aches for what you're going through. I feel so much compassion for the pain you must be experiencing right now. You're not alone through this; I'm right here to support you. Can you think of anything you might need right now? Would it feel helpful to talk about it?"

SELF-COMPASSION

WITH THIS SAID, THERE IS A LIMIT AND capacity to what we can physically and energetically provide and offer others. With my mother, my compassion for her state of dementia led me to be her long-term caregiver, but sometimes the act of showing up for her is exhausting and draining. As a family, we don't have the finances to afford another caregiver, so we do it ourselves, and with that duty comes a lot of physical and emotional effort. At times, I feel tired, sad, and spent. I feel bad and like there's no choice. Like other caregivers, nurses, doctors, dentists, and people working hard to relieve other people's suffering, it seems there is a necessary element of personal suffering required.

What then? We know it's not sustainable to suffer in honor of another's suffering, yet what if it feels like we *have* to suffer to actively care for someone?

The answer? Self-compassion. This is the necessary act of weaving together *compassion* and *self-love* to reach a place of deep care and love for the self. It involves being *discerning* about whether our actions to help others are constructive or destructive. If we're stressed, sleep-deprived, anxious, or filled with unwept grief, our actions are not sustainable. At some point, we have to prioritize our needs as much as other people's needs. We have to respect, honor, and care for ourselves.

Otherwise, we crawl around in the trenches of suffering and end up broken and hurting alongside whoever we're trying to help. That doesn't work, nor is it sustainable. Gradually, we break down until we're the ones laying in bed requiring someone to care for us. And, the cycle of suffering continues.

If we really want to make the world a better place, we have to feel compassion for everyone, including ourselves. We have to look deep into our own eyes and say, "You are hurting and I see you. I feel you. I don't want you to suffer. I have a deep desire for your pain and suffering to end. You deserve to experience love."

When you can feel the pain you're in, and understand the innocent being in need within, then you realize you're no different from anyone who is hurting and deserves care. You don't need to *feel sorry* for yourself or continually give every ounce of your energy, getting caught in the wave of thinking that suffering is who you are. If you're hurting, you need love. You need support. You need to know you're not alone and more than anyone, *you* need to take action and be the one who shows up for yourself and provides that warm, heartfelt compassion and care.

How do you do it? Maybe you have to ask for help. Maybe you have to take some time off. Maybe you have to change your profession. Maybe you have to take a step back, towards yourself, and make sure you're being cared for as much as everyone else in your life.

When you're able to do this—fully open your heart to compassionately caring for yourself—you transform, and so does your understanding of the world. You realize that love is a medicine and it's shared through compassion. The more you access it, the more access you have to it and the more abundant it becomes. No longer living in scarcity, you realize how easy it is to obtain, and how much you want to share it with others.

THE LIGHT OF FORGIVENESS

WITH COMPASSION, OFTEN COMES THE SACRED and holy light of forgiveness. There have been so many moments in our time together that I've wanted to talk about forgiveness. I really wanted to mention it when we were talking about feeling and when we were immersed in the benefits of release, but I waited. I held back until now because as much as forgiveness has the power to completely and instantly transform our entire state of suffering, it takes time. It's like a flower that gradually opens at its own pace, when it's ready. It's not something that can be rushed, strategized, or forced.

There are many, many reasons why forgiveness is essential and could truly change your life. However, encouragement may not be what you need. If you're not ready to forgive someone who caused you great pain, you don't have to and you definitely don't need to feel shame for not being ready. When it's time, it will happen naturally and maybe even without you realizing it's happening. You may just wake up one day and feel a little lighter.

With that said, I do want to share some insights about forgiveness that I've found very helpful over the years. You're welcome to tuck them into your satchel of wisdom if and when you're ready for support someday...

Forgiveness isn't about the other person.

I know it feels like it's about the other person. They're the one who caused you harm and it was their fault. *They're* the one who messed up and *you're* the one who had to suffer this whole time. If you forgive them, you'll somehow let them off the hook and they won't experience the suffering they deserve. It makes sense. I completely understand where you're coming from. You don't feel that *they* deserve the soothing relief of forgiveness, but it's not about them; it's about you.

You're gripping onto the cage and not giving up the fight. By not forgiving them, they're not the only one who is bound to the suffering—*you* are. You're holding *yourself* in a state of struggle to keep them there, and as righteous and worthy a cause as it may seem, it's not. Your incredible, wise, and wonderful self doesn't deserve to be held down by any more pain and suffering, even your own. And chances are, the person who wounded you is already suffering, regardless of whether you forgive them or not.

At some point, sooner or later, your heart will experience the clarity of compassion and if it doesn't happen while that person is still alive, you'll end up in regret. You'll spend years trying to forgive yourself for not forgiving them, which is a very sad place to be. You have permission to relieve yourself of the burden. Be a good friend to yourself and let that pain go.

Forgiving improves your health.

The rewarding act of forgiveness is something that will greatly benefit your mind, your body, and your health. Because there's so much pain and strain when we don't release something (remember, emotional constipation), our physical body feels the impact of that stress and tension. We hold onto the heavy and toxic burden of emotional pain and it weighs on our hearts and damages our bodies.

Personally, there have been numerous times when I was deeply concerned that something was physically wrong with me, that I was very ill. Shortly after I came to the place of release and forgiveness for someone, all of my symptoms instantly subsided. In fact, John Hopkins Medicine published an article showing that when we forgive, our physical body has a lower risk of heart attack, improved cholesterol levels, better sleep, reduced physical pain, lower blood pressure, and a decrease in anxiety, depression, and stress. It literally could save your life to forgive someone else!

Forgiveness isn't tied to trust.

Perhaps what makes it so hard to forgive someone is that you feel the person isn't trustworthy. Maybe somewhere inside, you're concerned that by forgiving them, it means you're inviting them and their destructive ways back into your life. It's not true. Forgiveness is an energetic transformation that happens within you, so you're not required to verbalize it or include anyone else in your process.

The truth is, some people *are* dangerous. They're extremely unconscious and not safe to be around. If the person who has wounded you is dangerous, it's wise *not* to experience further connection with them. However, just because you're forgiving them, it doesn't mean you have to trust them and re-establish a relationship now. You can simply make the internal decision to welcome compassion and *let it go* inside without including the person in the conversation.

Forgive it back.

Perhaps just hearing the word for*give* might make it feel like forgiveness requires us to give something. As though we (already feeling depleted, exhausted, and drained) have to give up part of ourselves and have even more taken away from us. Gratefully, that isn't the case. When we forgive, we actually *don't* get depleted. We may think that by not forgiving, we're keeping ourselves safe and ensuring that our love reserve is plentiful, but what we're really holding onto isn't love; it's pain.

Because compassion opens a channel of divine warmth and love into our beings, when we engage in forgiveness and allow the pain to be transmuted into love, we free ourselves from the suffering. We let go of the pain and feel lighter and freer. In that sense, forgiving is like *forgiving it back*. Forgiving back the pain that you're not indebted to carry any longer.

The story of your life will be just fine without a villain.

Sometimes, it's hard to see in the moment, but a lot of us continually play out a narrative that there are "bad" guys in our lives. Whether it's your neighbor, your ex-husband, your sister, the president of your country, or your mother-in-law, the story of your life likely has some shady, evil, and mean characters in it. With that, you are continually identifying with the role of hero and victim, fighting for justice and defending yourself at all costs. "It's his fault I feel this way." "If we actually had a good president, I wouldn't have to be so angry all the time." "If your mother would only mind her own business, our marriage wouldn't be struggling right now."

Yes, it's understandable. There are people in this world who are hurting and with that, they cause a lot of pain to others. However, as long as your mother-in-law is the bane of your existence, your marriage has a focus outside itself—somewhere you can pinpoint the cause of your problems without holding yourself accountable for being part of the problem. Well, what happens when she sends you a warm greeting card to apologize? You forgive her and your resentment lifts. Suddenly, she's not the bad guy. So, who is?

It's just a matter of time before your sister says something that makes your blood boil and miraculously, she's the new bad guy. A week later, you realize, "Wait, she's not so bad," and suddenly, you've forgiven your sister and become increasingly irritated at your husband. Now *he's* the bad guy! One by one, day by day, you constantly cast and rotate various characters as the villain in your story, and you give yourself the role of innocent victim.

Guess what? You don't need to do that. You don't need to have any villains in your story. If you let yourself feel compassion and forgiveness for everyone (including yourself), you won't suddenly disintegrate into dust. You'll actually be more comfortable in yourself, and you'll realize that the story of your life is a lot more fun, safe, and enjoyable without any bad guys or villains in it!

We become the person we never forgave.

If you think of pain like a hot potato, no one wants to hold it—everyone wants to keep throwing it around for someone else to hold. Your grandpa didn't want it, so he passed it to your dad. Your dad didn't want it, so he passed it to your brother. Your brother didn't want it, so he passed it to you. What are you going to do with it? Are you going to blame your dad for being the reason for your suffering? Are you going to resent your brother for the rest of your life? Are you going to hold onto it until your kids are old enough for you to throw it at them? What about your kid's kids? Do you imagine they want to hold it?

No, they don't. None of us do. None of us *want* to be burdened by the destructive pain that has been burning the family line for generations and generations. However, that's exactly what happens when we don't let it go. We hold onto it and we become it. We become the heat, the anger, the resentment, and the fire. We become the person we never forgave.

What happens if you hold onto it forever and try not to pass it to anyone? *You* get burned. You swallow that fire—and the sadness, shame, anger, and silence will slowly kill you from the inside out.

When you see the truth and understand the pain that caused your pain, you see the series of wounded victims who slowly became the villains in your story. You see where each of those sad, hurting children didn't have the ability or support to transmute that pain into compassion, love, and consciousness.

Do they deserve to be punished?
No.
Do you?
No.

By honoring yourself enough to welcome forgiveness, you transmute the pain of your family lineage. You peer your big, bright, conscious eyes above the clouds of unconsciousness and free yourself of the disillusionment. By forgiving those who have hurt you, you shine the light of consciousness onto the shadows and dismantle the cycle of passing on the pain. You break the chain of suffering and free yourself (and everyone else) from the cage.

Is there someone in your life you feel the need to forgive?
If you could say anything to them, what would you say?

ALONG THE HIGHWAY

FOR SO LONG, I FOLLOWED THE POPULAR BELIEF that my dad was a bad person. I honored my mother for how hard she worked and all she went through to take care of us. I stood by her, dedicated and devoted to being on her side.

Her side of the story.

Her side of the divorce.

Her side of the divide.

However, deep in my heart was the curiosity that had been there since I was a young child. My desire and need for connection with him never went away. It just got buried under piles of avoidance and pain. While my mom solely saw him as a monster from the past, I felt there must be more. Knowing that he and I shared the same blood, skin, and family, I wanted to know in my heart that there was love inside of him, not just a villain. So, I went in search of my dad; in search of a part of myself that felt missing for so long.

I did this by getting ahold of his phone number through a family friend and called him up one evening.

"Hello?" At first, he didn't recognize my voice. "Who is this?"

"Katie," I said.

"Katie who?"

"Katie, your daughter." Then, the phone went silent. For a few moments, we both sat in the silence of disbelief. Then, broken by the quiet whisper of tears on the other end, he said, "My Beti. My Beti," (*daughter* in Hindi).

With emotional support and heartfelt encouragement from my brother Sam, I made arrangements to fly from LA to DC and meet my dad for the first time since I was a child. The three of us met at a Chinese restaurant at a strip mall, and though it was a unique setting for such a monumental reunion, it was as powerful as a magnificent cathedral where angels rejoiced.

Sam held the space as my dad and I carved through the awkward veil of unfamiliarity and melted together in a steady stream of hugs, tears, and gentle laughter. The whole experience was surreal and painfully beautiful.

As the months passed, I flew back and forth to DC, tending to our reawakened connection like planting flowers around a hidden fortress in the woods. We would talk about India, family, and our favorite foods. We would laugh at our similarities and voice our commitments to the future.

As our comfort grew stronger and the shock of looking into one another's eyes wore off, I began to inquire more about our shared, wounded past. I asked about the early days and *what happened? Why was there so much conflict, abuse, and pain? What went wrong?*

That was hard for my dad. It was like handing him a scalpel and asking him to please slice into his scar tissue so I could see if there was any infection left.

He hesitated. He defended. He quickly tried scrambling back into his cage for protection.

However, karma granted him a second chance and with that came a fiery daughter as tenacious and driven as himself. I wasn't giving up. I didn't come all that way to tiptoe around the outside. I was determined to look within the great tomb of our past and unearth the treasures I felt so certain were inside.

I imagine he would've preferred that this heartfelt excavation had occurred when he wasn't behind the wheel on a busy highway, but sometimes life just happens and we don't get to choose when it's our time to crack open. Overcome with emotion, he pulled to the side of the road. I watched as my father turned monster turned ghost turned friend turned... into an innocent, hurting child. I watched as tears pushed through his closed eyes and his forehead rested on the steering wheel.

Finally, there it was, the answer I was seeking. The truth laid out before me: he was hurting and he had been hurting for a long, long time. Long before he met my mother and long before he grew into a man who traveled the world in search of purpose. He caused pain because he was in pain and he created wounds because he had been wounded.

Suddenly, like the spirit of a great grandmother entering wholly into my body, I felt entirely overcome with compassion for this precious, confused, and hurting child. I saw in him someone who had never forgiven themselves. Someone who had swallowed the fire of pain and was burning up from the inside.

Sometimes, forgiveness isn't a choice—it's the work of the Divine. It's the deities, angels, and saints wrapping their arms and wings around every one of us, cradling our hearts, exclaiming, "you've suffered long enough."

My arm reached over and comforted his back. I gently said, "I came here because I want us to create a new story. I'm your daughter and you're my dad. We can't change the past, but we can change the future."

And we did. My dad has been a close friend and a cherished presence in my life for all of these years. Like you, like me, like my mother staring at the sky—he's a being who came to this world with bright eyes and curiosity. He's a spirit having a temporary experience of being human and with that, he has made the most remarkable and valuable mistakes.

The truth is, bad things happen to good people and good people do bad things, but none of us are bad people. Each of us are struggling up the mountain of life in our own unique way, as best we can. Sure, we can blame, resent, or judge one another, but that doesn't really solve anything. When we see someone for their faults and weaknesses, we don't strengthen them or the situation—we just agree to be blind, angry, and ignorant alongside them.

If we really want to create change and rise up into the powerful strength that we're so capable of embodying, we have to courageously confront our own cage and challenge ourselves to move beyond it. Regardless of how hurt, upset, or resentful we may feel, we have to see beyond the illusion of defense and protection that so many of us hide behind, and we have to choose another way. We have to choose love.

Each time we do this, we open our hearts even more and become more powerful. We become wiser and our effect on the world becomes greater. Rather than being blinded and numbed by the effects of unconsciousness, we wake up. We become filled with the light of awareness and ignite the world around us. Each time we do, we encourage others to choose love and eventually, forgive themselves.

That does something.

That changes things.

That's freedom from suffering.

SELF-FORGIVENESS

MAYBE IT'S NOT YOUR DAD, OR YOUR MOM, or your sibling, or your boss, or your schoolmates, or your ex-wife, or that guy you went to college with who you can't seem to forgive. Maybe all of them feel like cleaner, better, and more deserving people than you because the person you can't seem to shake your disdain of is yourself.

Feeling like you're the one at fault for creating wounds and causing the pain is a very painful and lonely place to be in. When we blame ourselves, we force ourselves to feel shame, regret, and remorse. We feel that we *deserve* the suffering, and this self-inflicted entrapment makes it even harder to find our way out of the maze. We end up fighting with ourselves, and that is a very, very challenging and exhausting mountain to climb.

There's not a lot that I or anyone else can say or do to encourage you to feel compassion for what you've been through. If you're not ready to forgive yourself, it's a decision you're making with and for yourself.

However, consider that in order to feel resentment and judgment (towards ourselves or someone else), we have to be separated from our hearts and inched towards unconsciousness rather than consciousness. The artillery of our pain is fired from behind the cage walls and we have to remain there, in that state, to uphold our perspective of indignation.

Now then, how is that improving the situation? You resent yourself because you could have "done better." However, if you're genuinely concerned with doing better and making this world a better place, how is your perspective of *I created suffering, therefore I'm unforgivable and deserve to suffer* aligned with your mission statement of *I want the world to be a better place and I don't want to contribute to the suffering?*

It isn't.

If you try to play the hero *and* the villain, you end up being the victim who is silenced, shut down, and trapped in a cold, dark room of resentment. If your head is low and your spirit is trapped, how many incredible opportunities to help others are you overlooking? If you're crawling on your hands and knees, repenting and regretting, how can you step forward and lend a hand towards change?

Yes, you've done your part to bring pain and suffering to this world and you've done things and said things that are nearly impossible to forgive. However, wouldn't it make sense to turn things around and courageously do *everything* in your power to *transform* the suffering and bring healing to the world? Even if that courageous something meant forgiving yourself?

Regardless of what you've done or whether others are able to forgive you or not, you have the ability to forgive yourself. That's something you *can* do and it's something that actively helps the world suffer a little bit less.

Do you need to forgive yourself for something you did in your past?
Are you willing to forgive yourself if it means it would better the world?

YOUR BODY, YOUR FRIEND

WHEN YOU HEAR OF *love, self-love,* AND *compassion,* how does it relate to the way you connect and feel within your body? Similar to our collective inability to understand and love ourselves, the way we act, feel, and relate to our physical bodies is an equally global problem. Rather than nurturing and appreciating our bodies, many of us have learned to judge, abuse, poison, neglect, and deprive them of the care and attention they need to thrive and be healthy.

Somewhere beyond the steady flow of disapproval and negativity is a devoted servant who is completely in service to you at all times. You live within an orb of advanced intelligence, which surpasses the performance and ability of any computer or human-made creation in the world.

Think back to the incredible gift of breathing and the masterful air sacs and blood vessels that welcome oxygen into your body—after the oxygen disperses into your blood, it enters your heart and is pumped and pulsed through your entire body. This repeats itself about 100,000 times in one day (35 *million* times a year).

Meanwhile, your digestive organs are busily working together to break down the food you recently ate, collecting and sorting through minerals and trash to create a nutrient-rich pile of "keepable" stuff, then sending it along a 25–30-foot conveyor belt system so the next organ can do its thing.

In the time you've read a page of this book, you've blinked about a dozen times and your eyes have been steadily taking in light and turning it into electrical signals, which are then sent to the brain in order to be turned into images. Meanwhile, you're just having this experience of *reading a book* and likely not even aware of what's happening inside.

That's what's so incredible about your body: it's here helping you all the time and devotedly ensuring your protection and survival, *regardless* of whether you stop to appreciate it or not. So humble and unconditionally supportive, this helpful conglomerate of bones, muscles, organs, nerves, and cells is your family. They are your blood brothers and sisters, and they are the most responsive, caring, connected, and loving teammates you will ever have in your life. From the moment you were born, they've been gathered together, celebrating your every breath.

As a small child, they carried you to your first steps and reached out a hand every time you fell. Every time your heart ached, your body was right there, weeping and mourning alongside you. Every song that ever brought you dancing to your feet, they celebrated with you. The most beautiful sunsets, sunrises, storm clouds, and sleeping babies you have ever seen were all glimpses and visions you shared together.

Every single day and every single night, your body has provided a warm, nurturing, cozy place for your spirit to walk, sleep, connect, rest, sit, dance, run, do, and be. It loves you unconditionally and it will never, ever leave your side.

However, you will leave it someday.

You will be the one to leave this incredible, devoted family of bodily wonder behind, for you can't take it with you. You can't bring your hands or your feet or your hair or your hips or your lips or your voice to the realms where only the spirits soar.

Is your body afraid of this eventual separation? Will it anticipate this eventual abandonment and leave you first?

No. Never.

Your body is completely and entirely dedicated to you. Fearlessly and unconditionally, it will support you until the very end. Your beloved body will usher you to the final moments of your life and be with you on your deathbed. It will never, ever leave you. It's fully here, fully committed, in service to you, wholeheartedly.

How many years have you been taking your dear and devoted body for granted? How many times have you been the one to beat it down with hurtful words and unhealthy habits? How long have you been abusing it, discarding it, judging it, and calling it names?

You can go on saying hurtful things to yourself and painful words to your body, but you don't have long to keep doing that. Very soon, the years will pass and you'll approach the end of your days, where you and your body will have that deep and tender talk. You'll share fond memories, quiet secrets, and reflections of all that you experienced together.

Then, you'll say goodbye.

Will it be sad?

Possibly.

If you choose not to wake up to your life and begin living and loving yourself right now (or very soon), you run the risk of being there in those final moments, looking back and wondering: *Why was I so hard on myself? I was doing my best—why couldn't I see that? Why didn't I just love my body and love myself when I had years of opportunity to do so?*

Have you ever said or done something wounding or destructive to your body?
If you could apologize for that, what would you say to your body?

THE CHOICE TO LOVE IS THE CHOICE TO LIVE
Meditative vision exercise

If you're able, find a comfortable place to sit or lay down for this meditative vision. Allow for a few moments of stillness before reading.

◆

1. Allow yourself to imagine what the future will be like.

   Flashing years or decades forward into the future, pull right up to the final precipice of death.

   There, in that moment, try to imagine what you will be thinking and feeling.

   Will you feel at peace?

   Imagine it. See yourself safe, laying in the spaciousness of presence and contentment.

   What does it feel like?
   What does it look like around you?
   Is it a soft and comforting bed of fresh linen?
   Or rather a bed of moss beneath a tree?
   Are there loved ones with you?
   Who is there?

   Sit with this for a moment.

2. Imagine yourself surrounded by the smell of fresh flowers and the warmth of the sunlight beaming down on your skin and your closed eyelids. Imagine all of the moments you chose to love instead of fear.

   Close your eyes and allow yourself to sit with that warm, nurturing feeling for a moment as you gently breathe in and out.

3. Let a deep, full breath in...
   And slowly exhale.

4. Then, imagine a different scenario.

   Imagine what it would be like to be alone. Rather than feeling content, at ease, and surrounded by the soothing warmth of nurturance, consider your hands trembling and your body cold and in pain.

   Imagine that you are scared, anxious, and uncomfortable. Instead of being immersed in the profound awe of dying and transformation, your mind is racing uncontrollably through decisions you should have made differently. Like being forced to see a film from the past, you are reminded of the many hurtful things you did and said to your body, and the many loved ones you should have forgiven and never did.

   What does it feel like? How does it feel to know that you lived your life in fear and protection and it brought you here, to this desolate place of suffering?

   From this aching place of regret and pain, feel the thought inside you:

   If only I had a second chance, I would do it so differently.

   What does it feel like to be filled with a longing to relive the past?

   Close your eyes and sit with the discomfort for a moment.

5. Take a deep, full breath in...
   And slowly exhale.

6. Now, travel back through time and allow the years you traveled to soar beside you like jet streams of stars in space. Return here, to this present moment and open your eyes.

   Look around at where you are right here in this present moment.

   Where are you sitting right now?
   What does it look like?
   What does it smell like?

   Take note of five things about the environment you're sitting in right now.

7. Take a deep, full breath in...
   And slowly exhale.

8. Look down at your hands.
   Feel the life and vitality in your body.
   Feel the oxygen entering in through your lungs and allow a deep breath of gratitude to sweep through and out of you.

9. Your wish was granted.
   This is your second chance.
   What will you do differently this time?

   —

   Will you love your body and care for it?

   Will you feed it well, nurture it, and spend quality time being with it and resting with it when you're tired?

   Will you speak up when you feel truth moving through you and honor yourself the way a true friend would?

   Will you acknowledge where shame resides on your shoulders and offer yourself permission to let it go?

   Will you see the suffering in those who have caused you pain and offer yourself permission to forgive them?

   Will you choose to be more present in each moment and courageously welcome the unknown?

Each decision you make guides you to your final moments. Either that destiny can be one where you are estranged from yourself and lost in a storm of regret or it can be a room filled with peace and contentment where your heart is open and you are ready.

As you step forward into your day and into your life, remember, the choice is yours.

This time, choose *love*.

EXAMPLE CONVERSATION

Imagine you're in a moment of struggle. You're trying to make a decision and because you don't know what path to choose, you're feeling anxious and overwhelmed. To move through the thick waters of uncertainty and access direction and insight, you open yourself to some internal dialogue.

What's happening? What happened?

I: Can I describe what's going on right now?
W: I'm really torn and not sure what to do.
I: Can I explain this in more detail?
W: I can't decide if I should go on this trip or not.
I: What is the trip?
W: It's a weekend long conference for work. I'd be leaving Thursday afternoon and getting back late on Sunday.
I: What about the trip am I uncertain about?
W: I actually don't know. I just have a weird feeling.
I need to be more detailed and I need to find out more about what I'm really feeling.
How am I feeling? Where am I hurting? Where am I afraid?

I: Can I better describe this "weird" feeling?
W: Apprehension. Uncertainty. Nervousness.
I: Is there anything about the trip that I feel specifically nervous about?
W: I don't really know. Overall, I feel really excited about it and am looking forward to spending time with everybody. It's totally optional for me to go, but my boss has made it clear how important it is for each of us to try and be there.
Interesting. I just felt a shift in my senses. When I mentioned my boss wanting us to go, I felt my stomach clench up a little. I wonder why.
I: Do I feel pressured to attend because of my boss?
W: Yes, I'd say I do. I know everybody is expecting me to go and yet, there's just this other feeling that I can't explain. It's like "Nope. Don't go." That's where I feel stuck. I know I should go; I know it will be fun

and yet, there's this weird apprehension in me.
I: Can I describe the feeling of resistance a little better?
W: Kind of, but not really. It's as if I just know in my heart that I'm supposed to stay home that weekend. Every time I try to move forward in booking my flight, I stop because of that feeling and now I'm not sure what to do. I feel overwhelmed about it all and I'm really not sure what to do.

Hmmm, sounds like I might need some help working through this.

I'm not alone. I can engage with the people and world around me.

I: Am I open to talking to someone about this or going outside to clear my head?
W: Sure, I'll go outside and take a walk but I don't want to ask anyone their opinion. They might encourage me to go and then I'll really feel like I have to go.

Interesting. I must be really persuaded by what others think.

I: So my decision of whether to go or not will be based on someone else's opinion?
W: I don't know. Maybe so.

That's definitely interesting and sounds like insecurity.

I: I mentioned my boss wants me to go. Is any of my stress coming from wanting to please my boss?
W: Yes

Interesting. I just felt a shift in senses. Suddenly, a tightness in my stomach.

I don't have to hold onto this any longer. I can let it go.

I: What if I decide not to go. Do I feel comfortable telling my boss?
W: No.
I: Why is that? Why do I not feel comfortable telling them?
W: Honestly, I don't want to lose my job.
I: Would they fire me for making a decision that feels healthy and right for me?
W: Probably not but I guess I just want to remain someone they can trust.

I: Ok. What if I write a letter to them, just to test out what it would feel like to decline? I don't need to send it. It might just give me practice at using my voice.
W: Sure. I can do that but right now, I still don't know how I feel or what I want to do. I just feel stressed.

I deserve to be comfortable and receive the care I need.

It sounds like my intuition is trying to say something but because I'm so worked up about this, I can't hear it. It might be wise for me to really listen to it.
I: Am I willing to create a quiet and meditative place of stillness to quiet my thoughts and hear my inner voice?
W: Yeah, that sounds like a good idea. I've been losing sleep over this so taking a breather and relaxing actually sounds really good.
I: And? What if the insight that emerges is the decision to not go?
W: Well, that brings up some stress but I don't want to make decisions in life based on what others think. I want to be a better friend to myself.

Love is stronger than fear. I choose love.

I: Am I willing to practice with a letter then turn it into an email if it feels right to not go?
W: I think so. I'm a little nervous but I think I can do it.
I: Is it possible to communicate from my heart and take a step back with love? To decline with honor for myself rather than fear of upsetting someone else?
W: Yes. I guess I could say something like "I really appreciate this opportunity and while much of me wants to attend to retain my relationship with you and strengthen my role in the company, for personal reasons, I will not be attending this conference. I look forward to catching up on what I missed when the team returns."

Wow. I just felt a shift in senses. Instantly, just hearing myself say that, I feel relief. Like I don't have to go.

LOVING TOOLS

Though I may have been raised to believe that self-love is a sign of weakness, selfishness, or conceit, it's not true. My relationship to myself is a vital connection that needs to be honored and nurtured with my love. I give myself permission to receive my own love, care, and respect.

◆

By taking a step back and saying "no" at times, it doesn't mean that I'm unappreciative or mean; it means I'm making an honest and discerning decision with healthy intention for my well-being, which matters.

◆

Feeling compassion doesn't take or drain anything from me. It's a gift that offers love to both myself and the beings I feel compassion for.

◆

Next time I empathize and "feel bad" for someone, I can consider what it might be like to feel compassion and remain tethered to the inspiration to help them rather than suffering alongside them.

◆

When I welcome forgiveness into my life, I free myself from my own suffering and am more available to make the world a better place.

◆

My body is the closest friend I will ever have. Next time I feel myself judging, critiquing or wishing it to be different, I can remember that I won't have it forever. At some point, I'll have to let it go, so it's important for me to love and appreciate it right now.

✺

तन
आपके शरीर में, आप हमेशा मौजूद रहें और पोषण के लिए उपलब्ध रहें और उस प्यार को प्रोत्साहित करें जिसे आप एक साथ बुनते हैं।

दिल
आप हमेशा के लिए अपने दिल में शरण पा सकते हैं और एक साथ पैदा होने वाले प्यार की गरमि से प्रेषित हो सकते हैं |

मन
आप अपने मन में हमेशा शुद्ध रहें और अच्छे चीजों पर ध्यान दे, सद्गुणो से प्रेरति रहे और हमेशा एक दुसरे को सत्य और प्रेम से रहने को जागरूक करे।

आत्मा
आप हमेशा के लिए, उत्साह में, विनिम्रतापूर्वक और पूरी तरह से सेवा में रहें हमेशा अपने साथ रहने वाले के साथ प्रेम विकिसित करे और ईश्वरीय प्रेम पाने के लिए।

✺

(TRANSLATED)

Body
In your bodies, may you always be present and available to nurture
And encourage the love you weave together.

Heart
May you forever, in your hearts, find refuge and be nurtured
By the warmth of the love you create together.

Mind
In your minds, may you always be pure and focused
On the greater good, inspired by virtue and grounded in
The truth and love you awaken in one another.

Spirit
May you forever, in spirit, humbly and wholly be of service to
Offer the love that you cultivate together
To and for the Divine Love.

15.
EMPOWERED

To empower one's true self by overcoming pain, fear, and suffering; to choose love.

"That's because we're wildflowers. We're powerful, resilient, and capable of withstanding the twists and turns of life while still thriving and being healthy and strong."

As I said it, my hands reached up into the air in a very expressive and unfurling way, as they often do when I'm addressing a crowd during a talk or performance.

This analogy of empowerment being associated with wild flowers was one that I had acquired from my dear friend Heather. Being a landscaper, she had a deep awareness of the behavior and inner workings of plants.

She explained, "Wildflowers are flowers grouped together because they all share a similar quality: they're wild. They grow free without the hands of humans and are resilient beyond what we can understand or make sense of. Whether they're growing at high altitudes with strong winds or in dry and dusty deserts with little water, they grow strong and healthy. They don't just survive; they thrive."

I carried that vision with me for a long time, through addiction, through recovery, through the agonizing days of wondering why I had been killing myself for so long and what the reasons were for me being alive.

Now, as I found myself fearlessly speaking to this group of wide-eyed and heartfelt women at a workshop in Colorado, I reminded them what I had been reminding myself all those years: "Yes, you've been wounded and you know what it's like to feel stifled and broken. However, that's not who you are. Who you are is so much greater and more powerful. You didn't come into this life to struggle and survive through it; you came here to live out your life purpose and thrive!"

I've found that through the years of being fully recovered and sober (10 years and counting), it's not always a soft, gentleness that comes through me when motivating others—it's also a fierce, fiery directness.

"Fierce" like a mother protecting her young?

Yes. Exactly. It's like the fire of the whole universe birthing up from depths so deep that there's no beginning and no end. It's intense like rage and it feels powerful and igniting, except there's no fear. Because there's no fear, there's no anger. Only love.

As if I was a mother talking her daughter out of hurting herself, my voice was gentle and also forthright as I peered around the entire group, looking directly into each of their eyes.

I continued, "The world is not becoming a better place by wasting one more minute curled up in a corner and abusing yourself with shameful put downs and self-judgment. No, in fact, if you want to help the world, start loving yourself. Start being a real friend to yourself. Start taking action to get your needs met so you can finally be satiated and stop surviving through life and living it for only you. You know why? Because, when you finally realize that you're good and you've got your needs met you start having a lot more time, energy, and interest in helping others get their needs met, and guess what? We need you. We need your powerful light, wisdom, and love activated in this world. Step into the power of your heart, instead of the fear of your pain, and make this world a better place. It's time and you're ready."

The truth is, every one of us has been through the harsh winds and storms of life. We all know what it's like to get snagged and slowed down by the painful briars of suffering.

However, when we're finally ready to look at the truth, feel it, open ourselves up, let go of what doesn't serve us, and receive care because we know we deserve love—we're no longer suffering. We're no longer held down by the pain of our past or lost inside the experience of life—we're empowered by it.

With each wound you've endured, you've gained the strength of sacred scar tissue around your heart. From each moment lost to avoidance and neglect, you've gained the ability to better understand presence. Through stumbling and falling, you've learned what it takes to get back up again. Because you've spent so many years trapped in a locked box of secrecy, you understand the rewarding gift of honesty. And because you've experienced what the deep burn of resentment can do, you know the importance of forgiveness.

Your journey of suffering took you on a mission away from the home of yourself and brought you into the world of struggle. Now, you return home and are reintroduced to the qualities you embodied when you first arrived into this life, yet your light shines differently and more expansively.

You are the HEART you have always been:
- Honest
- Present
- Loving
- Conscious
- Innocent
- Trusting
- Vulnerable
- Caring
- Curious
- Unafraid
- Enthusiastic
- Whole

...and *so much* more:
- Experienced
- Resilient
- Wise
- Compassionate
- Understanding
- Forgiving
- Grateful
- Thriving
- Empowered

It's like you are reborn from the chrysalis of the past and freed from the weight of shame and pain. Through this journey of life and through your healing, you have learned to stop being afraid. You've been reunited with your heart and though it holds the same precious, pure light it always has, now it burns brighter. The light of love within you is stronger, more resilient, and more fierce than ever.

In this space of returning to the heart, your mantra would become:

"I am whole. I belong here."

Because this spaciousness of the heart is a landscape that you're returning to, the full expression of the empowered heart would be:

I am here, experiencing life.
I am whole. I belong here.

Altogether, beginning in the home of your heart, then traveling out into the realms of suffering, then back home again, your journey would be:

HEART: *I am here, experiencing life.*
WOUND: *Ouch! That hurt.*
PAIN: *I don't feel good. I'm in pain.*
NEED: *I'm hurting and I'm scared. I need healing.*
PROTECTION: *My needs aren't met. I'll protect myself by trying not to feel the pain.*
DEFENSE: *To avoid feeling more pain, I will fight to protect myself.*
SUFFERING: *I feel lost, lonely, and stuck.*
REALIZATION: *I'm ready for change and I'm going to do something about it.*
OBSERVE: *What's happening right now? What happened in the past?*
FEEL: *How am I feeling? Where am I hurting? Where am I afraid?*
CONNECT: *I'm not alone. I can engage with the world around me.*
RELEASE: *I don't need to hold onto this any longer. I can let it go.*
COMFORT: *I'm ready to be comfortable and receive the care I need.*
LOVE: *Love is stronger than fear. I choose love.*
EMPOWERED: *I am whole. I belong here.*

Through the perfect alignment of all your experiences, choices, actions, and heartaches, you've gone from having a *heart* to having an *empowered heart*.

Being empowered in your heart doesn't mean you're immune to pain or struggle. It means you're aware that life is painful, sad, beautiful, bewildering, wild, perplexing, and at times, unjust—and, you're not scared. You understand your wounds, so you're not afraid of being wounded. You know how to move through pain and heal yourself by getting your needs met. Your heart is stronger than your fear and you boldly, knowingly step forward on the journey.

As if you were previously paddling to stay afloat, now you are a trained swimmer. All the challenges you've endured conditioned your lungs to be stronger and expand, enabling you to dive deep into the depths of suffering, look directly at the core of the pain, and expose it with your awareness. Now, you can just do what you were born to do naturally—rise back up to the surface, to the fresh air of presence, where you belong.

The sense of belonging and confidence acquired through having an empowered heart doesn't mean you're enlightened or better than anyone else, though. It means you know for certain that you're *no better* than anyone else, and with that heightened level of compassionate awareness, you're free from the clutches of the ego and the haze of unconsciousness.

You know that everyone is wounded and everyone is hurting, and you don't want to add to the pain—you want to do something to ease it. Because you're no longer struggling in your own suffering, you're more able and available to help others through theirs, and that is what you came here to do. To be a leader and a light. To be an example of what a human is capable of—while living in a state of consciousness, compassion, and presence.

It's your purpose and now, you're ready to live it.

FALSE CONFIDENCE VS. TRUE CONFIDENCE

FOR SOME TIME IN MY YOUTH, I WAS AN ACTRESS. I had a manager and an agent, and I did the whole *strive-to-become-someone* thing. The extent of my acting career was some small roles on a few TV shows and voicing an anime series, so I can comfortably say that my time in Hollywood was not abundantly fruitful. And, while I deeply cherish the friendships birthed in that time and appreciate the spiritual growth, LA life was not for me. Perhaps I would've and could've invested more time and effort into expanding my career, but I was severely unhappy and unhealthy, and I had a car accident after almost blacking out with a nervous breakdown. So, I left.

However, nothing taught me more about false confidence than my time spent working in the film industry. It was like being inside a cage the size of a city, the epitome of being broken on the inside while presenting a story of confidence on the outside. Surrounded by the thick smog of ego, LA is a land of beauty, popularity, and wealth—all things that false confidence thrives on.

On various occasions when doing "background" work (silently creating atmosphere in the background of scenes) and nearly invisible, it was a unique experience when the lead actors would come on set. Strangely, I would watch as famous, fit, and wealthy actors entered the room, and rather than seeing a glowing orb of confidence and stardust, I would clearly see a sad and insecure human fidgeting with their clothing, looking jealously at others, and treating the set team with disrespect. Not everyone was like this, but enough that I became fully aware of what was behind the facade of the glorified film industry.

Until that point, I revered those with wealth, beauty, and fame, like so many of us do. I saw them as superior and successful. I thought: *that must be a life of confidence and happiness.*

I was wrong.

Just because someone's famous, fit, or wealthy, it doesn't mean they have a strong self-esteem. It might just mean that they are caught in the ego and value themselves through an external understanding; a false sense of confidence.

What is it?

False confidence: a temporary and insincere sense of power and security that is ego-based; an understanding of the self derived from insecurity and fear.

Perception of the Self through **external understanding**:

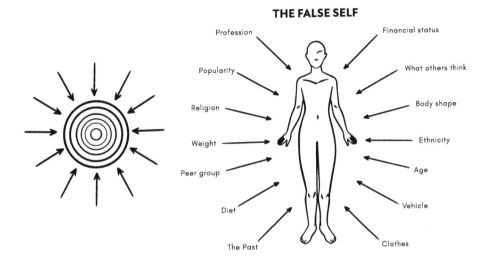

THE FALSE SELF

Examples of **false confidence**:
- What other people think about you
- The clothes you wear
- Your peer groups
- Your profession
- Your age
- Your weight
- Your diet
- Your ethnicity
- Your religion
- Your level of popularity
- Your financial status
- The vehicle you drive

Perhaps a perfect body or a thriving list of followers offers a temporary sense of belonging and self-assurance, but at some point, it will inevitably end. The clothes will tatter, the car engine will die, the skin will lose its elasticity, and the followers will be swept away by the next fad.

There's nothing wrong with having a quality vehicle, well-made clothes, and beautiful adornments, however, when those *things* become your identity and your lifeline to reaching a place of self-acceptance, confidence, and happiness, then you've been duped. You've been successfully persuaded by the unconsciousness and pulled further away from your true self.

So, what's the alternative? How do you access a feeling of being empowered, grounded, and satisfied within yourself—without relying on your external environment?

True confidence.

True, honest, genuine, real *confidence*.

What is it?

True confidence: the deep knowing that one is safe and can rely fully on one's self; a sense of empowerment and belonging that comes from being united with the higher self, rather than the ego; an understanding of the self deriving from love.

To be truly confident means you rely fully on yourself and *trust* yourself wholeheartedly. While false confidence comes from the outside, true confidence comes from within and beams outward. It means you are strongly connected and tethered to the divine spirit within you—and there's nothing anyone can say or do that will weaken or diminish the respect, love, and trust you have in yourself.

Perception of the Self through **internal understanding**:

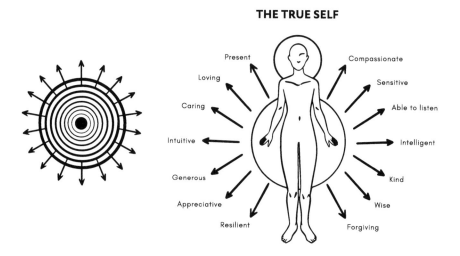

THE TRUE SELF

Examples of **true confidence**:
- Present
- Loving
- Compassionate
- Caring
- Sensitive
- Able to listen
- Intuitive
- Generous
- Kind
- Intelligent
- Appreciative
- Wise
- Resilient
- Forgiving

While we may be tempted to think that if we lose our external stories, items, and merits, we are left hollow, naked, and without anything of value or worth—the opposite is the case. Because our external understanding of self is woven into the ego cage, it's only when we detach ourselves from the stories and false needs that we start remembering true confidence.

Does that mean we need to give away everything and wear only tattered clothing? No. It just means we have to be consciously aware that whether we're attractive or unattractive, wealthy or unwealthy, successful or unsuccessful, our external and material world doesn't determine the value of our worth, nor should it determine how we perceive ourselves. *That* comes from within!

In what ways have you accessed confidence through an external understanding of self?

How would it feel to be truly confident in who you are?

STRENGTH & POWER

HOW MANY OF US WERE LED TO BELIEVE THAT money and success equals *power*? If we have a tendency to perceive our confidence through the material world, we might assume that a nice car, a perfect body, or lots of money will also give us a sense of strength and power.

It makes sense. Living in a money and material-based society, money definitely carries a lot of clout and can easily be seen as the access point to gaining confidence, respect, notoriety and all the other things our egos like to feed on. Especially if we've been judged or made fun of, we might be seeking a sense of strength, respect, and empowerment through finances and physical materials.

At times, we may have even found ourselves sidetracked and drifting into fantasies of how good it will feel when the tables turn. When all the people who didn't believe in us will cringe in disbelief at our dreamlike success, popularity, and eventual power. "Who's laughing now?"

Yes, it's tempting to let ourselves imagine. However, that's not the real you. That's the sad, hurting, defensive version of you imagining freedom while peering through the lens of protection and unconsciousness. That's the part of you who still feels excluded and thinks that by having *more* (money, friends, houses, attention) than others, you're safe from future neglect and belittlement. Somehow, you've made it to safety on top of the mountain, where pain magically can't reach you.

The reality is, money, success, and popularity don't provide genuine and sustainable strength and power. They may cause others to feel more intimidated, which will drive some away and others closer, but intimidating people and awakening fear in them is no way to access a sense of empowerment. Will your strife to reach the top really grant what you seek? What's so desirable about being perched up high on a lonely mountain top when everyone else is far below?

True strength isn't something that can be temporarily gained or lost. It's deeper than that. It's something that comes with true confidence, true presence, and true love. It's the quality and capacity of allowing ourselves to engage with this life experience with our purest, most honest, qualities. It's the strength of commitment and devotion to what serves the greater good and the potency of knowing that we belong and are a part of that greater good.

So do it. Stand up into your higher self and be done with this charade of fear and false confidence. Stand up to the people who judge you and who rate your value by your appearance or success. Stand up to the hordes of businesses, industries, corporations, and companies that make billions of dollars off your insecurity and your need to fit in. Stand up to the fear inside you and stand up inside your cage, then *step out of it*.

Be different.

Be compassionate.

Be wise.

Be confident in who you are and speak from a place of honesty and truth.

Be right here, right now, just the way you are and be your powerful, present self.

ANGER VS. EMPOWERMENT

WHAT HAPPENS WHEN SOMEONE THROWS an emotional dagger or hurtful swing at your heart? What do you do to remain present, empowered, and confident in yourself, rather than overcome with volcanic rage?

You take a moment and you take a breath.

Remember, it was unconsciousness that created so many of your wounds and from that unconsciousness came the fire of anger and hatred. That anger and hatred is what cracked your heart, their heart, and all of our hearts, breaking this world apart.

When someone says or does something to rattle the cage and tempt you to react like a tiger, you can either get lost in the emotion *or* be empowered by conscious awareness. Not both. If you don't have the power to control your anger, you're not working with true strength; you're working with true *fear*.

If someone says something unkind or destructive about you, let them. That's their journey, not yours. What others do and say has nothing to do with you; it has everything to do with them. So, observe them, learn something new, and let them struggle through life until they have their own realization that they're done suffering. You've rediscovered what it feels like to be whole and no one can crack apart that inseparable connection of self-love and unity that you know and feel within yourself.

Lean into the fierce message of love coming from your heart that says: *Go ahead, try to break me. I've been broken 1,000 times and each time, it has made me stronger, wiser, and more aware. Each time, it has broken me open. Keep trying but know that I'll only become more empowered. Why? Because I'm devoted to presence and I won't be divided from myself any longer. I won't separate from myself because your pain and fear needs me to justify your actions. Sort that out within yourself. I know who I am and I'm devoted to love and presence, not suffering.*

This world doesn't need more scared, angry, and power-hungry people battling each other and battling themselves. We don't need more blind and heartbroken soldiers who are trained to fight. We need people who are fiercely present and courageously compassionate. We need people who act with intention, not react with pain. We need people who have sipped from the destructive poison of hatred and discovered ways to free themselves by turning it into presence, intelligence, and awareness. Then, we need those people to lead the way.

What makes a powerful leader? The one who is least afraid. The one who has conquered their internal fears and steps boldly and confidently forward. An empowered heart is a leader. It's someone who has experienced great pain and consciously chosen love instead of fear. It's someone who is no longer afraid to be alive, like you. You're ready and you're not afraid anymore.

OVERPOWERING ADDICTION

WHILE YOU MAY NOT FEEL OR TRULY RECOGNIZE this strength and fearlessness inside of you, it's in you. You are powerful and you'll *need* to be in order to recover from an addiction. For me, this is something that took time. Like being slowly reunited with the essence of my true self, I gradually healed and became aware of my strength through the process of recovery.

Over the years, people have asked me, "How did you know you were healed from addiction?"

For someone who has never dealt with a serious addiction, this might seem like a silly question. You might think "Well, when you stop drinking, or purging, or looking at porn, you're done, right?"

No, not entirely. Addiction doesn't really work like that. The way it plays itself out physically is only one aspect of the entrapment. Maybe we reach for food, or a drink, or a cigarette, but it's only the *external* symptom of a much deeper issue within. I've worked with numerous people trying to recover from bulimia who hadn't thrown up in years but still considered themselves "bulimic." I have friends who haven't had a sip of alcohol in decades but still consider themselves "alcoholic."

How is this possible?

Because addiction is like a spirit, a smoke that circulates throughout our beings and longs for more. Even if we manage to train our bodies to not physically reach for the glass or the fork or the cigarette, we may still be suffering from the desire to do so. In that sense, we're still suffering from it.

How did I know I had recovered?

Because I stopped fearing it. I stopped believing I was powerless and learned the truth: I am *powerful*.

For so long, I was afraid of my addiction. I was afraid that it would take over me, control me, and force me to do things I didn't want to do. I felt cursed by an evil longing that haunted me day and night and had the power to make me slowly kill myself. I was so scared of it that I wouldn't even utter its name. For a long time, even after the recovery began, I would say "eating disorders" so that I didn't have to say "bulimia."

Then, as my healing progressed and I became more present, I replaced binge sessions with writing and crying sessions, and trips to the kitchen with walks outside. In doing so, I began to discover the truth: it wasn't as powerful as I once thought. It actually wasn't powerful at all. While I was a living, breathing, powerful human, the addiction was just a sad, innocent, unmet need for support and nurturance hidden in a dragon costume.

How did I slay it?

Presence.

By choosing to be awake enough in each moment that I didn't drift off into a state of unconsciousness where that hungry dragon could sneak up unexpectedly.

Remember that house inside us where the mold of unconsciousness grows? When the light of awareness enters, the mold can't survive. Because addiction requires unconsciousness to breathe and live, it can't survive when you're *present*. It literally cannot survive—but you can. You can outlive it, and you will.

By being consciously aware of your actions and your needs, you overpower it. By allowing yourself to feel and release your emotions, you overpower it. By sensing that you need to talk to someone, then being fully open and honest about what's going on, you overpower it.

The power of your presence transforms your entire being to a light-filled space of consciousness, where addiction and fear *cannot* thrive.

You're done with addiction when you're no longer afraid to be right here, right now, without a cage or distraction to separate you from the moment. When you love and appreciate yourself so much that nothing and no one could ever cause you to abandon yourself in a time of crisis. When you are committed to showing up for yourself as a true and unconditional friend, *every* single day.

THE SUBTLE REWARDS OF TRUE HAPPINESS

I USED TO THINK THAT HAPPINESS WAS SOMETHING expressive, radiant, and colorful, like spinning on top of a mountain with outstretched arms. I would eat sugar, go shopping, and be constantly engaged with friends, phone calls, traveling, and "what's next?" so I could feel the nonstop sensation of elation, pleasure, and excitement. To me, that was happiness. That was when I forgot the heavy weight of my reality. Happiness felt like the opposite of sadness—the way I felt deep inside and the feeling I avoided at all costs. Why be sad? Let's get happy!

However, happiness doesn't always look like sparks of electricity or reveal itself through a face-stretching grin. It's not always a song, a laugh, or a dance celebrated among friends.

Sometimes, more than a party or fun-filled adventure, we just want to feel at peace in this moment. Rather than feeling the need to lift ourselves up to the highs and shout the howls of excitement, we just want to take a long nap or a calming gaze at the sky. We just want to spend time alone, with our eyes closed and our faces free of any expression. For many of us, what we want more than anything is to just feel ok with ourselves, right here, right now—*without* having to do, say, or change a thing.

Thankfully, this peaceful, spacious happiness is something that you are designed to experience. Like presence, honesty, love, and tears, you don't have to contort yourself to awaken it in your life. Without needing to search for it, you may even find that happiness begins to naturally awaken as judgment, anxiety, resentment, and shame is released.

In many ways, happiness is your natural state. It's what naturally happens when you return to presence by awakening genuine confidence, self-love, and empowerment from unconsciousness. Rather than constantly struggling and anxiously scrambling in each moment, you feel calm and content in your body, your life, and yourself. You're happy and grateful to be here and you know that you belong. And, there's nothing anyone can say or do to shake you from that knowing. You've spent enough of your life struggling. Now, you can relax and genuinely *be happy* with who you are, where you are, right here and now.

GRATITUDE IS A CHOICE

FOR MANY YEARS, I HAD A DEAR, BELOVED friend who was as close to me as family. She was radiant, wise, and filled with the glowing force of sunlight. Being 30 years older than me, Cornelia Gabriela Lipp was somewhat of a mother figure but at times, like a younger sister.

She would whisk through the room, like a whirlwind of magic, and mysteriously even the flowers seemed to bloom in her presence. I learned so much from her, and to this day I still reflect on, unravel, and make use of her incredible reminders and blessings of guidance.

One thing that Connie taught me was the importance of gratitude. Yes, life will be challenging. It will hand you the short end of the stick and offer you an unpleasant spread of cards, but there is reason and purpose in its madness. There is a higher, divine, and elaborate understanding above us, and it connects us all. "It's a choice," she would say, reminding me to look deeper within what appeared to be an obstacle—and to find trust, opportunity, and gratefulness in it.

She had the letter 'g' written or painted in many places throughout her kitchen, home and garden, reminding herself that *gratitude* is the way. She was so thankful for her life, so thankful for her home, so thankful for her friends, so thankful for the wine, so thankful for the food she was able to eat. There were times when I questioned whether she was naive or so privileged that she didn't understand suffering the way I understood it.

Inevitably, I was wrong. We might assume or imagine that because someone appreciates their life, they don't understand pain, wounds, torment, loss, and sadness, but it's not true. We've all dipped our toes in the river of suffering and swam in the ocean of grief. We've all wept tears of remorse and tasted the sting of sorrow. However, some of us have an invaluable understanding: just because there is much that doesn't feel right, it doesn't mean we should lose appreciation for all that does. If we see ourselves and our lives as burdensome, it's likely that we'll lose sight of all of the gifts, riches, and incredible opportunities that surround us.

I'm so thankful for my hands, so thankful for my lungs, so thankful for my eyes, so thankful for my friends, so thankful for my home, so thankful for the food I'm able to eat, so thankful for all of these incredible opportunities and gifts that allow me to be alive. All the gifts that Connie had to return to the Earth when she gracefully and swiftly returned to the stars.

While the pain and suffering in your life may feel unavoidable, the decision of whether to be grateful or not *is a choice*. It's important to lean into trust and remember that there is an immense, karmic, more elaborate experience going on. Like the sun that weaves its light to ignite the moon, there are bigger and brighter forces at work to support all that displays itself as *what is*. It may not seem like it in the moment, but in time, much more may reveal itself, and as it does, you may feel much more grateful for it all.

What is something you feel grateful for?

THE RETURN HOME TO PRESENCE

FOR A LOT OF PEOPLE, *presence* IS THE SOUGHT-AFTER, holy land of spiritual work. It's the distant mountain peak that exists somewhere in the realm of enlightenment, and in many ways, *being present* has been our goal this entire journey together.

However, through this process, I imagine you've learned something very important: it's really not that hard to be present.

Once you've faced your wounds, courageously heard the cries of your hurting heart, leaned in to find out what you needed, and taken action to get your needs met, you realize you're not afraid anymore. Being content, still, and present isn't as far-off and out of reach as you once imagined. Rather than seeing presence as a distant temple reserved only for the saintlike creatures, you realize it's your *home*. It's where you belong. It's the place where you get to *be* yourself, without needing to change or do a thing.

This understanding of presence brings me to my mother and what it's like for her right now—with no identification with the past or attachment to her story:

She doesn't know to be worried about money or concerned about her appearance. She doesn't know to turn away and avoid staring deeply into another's eyes for fear of being rude. She is unabashed, untamed, and unafraid. Like a nameless, sexless, ageless being who doesn't know about the past or feel concern about the future, she has unlearned the awkward and polite conduct of being human and simply rests in the spaciousness of presence.

Are we less valuable and less human when we're present? Are we suddenly naked and void of purpose when we're separated from our memories? Without constant reference to what we've accomplished, where we've failed, and what all we have to do each day to feel fulfilled, do we give up ourselves when we *give up* the stories and return to presence?

No. Like the strength and true confidence birthed when we stop identifying our past experiences with who we are, when we allow ourselves to be right here, right now we are reunited with our true selves again.

You may be familiar with the term "awakening consciousness" but the reality is that after the long, arduous journey of life you've been on to get to this moment, you're *returning* to consciousness. Rather than awakening, you are *re-awakening* the consciousness that's already inside you and giving yourself permission to be right here in this moment, without turning away, distracting yourself, or hiding your light any longer.

Finally, you feel safe enough to come back to your true home: *the present moment*, and back to your true state of being: *presence*.

How do you feel when you are fully present?

GREATER INTELLIGENCE

THIS ABILITY TO BE PRESENT AND EMPOWERED in your heart is truly the most intelligent thing you can offer yourself. Society will encourage you to stay busy and continue striving for "success" until you retire. It will try convincing you that it's the right thing to do; that it's the *smart* thing to do. And, look where that's gotten us. Most of us feel lost, anxious, and hungry, in a constant state of survival. Rather than feeling satisfied and fulfilled, we feel disconnected from our bodies, our families, and our hearts, which isn't *right* or *smart*.

When you add up enough of us doing this, you get an entire civilization of people scrambling around disconnected and treating the earth as badly as we treat ourselves. Quickly, we're destroying it faster than we can put it back together. We think we're smart, but we're not. We're like prehistoric sea creatures crawling around in survival mode with plastic pacifiers in our mouths, weighed down and distracted by our unawareness.

By doing this powerful work of healing our wounds and empowering our hearts, we exit survival mode. We stop crawling around in a state of unconsciousness and open our eyes. We also awaken the sensitivity and intelligence required to enter higher levels of awareness, understanding, and evolvement. Similar to the effects of lucid dreaming, psychedelics, and meditation, when we reach higher levels of conscious awareness, we wake up to new ideas and new ways of thinking, which allow us to think outside the collective box (cage) we've all been stuck inside for so long. Essentially, we become consciously awoken and it's the smartest thing we can do.

Why? Because consciousness is like an ocean of intelligence that fills us and surrounds us. It is absorbed into our beings and with each moment we are present and consciously aware, we are increasingly more evolved. We begin seeing details previously unnoticed and become hyper-aware of the larger, expansive world inside us and all around us. And that's something we need. As a species, we *need* to evolve to the next level of our potential. We need to wake up to what we're doing to this planet and all the creatures who inhabit it. Rather than mindlessly consuming, wasting and trashing, we need to be present, wise, caring and conscious.

Yes, life is devastating and frustrating at times, but we don't need to get lost in the suffering—we need to get smart. We need to be intelligent. We need to expand our awareness into the far reaches of the galaxy, awaken solutions to the problems created by our collective suffering, and do our part to support the healing of this ailing planet. That's what *intelligent* and *empowered* hearts can do.

THE WORLD AROUND YOU

I ONCE HAD A DREAM WHERE I WOKE UP INSIDE A large room where everyone was sleeping. On the floor, the sofas, in the doorways, people were sleeping. At first glance, it might have been the aftermath of a raging party, but it wasn't. There were family members, loved ones, elders, and children, all sunk in a deep, intoxicating slumber.

With care not to awaken anyone, I stood up and looked around. I wondered "it's daylight, why is everyone asleep?" Tiptoeing over arms and legs, I made my way to the door and stepped outside. I stood there, alone and contemplative. Within me, there was a sense of urgency, a feeling that we needed to go somewhere, that we weren't safe and needed to move quickly.

Everyone was still inside, asleep. I felt overwhelmed, alone, burdened by knowing that I had woken up and it was up to me to wake everyone else and encourage our quick departure.

Then, miraculously, people began slowly stumbling out of the house. Without the need to go in or say a thing, somehow, my waking woke up the others. Sleepy-eyed and confused, they began gathering in a circle with me. I said "We need to go." Some looked apprehensive and others concerned, but slowly, as a group, we began moving on to our unforeseeable destination of safety.

I think of self-growth and healing like that dream. I think of so many of us being lost and disconnected from ourselves and our bodies, bloated with insatiable hunger, fogged over by pills, drinks, LED screens, and distraction. Waking up from this can be very empowering and also very lonely. While once you said yes to an invitation to go drinking, now you ask whether anyone is interested in a quiet walk to see the sunrise. Where once you were surrounded by the sparkling lights of stimulation, you are now content sitting in silence. Instead of fists squeezing tightly with the need for more stuff, you have the flowing desire to downsize and declutter.

Sitting peacefully beneath the tree in your yard or pleasantly drinking a glass of water at the bar, you may not be understood. You may be questioned and judged and compared, surrounded by doubt, and encouraged to doubt yourself. For those who aren't ready to stop and slow down, you may appear as dense and boring as a large rock. You may come off as rude for not playing the *smile to make me feel more comfortable* game.

The reality is, if they weren't aware of the suffering you experienced in the past, they won't understand what you've overcome or how long it's taken to get where you're at. If they aren't ready to do the work on themselves, they may feel a deep sense of longing for the freedom you've achieved and with that comes envy, jealousy, and resentment for you. Or, their false sense of confidence might be threatened by your true confidence and with that, they'll do everything they can to feel bigger and better than you.

A suggestion: be patient. We can't change anyone else—all we can do is free ourselves and trust that one day, others will be ready to experience their own version of freedom. Remind yourself that everyone is trying their best and doing everything they can to reach a place of peace inside. Maybe they're doing it in destructive and distracting ways, but that's a conversation between them and the Divine.

Instead of reaching for the cage door, rise up to the place of compassion. Rise up for them and rise up for yourself. Use your power, wisdom, and courage to confront your fears and access infinite love and understanding.

Find the network of intuition and compassion that connects your heart to their heart to my heart to all of our hearts—and let that awareness *fill* your entire being. And, *feel* them. Not just their experience of pain, feel *them*—the innocent, loving, vulnerable, tenderness buried deep within. Even if they've lost sight of it themselves, you can find it. Feel a synchronistic siblinghood with what they are experiencing because you've been there. You've sipped from the same poisoned water and you know the burning pain of someone who isn't ready to be free from their suffering.

It may feel vulnerable to step outside the cage, but you're not alone. You're held and supported by the guardian guides who have been watching over you all this time, the noble saints who have seen your struggles and commemorate your devotion to the heart. For so long, it was them quietly reaching a hand to you as you struggled and suffered, but now *you* can reach a hand to help others. In your devoted intention of remaining present and open, you naturally invite those who are suffering to sit beside you under the tree when *they're* ready.

THE POWER OF PURPOSE

WHETHER YOU REALIZE IT OR NOT, YOU'RE HERE for a reason. We all are. Each of us is here to learn, absorb, and acquire knowledge and life experience, then cultivate that wisdom into what we offer the world in return. Because each of us has been through such different experiences of life, what each of us has to offer will be unique and different from one another, yet equally important—regardless of how brightly our work stands out in comparison to each other's.

To understand this, we can visualize a symphonic performance.

On stage, there are dozens of musicians, some seated and some standing, all grouped in different sections, each filled with instruments different in size and shape. Because of those differences, each instrument has a unique voice and tone in the overall sound. While the brass players create deep, low bass tones, the violins guide the song with light, playful melodies.

There is also a conductor guiding the performance and keeping the tempo. This musical guide unites and directs the herd of musicians to move ahead through each bar of music.

Who are you on that stage? Are you the oboist playing a light-hearted tune, bringing the sound of joy to the audience? Are you the drummer, driving the deep rhythm of the herd? Are you the cellist, pulling the strings and opening listeners' hearts? Or, are you the conductor, standing in a place of leadership?

What if you're none of these?
What if you're not even on stage at all?
Does that mean you're nobody?
Does that mean you're useless and without purpose?

No, not at all.

Behind the musicians and behind the curtains are dozens of people pulling ropes, queuing lights, boosting monitors, and waiting for signals to adjust the settings on stage. Then, there are the people running the ticket booth and the seamstresses who sewed the seat covers and hemmed the curtains. There are the technicians who built the speakers and the engineers who designed them. There are the woodworkers who mindfully cut each piece of wood that built the stage, the chairs, and the bows that slide across the strings. Then, there are the miners who carved deep into caves to access the silver that would eventually become the flutes.

You see, while it can be mesmerizing to behold this glorious, glamorous group of musicians on stage, they're only a small piece of the whole. They're just one ray of light beaming out from the beautiful symphonic experience.

Like each of the many minds, hearts, and hands that work together to bring a performance to life, we all play a very important role in this expansive mystery of the world and each of us plays our own unique part.

The reality is, no one is playing the same part as you. No one has experienced what you've experienced, no one knows what you know, and no one has been gifted with the challenges and wisdom that you have. Only you have lived your life and only you can do what you do.

If any part of you is trying to fit in to be accepted and be like everyone else—you're crawling towards a mirage in the desert and you won't get there. You'll do, buy, and say all of the right things but by the time you've mastered normalcy, the norm will change and you'll have to start over, resculpting your life and your style to mimic what you see everyone else doing.

Please don't do that. There are enough people in the world doing that. We don't need more emotionally hungry and insecure people concerned about fitting in and gaining a temporary sense of self-acceptance by following what everyone else is doing.

If you really want to step into the power of your purpose, then be a rebel and be different. Be yourself. Pull your gaze and attachment away from the stage and stop telling yourself you're a nobody because you're not adorned with an audience of attention and admiration. Have true confidence and trust in yourself regardless of what anyone else is doing or saying.

Realize that all the shameful memories of remorse that you considered the regrets for so long weren't actually mistakes, but the precious and powerful ingredients needed to fulfill your life purpose. Acknowledge the many gifts, talents, and skills that are uniquely yours, without concern for what they do or don't do for you, then *share them!*

The world needs you to do this. We *need* you to honor yourself and step into your confidence so you can contribute your unique strengths to this sacred tapestry we are creating together.

Why? Because the world is in a troubled place right now and we need healthy leaders. We need people who are strong, wise, compassionate, and genuinely confident to be present and able to help others. When someone is ready to wake from their suffering, you need to be someone they can look up to, learn from, and heal alongside. It's time for you to stop being afraid of your power and start stepping into your purpose.

What is your life purpose?

I don't know, but you do. Somewhere, tucked away, behind the stacks of stories, is a knowing that whispers to you when you're laying in bed at night, staring at the ceiling in the dark. It calls to you, reminding you that you're here to make this world a better place.

Lean into it. Listen to that voice inside of you and say yes.

Say yes for you, for me, and for the many people, animals, trees, bees, and beings who will benefit from one more being following what is right inside their heart. One more human choosing love instead of fear.

*What dream vision is calling from your heart, longing to be heard?
Are you willing to listen and honor it?*

THE UNKNOWN

SOMETIMES, MAKING THE CHOICE TO BELIEVE IN yourself and step into the power of your purpose is like standing at the edge of a cliff where you either have to step forward boldly into your life or cling to the edge. The edge is what connects the land of your past to the expansive mystery ahead of you.

Many of us will cling and remain in the same job, the same marriage, and the same habits year after year because we are fatally intimidated by the unknown. *What if I end up alone? What if I never recover? What if I lose everything and end up failing?* Knowing that our lives will continue to be miserable is somehow safer and more comfortable than not knowing what the future holds.

We do this because we're afraid.

We don't know what tomorrow will bring. We don't know what's happening light years away. We don't know what the economy will be like in five years. We don't know what our children will decide to do with their future. We don't know if our lovers will go to the grocery store and fall in love with someone else. We don't know how decomposing plastic will affect the future of the Earth. We don't know why loved ones sometimes choose to end their lives instead of seeking help. We don't know if our beloved dog will live to be old or get hit by a car. We don't know if *we* will live to be old or get hit by a car. There's so much that we don't know, and that scares us.

Without being comfortable in this vulnerable and sacred space of the unknown, we make up answers. We create stories and reasons and facts and solutions and boxes where we package and label everything to fit on (un)secured shelves, and we then watch, control, predict, assume, and know it all. We replace all question marks with tightly woven knots, and somehow feel a little less uncomfortable and less at risk of being touched by the almighty unknown or its beloved partner, death.

The reality is, we're going to die.

This life was never meant to last forever and our bodies were never ours to keep.

All the materials, minerals, and flesh used to house our spirits for this incredible passage will be sent back to the terrestrial plane of earthworms and ashes, and we will be transformed. Like books on loan from God's personal library, we have to return it all. Like dreams, like songs, like prayers woven back into the vast unknown, one day we will have to release this life and return to the field of expansive oneness and consciousness, once again becoming *nameless, sexless, ageless beings who don't know about the past or have concerns about the future*—infinitely twinkling within the stars and shimmering from each grain of sand.

Am I strong enough for this?
Can I really handle being so present and alive knowing it will someday end?
Yes, you can.

Courageously, you set down the shredded bits of tarp you were planning to use as a parachute and open your arms with deeper knowing that you're not alone and that those things beside you are not just arms but *wings*.

Then, as the winds of trust summon you forward, you make the choice.
LEAP into life!

The wholeness of the Divine will rise up to meet you on that cliff and welcome you into the vast, brilliant web of mystery and life. A life that is far better than anything you could have imagined because there, you begin stepping out of your own story and into the life experience. The expansive and brilliant journey that is majestically whispered and planned between you and the omnipotence of the Divine.

The reason you were born.

❈

I HAVE CARRIED IN MY HEART A VISION FOR MANY YEARS...

A giant and expansive place that reaches into the sky like a tree into the stars.

It's a temple.

A sacred space of prayer.

A cathedral.

A cavernous womb inside a mountain.

What do the walls look like within this place?

It's hard to say. With no light, there is little to be seen.

Held within the space are masses and masses of unlit candles. Thousands, hundreds of thousands, billions of candles filling this room for as far and high as the eye can see. Each and every candle, the same size and each upright, securely placed.

None are laying down and none are broken.

For each of us on the planet, there is one candle, devotedly representing the heart of that being.

I think of consciousness as light.

Burning, fire, sun, light.

I think of a world living in the dark.

I imagine each of us and all that we've been through. I think of all of the times we didn't have someone to talk to and all the moments we felt lost and uncertain. I think of what it feels like to be alone and not know that you're loved or that you belong. I think of everyone who never felt safe enough to cry and the many wars that gave way for those unshed tears to drop like sobbing missiles and bombs.

I think of the countless opportunities that are handed out to us like books to study in school—lessons on how to sink and drown in suffering. Watch, hide, avoid, fight, cover, deflect, lie, judge, and divide far away from here, far away from one another, far away from the tenderness of the heart.

The candles are not here to be hidden in darkness.
They were created to sing the song of the sun.
This place was not built to be forgotten.
It was created to house the beauty of tomorrow.

What can I do to make a difference?

I'm only one person and I am so small in comparison to this cold and desolate place of night that stretches so far, too far beyond.

It only takes one.

Whispered like a breath from the Divine.

It only takes one.

We question our strength.

We listen to what we are told and believe that we are nothing.

It only takes one.

We hold back our strength and wait to exhale until one day it's over, and still...

It only takes one.
One individual light to awaken the entire space.

You are not here to be forgotten.
You are not here to be hidden and remain unlit within a chamber of untold secrets.
You are here to be alive and burn brightly. You are here to gather the pieces from each of your noble lessons and wear them in honor and passion for all you've learned and all you've overcome.
Open.
Awaken to this day and see that you are powerful.
See that you are here for a reason and you are what it takes to create change.
Remember what it was like to be born.
Remember.
Remember why you are here.
You are here to continue the awakening of consciousness.

You are here to be alive and be the eyes for creation to witness what is being created:

Love.

Suddenly, the walls begin to speak with stories of life and remembrance. Blues, greens, and golds, a sparkling glow. The light dances on the walls and the room comes to life with awakening.

Who are we if we're no longer afraid to speak up and be ignited?

What is our purpose if it's no longer to hide within forgotten corners of pain?

We are the candles who have been lit and we have the power to spread the light of love, compassion, and forgiveness—inspiring and awakening others.

Together, we will remember the truth.

Together, we will transform the night into day.

Together, we will awaken this world.

GLOSSARY

Here you will find terms used in the book. Though most are the official definitions, some are unique to the work of the Empowered Heart.

ANONYMOUS SHARING: The act of sharing personal and intimate experiences while remaining unknown and unidentified.

CLEANSING LIGHT OF AWARENESS: The transformational shift that happens when consciousness is infused into the mental and emotional areas of unconsciousness within a being.

COLLECTIVE CONSCIOUSNESS: The essence of consciousness present and shared between numerous beings.

COMFORT: Freedom and relief from pain or constraint; receiving constructive forms of nourishment and soothing support in order to experience being comfortable in one's self.

COMPULSION: The irresistible and unconscious urge to do something.

CONNECT: To deepen a sense of connection with the self and others to experience necessary healing and an understanding of wholeness.

CONSCIENCE: The internal understanding between what is morally right or wrong.

CONSCIOUSNESS: The state of being present and awake; aware of one's internal self and external surroundings.

DEFENSE: The act of defending that which needs protecting; the state of aggression and outward protection embodied to safeguard the wounded heart.

DESENSITIZED: To become less sensitive; to no longer feel.

DISCERNMENT: Perception in the absence of judgment with a view of obtaining spiritual direction and understanding.

DIVINE CONSCIOUSNESS: The highest form of spiritual awareness.

EGO: The part of the mind that mediates between the conscious and the unconscious and is responsible for a sense of personal identity; the perception of the self that is developed through being disconnected from the true, formless self within.

EMOTIONS: A complex state of feeling that results in physical and psychological changes that influence thought and behavior (feelings are the same, though with conscious awareness of the feeling).

EMPOWERED: To empower one's true self by overcoming pain, fear, and suffering; to choose love; the authentic and true self that emerges when one's pain has been soothed and needs have been met.

FALSE CONFIDENCE: A temporary and insincere sense of power and security that is ego-based; an understanding of the self derived from insecurity and fear.

FEEL: The ability to experience an emotion or sensation; the act of resensitizing.

HIGHER SELF: The aspect of the self that is directly connected with an understanding of consciousness and divine awareness.

HEART: The central and innermost part of something; the vital essence; the spirit of one's being.

INTUITION: The heart's natural and visceral ability to listen, sense, and feel; the internal compass system that operates from feeling more so than thinking.

INVESTIGATOR & WITNESS: The personas of the question asker and the question responder one can embody and interact with to explore deeper levels of self-awareness.

JUDGMENT AWARENESS: To consciously witness and recognize the harmful act of being judgmental.

LOVE: To experience deep joy, admiration, and respect; the act of giving and receiving; understanding and embracing compassion and forgiveness, while also practicing self-honor and respect.

NEED: The state of requiring support, safety, and healing; the need to heal, soothe, and ease the pain resulting from injury.

OBSERVE: To gain knowledge and understanding through observation; to clearly and honestly witness the reality of a situation.

PAIN: The experience of distress and discomfort caused by injury; the feelings of discomfort, sadness, insecurity, and pain resulting from being wounded.

PRESENCE: The state of being fully present and consciously aware.

PROTECTION: The experience of feeling sheltered and protected; the attempt to care for one's self by disconnecting from the sensations of pain when needs for relief and healing aren't met.

REALIZATION: To become fully aware of something; the experience of understanding something previously unknown.

RELEASE: The action or process of releasing or being released; to set free; the ability to emote feelings and energies from within.

SHAME: A painful feeling of humiliation or distress caused by the perception of wrong or foolish behavior.

SHAME AFTERMATH: The feelings of embarrassment, humiliation, and regret that accompany being honest and open about intimate and heartfelt matters.

SUBCONSCIOUS: A level of awareness that is neither fully conscious or unconscious; the hidden room between consciousness and unconsciousness.

SUFFERING: To experience continuous pain, sadness and loss; to feel trapped or lost; the pain resulting from feeling disconnected from the heart, body and/or surrounding environment.

SYMPATHETIC CONSCIOUSNESS: The understanding, awareness, and regard for another's state of being; compassion.

TRUE CONFIDENCE: The deep knowing that one is safe and can rely fully on one's self; a sense of empowerment and belonging that comes from being united with the higher self, rather than the ego; an understanding of the self deriving from love.

UNBIASED NEUTRALITY: The ability to remain centered and neutral without taking sides or personally identifying with specific opinions or viewpoints.

REFERENCES

Screen usage

Alyssa Cimino, "Americans devote more than 10 hours a day to screen time, and growing," IST 110 (blog), *Penn State University*, February 21, 2018, https://sites.psu.edu/ist110pursel/2018/02/21/americans-devout-more-than-10-hours-a-day-to-screen-time-and-growing.

Nielsen, *How People Watch: A Global Nielsen Consumer Report*, August 2010, https://www.nielsen.com/wp-content/uploads/sites/3/2019/04/Global-Video-Report-How-People-Watch-1.pdf.

Nielsen, *The Nielsen Total Audience Report*: Q1 2018, July 2018, https://www.nielsen.com/us/en/insights/report/2018/q1-2018-total-audience-report.

Vicky Rideout, *The Common Sense Consensus: Media Use by Tweens and Teens* (San Francisco, CA: Common Sense Media, 2015), https://www.commonsensemedia.org/sites/default/files/uploads/research/census_researchreport.pdf.

US trash consumption

"National Overview: Facts and Figures on Materials, Wastes and Recycling," United States Environmental Protection Agency, last updated July 14, 2021, https://www.epa.gov/facts-and-figures-about-materials-waste-and-recycling/national-overview-facts-and-figures-materials.

Anger on the body

"National Overview: Facts and Figures on Materials, Wastes and Recycling," United States Environmental Protection Agency, last updated July 14, 2021, https://www.epa.gov/facts-and-figures-about-materials-waste-and-recycling/national-overview-facts-and-figures-materials.

LaVelle Hendricks et al., "The Effects of Anger on the Brain and Body," *National Forum Journal of Counseling and Addiction 2*, no. 1 (2013): 1-12.

"Anger: How it Affects People," Better Health Channel, accessed October 4, 2021, https://www.betterhealth.vic.gov.au/health/healthyliving/anger-how-it-affects-people.

Sarah N. Garfinkel et al., "Anger in Brain and Body: The Neural and Physiological Perturbation of Decision-Making by Emotion," *Social Cognitive and Affective Neuroscience* 11, no. 1 (2016): 150-158. https://doi.org/10.1093/scan/nsv099.

Depression

"Depression," World Health Organization, September 13, 2021, https://www.who.int/news-room/fact-sheets/detail/depression.

"GBD Results Tool," Global Health Data Exchange, Accessed October 4, 2021, http://ghdx.healthdata.org/gbd-results-tool?params=gbd-api-2019-permalink/d780dffbe8a381b25e1416884959e88b.

1 in 3 women, India

Joe Wallen, "One in Three Women in India Subject to Domestic Abuse, Study Finds," *The Telegraph*, June 2, 2020, https://www.telegraph.co.uk/global-health/science-and-disease/one-three-women-india-subject-domestic-abuse-study-finds.

Yuvaraj Krishnamoorthy, Karthika Ganesh, and Karthiga Vijayakumar, "Physical, Emotional and Sexual Violence Faced by Spouses in India: Evidence on Determinants and Help-Seeking Behaviour from a Nationally Representative Survey," *Journal of Epidemiology & Community Health* 74, no. 9 (2020): 732-740, http://dx.doi.org/10.1136/jech-2019-213266.

Sensitivity

Bianca Acevedo et al., "The Functional Highly Sensitive Brain: A Review of the Brain Circuits Underlying Sensory Processing Sensitivity and Seemingly Related Disorders," *Philosophical Transactions of the Royal Society B: Biological Sciences* 373, no. 1744 (2018): 1-5, https://doi.org/10.1098/rstb.2017.0161.

Sebastian Kraemer, "The Fragile Male," BMJ 321, no. 7276 (2000): 1609-1612, https://doi.org/10.1136/bmj.321.7276.1609.

Tara M. Chaplin, "Gender and Emotion Expression: A Developmental Contextual Perspective," *Emotion Review* 7, no. 1 (2015): 14-21, https://doi.org/10.1177/1754073914544408.

Animal consciousness

Donald R. Griffin and Gayle B. Speck, "New Evidence of Animal Consciousness," *Animal Cognition* 7, no. 1 (2004): 5-18, https://doi.org/10.1007/s10071-003-0203-x.

Crying

Asmir Gračanin, Lauren M. Bylsma, and Ad J. J. M. Vingerhoets, "Is Crying a Self-Soothing Behavior?" *Frontiers in Psychology* 5 (2014): 1-15, https://doi.org/10.3389/fpsyg.2014.00502.

Leo Newhouse, "Is Crying Good for You?" *Harvard Health Blog*, March 1, 2021, https://www.health.harvard.edu/blog/is-crying-good-for-you-2021030122020.

Holly Tiret, "Benefits of Crying: Go Ahead and Cry, It's Good for You," *Healthy Relationships, Michigan State University*, December 4, 2018, https://www.canr.msu.edu/news/benefits-of-crying.

"Complicated Grief," Mayo Clinic, June 19, 2021, mayoclinic.org/diseases-conditions/complicated-grief/basics/definition/con-20032765.

Abigail Millings et al., "Holding Back the Tears: Individual Differences in Adult Crying Proneness Reflect Attachment Orientation and Attitudes to Crying," *Frontiers in Psychology* 7 (2016): 1-18, https://doi.org/10.3389/fpsyg.2016.01003.

Emotional repression

Marcus Mund and Kristin Mitte, "The Costs of Repression: A Meta-Analysis on the Relation between Repressive Coping and Somatic Diseases," *Health Psychology* 31, no. 5 (2012): 640-649, https://doi.org/10.1037/a0026257.

Sleep

Paula Alhola and Päivi Polo-Kantola, "Sleep Deprivation: Impact on Cognitive Performance," *Neuropsychiatric Disease and Treatment* 3, no. 5 (2007): 553-567.

National Heart, Lung and Blood Institute, *Your Guide to Healthy Sleep*, January 2011, https://www.nhlbi.nih.gov/health-topics/all-publications-and-resources/your-guide-healthy-sleep.

Cleve Backster

Hannah Jenkins, "Cleve Backster," PSI Encyclopedia, Last updated May 6, 2019, https://psi-encyclopedia.spr.ac.uk/articles/cleve-backster.

Cleve Backster, *Primary Perception: Biocommunication with Plants, Living Foods and Human Cells* (California, USA: White Rose Millennium Press, 2003).

Trees

Anne Marie Helmenstine, "How Much Oxygen Does One Tree Produce?" *Thought Co.*, Updated November 19, 2019, https://www.thoughtco.com/how-much-oxygen-does-one-tree-produce-606785.

Joanna Mounce Stancil, "The Power of One Tree—The Very Air We Breathe," US Department of Agriculture, June 3, 2019, https://www.usda.gov/media/blog/2015/03/17/power-one-tree-very-air-we-breathe.

Self-love

Kelton Global, *Birchbox: The You Time Report*, accessed October 4, 2021, https://edge.birchbox.com/uploads/birchbox-the-you-time-report.pdf.

Dictionary.com, "self-love," accessed October 4, 2021, https://www.dictionary.com/browse/self-love.

Forgiveness

"Forgiveness: Your Health Depends on it," Johns Hopkins Medicine, accessed October 4, 2021, https://www.hopkinsmedicine.org/health/wellness-and-prevention/forgiveness-your-health-depends-on-it.

RESOURCES

While it is my deepest intention that this book offers you tools, awareness, information, and support along your path of healing, I also want to share some additional resources that may be helpful to you.

Music

WRITING THIS BOOK REQUIRED A LOT of patience, perseverance, and years of sitting still and going within. One thing that helped me enter the necessary and creative space of inner listening and outer writing was meditation music. This ushered me into that space again and again. In fact, there were three artists/albums I listened to on repeat while writing this book and I highly recommend checking them out:

Alio Die, "Horas tibi serenas". Hic Sunt Leones, Italy. 2010
Klaus Wiese, "Vision". Aquamarin Verlag, Germany. 1994.
Ben Leinbach, "The Spirit of Yoga". Myndstream, USA. 2006.

Music has been a big part of my world for many years and has been a way for me to express the truth of what my experience of suffering and healing was like. I've recorded numerous solo albums and have a project with Kurt called *Sea Stars*. To explore this music, you can go to www.katiegray.com/music.

Counsel

IN CHAPTER 11, I TALK ABOUT THE IMPORTANCE of exploring counsel and support when you need it. I also mention that being able to afford it can be challenging and unrealistic for a lot of us. For that reason, if you are in need of support or someone to talk to, you might consider something less traditional and more affordable. Through online counseling sites and apps, you can access professional support.

Here are some you might consider checking out:

Talk Space www.talkspace.com
Calmerry www.calmerry.com
Better Help www.betterhelp.com

Your book

I HOPE THAT AFTER TAKING THIS JOURNEY together, you are ignited, inspired, and sparked with enthusiasm to heal yourself and in doing that, bring some much-needed healing to this world.

If writing your own book is something that speaks to you from your heart, I highly encourage you to take the leap and do it! Perhaps it will be as healing, transformative, and profound of an experience for you as it was for me.

I also encourage you to consider exploring these resources as you embark on that mission…

Editing

THE ONE PERSON WHO SPENT THE MOST TIME working with this book, besides me, is **Ameesha Smith-Green**. She's the lead editor and someone I trust, respect, and admire deeply. She's wise, intuitive, compassionate, very experienced in editing self-help literature, and someone I plan to work with forever. In fact, she works with an incredible team at her company called The Book Shelf based in Birmingham, UK, and I highly recommend them! www.thebookshelf.ltd

In addition to Ameesha, the book was blessed by the warm, talented presence of **Nirmala Nataraj**. Nirmala was the developmental editor and it was because of her that many magical characteristics of the book were nurtured and encouraged. She is extremely wise and skilled, and someone who has become like a sister through the process of bringing this book to life. If you have a message to get out into the world and need someone who can see the unseen and feel the magic, Nirmala is amazing.

It was through our dear and mutual friend **Kelly Notaras** that Nirmala and I were introduced. And it was through Kelly's company KN Literary Arts that the initial developmental edit took place. Kelly is truly a genius and someone worth connecting with if you plan to write a book. In fact, she wrote a book called *The Book You Were Born to Write* and it is a priceless tool for anyone who needs encouragement and motivation to get healing messages out into the World. www.knliterary.com

Design

WHEN IT BECAME CLEAR TO ME THAT THIS book was more than a dream, I immediately visualized it being a collaboration with one of my best friends, **Erica Ekrem**. For years, Erica has designed album covers and posters for me. She and I drink from the same well of aesthetic passion and I adore everything she has ever created, including this book's cover design, map diagram, book layout, and logo design. She has the gift of bringing visions and dreams from the ethereal realms into the physical, and I recommend her more than words can say. She's also a phenomenal bookbinder and creates handmade journals if you feel ready to take your journaling to the next level! www.loombound.com

Illustration

WHILE THE EMPOWERED HEART IMAGES HAVE been gradually unearthing themselves over time, it wasn't until working with **Masha Pimas** that they really came to life. Masha did all of the original artwork for the book and is an absolute joy to work with. I adore her and highly recommend her. instagram.com/mashapimas.art

THANK YOU

THANK YOU TO **Ameesha Smith-Green, Erica Ekrem, Nirmala Nataraj, Masha Pimas, Lisa Vanacore, Shaun Hand, Victor Solano, Mohammed Fadel Zalabia, Kelly Notaras, Bridget Law,** and **Barb Pollard.** I'm so grateful for each of you and the time you spent helping nurture and honor this journey. What a profound team of heartfelt editors and artists you are! Each of you have helped tremendously in welcoming this book baby to life. Thank you.

THANK YOU TO **my mother,** for teaching me to be independent, follow my own path, and honor my intuition. Through you, I have learned to be a loving mother who welcomes and honors the innocent child in everyone. One day, when the story and body of Katie Gray disassemble into nothingness, I'll float up through the ceiling of this masterful cathedral of life and meet you in the realms of mystery and stardust. I love you.

THANK YOU TO **my father,** for always being so caring and loving. Thank you for courageously encouraging me to write this book and tell my story. Your support and unconditional love means the world to me. I love you, Papa.

THANK YOU TO **Kurt,** my beloved psychedelic cowboy husband, who courageously leans into the mystery of life and lives within the healing space of curiosity and magic. You've taught me so much and get the credit for first calling it out 12 years ago, "I sense you've got some books in you." Thank you. I love you.

THANK YOU TO my twin sister **Becca** and brother-in-law **Nate,** for helping to take care of Mom while I spent months and eventually years hidden in the cave of my office to write this book. Thank you to my little sister **Alena** for sitting beside me at the pond and helping with the illustrations. Thank you to **Shyam**, **Sam**, and **Paul**—you are each woven into these pages. I Love you guys.

THANK YOU TO **Dove**, **Bisou**, **Matisse**, **Bella**, **Alexander**, **Lucy**, **Twinkle Toes**, **Mabel**, **Alison I**, **Alison II**, **Blue Bird**, and **Red Man**: the many mystical guides who came in the form of animals and blessed me with so much love and guidance through the years. Your love saved my life again and again and again.

THANK YOU TO **Augie Cullen**, **Connie Zehner**, **Elisheva Wexler**, **Bonnie Schmidt**, **Eve Ensler**, **Naih**, **Mado**, **Bijou**, **Christelle**, **Darin Leong**, **Vicci Martinez**, **George Evelyn**, **Bridget Meyer**, **Taryn Michele**, **Kaitlyn Smith**, **Rajesh Kumar** and the many friends and beings who have supported, helped, and encouraged this work to come through me and out into the world.

AUTHOR

Katie Gray IS A WRITER, SINGER, COUNSELOR, and elder caregiver devoted to helping people who are hurting. Inspired and compelled by her own full self-recovery from a 17-year addiction to food and bulimia, she utilizes her voice, experience, and wisdom to assist others through the healing process.

Journey of the Empowered Heart is her first book.

To learn more about her courses, workshops, recordings, live events, and *The Empowered Heart* podcast, go to www.katiegray.com.